HARVARD STUDIES IN ENGLISH

VOLUME III

THE DRAMA OF SENSIBILITY

BY

ERNEST BERNBAUM

THE DRAMA OF SENSIBILITY

A SKETCH OF THE HISTORY OF ENGLISH SENTIMENTAL COMEDY AND DOMESTIC TRAGEDY
1696–1780

BY

ERNEST BERNBAUM

Mrs. Dangle: There was some edification
to be got from those pieces, Mr. Sneer!
Sheridan, *The Critic*, I, i.

GLOUCESTER, MASS.

PETER SMITH

1958

TO
GEORGE PIERCE BAKER
PROFESSOR OF DRAMATIC LITERATURE
HARVARD UNIVERSITY

PREFATORY NOTE

The sentimental comedies and domestic tragedies composing what I venture to term the drama of sensibility have heretofore been dealt with chiefly in monographs upon one play or one author, and in rather brief portions of general literary histories. This is, I believe, the first attempt to deal in one volume with all the English dramas of sensibility from the time of their rise to the year 1780. The work is, as its subtitle states, a sketch, not a history. In the present state of learning, when there may be said to have been much soliloquy upon the subject but little discussion, a real history, — recording the facts that are by general consent considered important, and weighing judicially the conflicting arguments about their significance, — can hardly be written; and, were it possible to write, it would require greater space than this volume affords.

Even a sketch of the subject can be kept within these limits only by omitting matter that some students might expect and desire. The inclusion of a full bibliography would enlarge this book by one-half of its present size. What I have given instead are references in the footnotes to passages of special importance, and occasionally to general works likely to be overlooked. Other bibliographical information may be readily found in Professor G. H. Nettleton's *English Drama of the Restoration and Eighteenth Century* and in *The Cambridge History of English Literature*.

In order to keep within my compass, I have, even at the risk of seeming dogmatic, tried to avoid so far as possible all controversy. My definition of the drama of sensibility, my inclusion and exclusion of plays in accordance therewith, and many of my historical statements, differ from those of other writers; but I have made them upon the best of my knowledge and belief, and have rarely turned aside from my course to engage in dispute. In cases where opinions contrary to mine are prevalent, however, I have called attention to the fact in a footnote and given references that will enable anyone to check my statements and correct my errors of judgment.

The nature of the subject has compelled me to include some matter that would be unnecessary in dealing with better known works. Nearly all the dramas of sensibility are unread to-day, and are likely to continue unread forever. I could therefore not assume any knowledge of them on my readers' part, and had to outline their contents (and that of some better known plays, for purposes of contrast) in order to discuss them intelligibly. "Some books," says Bacon, "may be read by deputy, and extracts made of them by others." Of just that sort are the playbooks herein described. I do not indulge the vain hope that I shall lead modern readers to peruse many eighteenth century dramas of sensibility; I hope, however, that I have explained why they were once enthusiastically admired.

For the thorough student of literature, I have tried to furnish a convenient introduction to the whole subject, in place of the many separate articles on portions thereof. To the general reader I offer an historical and descriptive account, accompanied by a critical interpretation, of a large group of plays which were once thought entertaining and inspiring, and which, though themselves dead beyond resurrection, have left to an extent little realized the impress of their ideals upon our contemporary literature.

In the preparation of this book, I have been aided by many helpful suggestions from Professors Bliss Perry and Chester Noyes Greenough. To the latter I am indebted also for reading all the proofs.

                                                                    E. B.

CONTENTS

THE DRAMA OF SENSIBILITY

CHAPTER I

THE NEW ETHICS OF THE DRAMA OF SENSIBILITY

On an evening in January, 1696, the usual audience at Drury Lane Theatre gathered to attend the first performance of a comedy by a new author. They saw nothing in its title, *Love's Last Shift, or the Fool in Fashion,* to pique extraordinary curiosity. They expected to be entertained by some ingenious lover's trick, and by the manners of some sort of modish coxcomb,—in any case by something that reflected the absurdities and intrigues of London society. They had no warning that they were to witness the beginning of a new epoch in English dramatic history. Since the play was not a tragedy, nor a romantic drama, they could not suppose that their sensibility, their sympathy for the virtues and distresses of beings like themselves, would be appealed to. They came, as usual, to laugh; they remained to dissolve in tears. They themselves furnished a spectacle that must have amazed the cool observer even more than the play itself.

The principal characters in *Love's Last Shift* were a sorely tried wife and a husband who, after being led astray into fashionable dissipation, sincerely repented and was reunited to her. "The joy of unexpected reconcilement," we are told, "spread such an uncommon rapture of pleasure in the audience that never were spectators more happy in easing their minds by uncommon and repeated plaudits," and by "honest tears." [1]

[1] Thomas Davies, *Dramatic Miscellanies* (1784), III, 411–412.

Their enthusiasm, it is important to note, was aroused by the virtues of the characters. To them the play was an astonishing novelty, not merely because it was a comedy at which they wept, but also because it aroused admiration for persons like themselves. It exhibited faith in the natural impulses of contemporary middle-class people.

Confidence in the goodness of average human nature is the mainspring of sentimentalism. That confidence became in the eighteenth century the cardinal point of a new gospel, and the underlying ethical principle of a new school of literature. It was the fundamental assumption of the dramatists of sensibility. Richard Steele recommends one of his sentimental comedies because it "makes us approve ourselves more." [1] Denis Diderot, the enthusiastic advocate of sentimentalism in drama and in life, writes:

> I repeat it, — the virtuous, the virtuous. It touches us in a manner more intimate and more sweet than whatever excites our contempt and our laughter. Poet, are you a man of sensibility and of tender feelings? Then strike that note, and you will hear it resound or tremble in every heart.
> 'Do you mean to say that human nature is good?'
> Yes, my friend; it is very good. Water, air, earth, fire, — everything in nature is good. . . . It is wretched conventionalities that pervert man. Human nature should not be accused.[2]

To-day the power of such faith in human nature is manifest. Sentimentalism is pervasive, and unites social and literary phenomena that have apparently little connection with one another. It has encouraged religious sects that deny the reality of sin. It has led us to entrust the slave with freedom, and to bestow upon the average man unprecedented political responsibilities. It has revolutionized education by insisting that the child, whose instincts it regards reverently, shall not be hampered by discipline.

[1] Epilogue of *The Lying Lover* (1703).
[2] Diderot, *De la Poésie dramatique. Œuvres*, ed. Assézat (1875), VII, 312.

It remains the animating impulse of our most conspicuous movements towards social reform. It asserts that the poor are not responsible for their poverty, nor the criminal for their offenses. It supports the socialist and the pacificist in their hope that the world order they desire, based on universal benevolence, will survive the test of actual practice.[1]

Immersed as we are in the sentimental spirit, we take it for granted that a modern comedy shall portray humanity as amiable. Astonishment, if not disgust, would be created in us by a play from which virtuous characters were totally excluded. We go to the theatre, as we carelessly say, "to get away from life,"—that is, to live in imagination for a brief time among persons more lovable than ourselves. We go to admire; and such is our trust in the possibilities of human nature that we feel our admiration to be justifiable. If the wisest men of the seventeenth century could be made to comprehend our attitude towards life, they would consider us dwellers in a fool's paradise.

Sentimentalists have existed in all times and nations; but in seventeenth-century England there was no organized body, except the Quakers, devoted to sentimental principles, — and the Quakers were as uninfluential in literature as they were weak in political affairs. The dominant men of action, of thought, and of letters, profoundly distrusted human nature. To them it was a dual entity: its baser passions were constantly at war with its nobler, and too frequently victorious. In this world, moral perfection was quite unattainable. What both Cavalier and Puritan had conceived mankind to be was summed up by Alexander Pope, who so often expressed seventeenth-century sentiment with finality, in the following notable lines:

---

[1] Cf. Paul Elmer More, "Humanitarianism," in *Shelburne Essays*, First Series (1907), pp. 225–253; and Agnes Repplier, "The Cost of Modern Sentiment," in *Atlantic Monthly* (1913), CXI, 610–617.

Placed on this isthmus of a middle state,
A being darkly wise, and rudely great,
With too much knowledge for the sceptic side,
With too much weakness for the Stoic's pride,
He hangs between, in doubt to act or rest,
In doubt to deem himself a god or beast,
In doubt his mind or body to prefer,
Born but to die, and reasoning but to err.
Alike in ignorance, his reason such,
Whether he thinks too little or too much.
Chaos of thought and passion, all confused,
Still by himself abused or disabused;
Created half to rise and half to fall,
Great lord of all things, yet a prey to all;
Sole judge of truth, in endless error hurled,
The glory, jest, and riddle of the world! [1]

Such was the orthodox doctrine concerning Man, and in the seventeenth century it guided every thought and activity relating to him.

The influence of that ethical conception upon the various types of dramatic literature is unmistakable. Whenever the human aspiration toward goodness was to be gratified by the presentation of ideally virtuous persons, these were placed in a background remote from the usual course of human experience. In other words, the place for perfect characters was romantic drama. There, as a distinguished historian of the drama has well observed, " the conditions of each dramatic action are taken out of the control of moral or even social laws of cause and consequence, although the art of the poet wins our sympathy for the personages by whom that action is conducted." [2] In that obviously unreal atmosphere, nothing was impossible, — not even a human being without blemish. Such virtuous characters

---

[1] *Essay on Man*, Book II, ll. 3–18.
[2] A. W. Ward, *A History of Dramatic Literature to the Death of Queen Anne* (2d ed. 1899), II, 277.

as the eighteenth-century drama of sensibility was to place in the environment of ordinary life, were, previous to its rise, placed in romantic comedy, pastoral drama, and heroic tragedy, — types which did not profess to hold a true mirror up to nature.

The principles governing the characterization of the chief figure in a tragedy, — a type of drama regarded as of higher rank than those just mentioned, — were in harmony with the orthodox ethics. Aristotle had laid down the law that "the change of fortune presented must not be the spectacle of a perfectly good man brought from prosperity to adversity." The principle was accepted and emphasized by Rapin, Rymer, and Dryden, — Dryden saying, "All reasonable men have long since concluded that the hero of the poem ought not to be a character of perfect virtue."[1] It is true, of course, that the reason given by Aristotle to support this principle was an æsthetic or psychological one, — namely, that no other type of tragedy would give the human mind the proper tragic pleasure; but the doctrine would hardly have established itself so firmly if it had not been upheld by the ethical ideas of the age. Addison mentioned the current ethical assumption when, in commenting on Aristotle, he declared that the tragic hero should not be "perfect or faultless, not only because such a character is improper to move compassion, but because there is no such thing in nature."[2] Thus the seventeenth century saw in its tragic heroes, which, though endowed with noble qualities, were subject to grievous weaknesses or sins, figures that typified the moral constitution of mankind.

In Aristotle's laws, rightly interpreted, there was nothing to forbid tragedies concerning persons who were not of the upper

[1] Preface of *All for Love* (1678). Dryden is here speaking of Antony, but the words express his attitude in general.

[2] *Spectator*, No. 548. Cf. Dryden, Preface to *Troilus and Cressida* (1679): "As for a perfect character of virtue, it never was in nature."

class of society; and such tragedies, for example *Arden of Feversham*, had been written in the Elizabethan period. During the Restoration period, however, a misunderstanding of Aristotle's words led, as is well known, to the convention that tragedy must present only persons of very eminent station. This rule, which was far easier to observe than that requiring some fatal weakness in the hero's character, combined with it to put the average human being into a curious position so far as his appearance in drama was concerned. He could not become the hero of a tragedy because he was not of princely rank. He could not become the hero of a romantic drama because no one thought of him as good enough to be a moral exemplar. He was thus reduced to the comic class. Honorable conduct in a commoner could not appear upon the stage. It was almost as if the sarcastic words of Parly, in Farquhar's *The Constant Couple*, were to dramatists a serious maxim, — "Leave honor to nobility that can support it; we poor folks have no pretense to it."

The ethical basis of comedy was the belief that the majority of men and women in ordinary life were very imperfect creatures. The comic dramatists made it their main business to show the worldliness of society, to strip it of its disguises, and to exhibit the ridiculous contrast between its pretended respectability and its actual folly and vice. They seemed, like Congreve's Hartwell, to be "entertaining company like a physician, with a discourse of their diseases and infirmities."[1] Like Wycherley's Manly, they "spoke ill of most men because they deserved it."[2] Neither social rank nor sex was any protection against the comic lash. "Damn the poets," says Wycherley's Sparkish, "they make a wise and witty man in the world a fool upon the stage, you know not how."[3] The gentleman of the

---

[1] *The Old Bachelor*, I, iv.   [2] *The Plain Dealer*, I, i.
[3] *The Country Wife*, III, ii.

court differed, in their representation of him, from the country squire only in the manner of his affectation and the degree of his folly. All were ludicrously inferior to the best possibilities of human character.

Sympathy for such characters was not expected, and pathetic scenes were banned. The predicaments into which the personages occasionally fell were often distressing to themselves, but must never appear other than amusing to the audience. When the follies and vices were punished at the conclusion of the play, the punishment must appeal, not to the sense of fear or horror, but rather to that of scornful humor. "The characters in comedy," says John Dennis, "may be chastised at the catastrophe for faults which they have committed; but that very chastisement ought to be wrapped up in the *ridiculum*, or the catastrophe cannot be truly comical."[1] Accepting the classical principle of unity of tone, the comic dramatists subscribed to Boileau's dictum :

Le comique, ennemi des soupirs et des pleurs,
N'admet point en ces vers de tragiques douleurs.[2]

Since comedy revealed the frailties of men, and showed the consequences of indulging them to be ridiculously contemptible, it professed a moral aim and an important moral effect. This moral pretension so ill accords with modern notions about Restoration comedy that the historical proofs of it must be presented in some detail. From Elizabethan times onward, comic dramatists and the critics who defended them asserted the moral purpose of comedy. They insisted upon it partly because the Puritans attacked drama not on æsthetic but on moral grounds, and the defenders took up the issue as it was presented to them. Irrespective of the controversial circumstances, however,

---

[1] John Dennis, *The Advancement and Reformation of Modern Poetry* (1701), p. 55. [2] *L'Art poétique*, Canto III, ll. 401-402.

the characteristically English preoccupation with the moral aspects of literature tended in this direction.

The most notable seventeenth-century definitions of comedy, whether made by critics or by dramatists, emphasize its ethical value. " Comedy," says Sir Philip Sidney on the eve of that century, " is an imitation of the common errors of our life, which he [the playwright] representeth in the most ridiculous and scornful sort that may be ; so as it is impossible that any beholder can be content to be such a one." [1] Dryden, after some toying with the notion of art for art's sake, shows in his criticism a growing tendency toward the ethical point of view. "Moral truth," he says, "is the mistress of the poet as much as of the philosopher ; poesy . . . must be ethical." [2] " Comedy," as he defines it, "presents us with the imperfections of human nature ; . . . [it] causes laughter in those who can judge of men and manners, by the lively representation of their folly and corruption." [3] Rapin, translated by Rymer, declares : " Comedy, which is an image of common conversation, corrects the public vices by letting us see how ridiculous they are in particular." [4]

Shadwell scorned the heretical notion that plays were written merely to entertain, and against it invoked the powerful aid of Ben Jonson's authority. In the prologue of *The Squire of Alsatia* he writes :

> Our author, ever having him [Jonson] in view
> At humble distance would his steps pursue.
> He to correct and to inform did write :
> If poets aim at naught but to delight,
> Fiddlers have to the bays an equal right.

[1] *An Apology for Poetry* (1595), ed. Edward Arber, p. 44.
[2] *Defense of an Essay of Dramatic Poesy* (1668).
[3] Preface of *The Mock Astrologer* (1671).
[4] Thomas Rymer, Translation of Rapin's *Reflections on Aristotle's Treatise of Poesy* (1674), II, 144.

The proper function of comedy is, according to him, "to repre-hend some of the vices and follies of the age."[1] Wycherley has nowhere formally defined comedy; but that his intention was in this respect identical with that of his fellow dramatists appears clearly enough beneath the superb irony with which he attacks hypocrisy in his dedication of *The Plain Dealer*. Congreve, in the important preface to *The Double Dealer*, remarks: "I de-signed the moral first, and to that moral I invented the fable." Elsewhere he says: "Men are to be laughed out of their vices in comedy. . . . As vicious people are made ashamed of their follies or faults by seeing them exposed in a ridiculous manner, so are good people at once both warned and diverted at their expense."[2] Vanbrugh asserts:

> 'Tis th' intent and business of the stage
> To copy out the follies of the age,
> To hold to every man a faithful glass
> And show him of what species he's an ass.[3]

When vindicating *The Relapse*, he writes:

> The business of comedy is to show people what they should do by representing them upon the stage doing what they should not do. . . . What I have done is in general a discouragement of vice and folly. I am sure I intended it, and I hope I have performed it.

The most important foreign master of these authors, Molière, described his aims as follows:

> The business of comedy is to represent in general all the faults of men, especially those of our own time. . . .
> The duty of comedy being to correct men while amusing them, I was of the opinion that in my position I could do no better than to attack, by means of ridiculous portrayal, the vices of my age.[4]

[1] Preface of *The Humourists* (1671).
[2] *Amendments of Mr. Collier's False and Imperfect Citations* (1698), p. 8.
[3] Prologue of *The Provoked Wife* (1697).
[4] *L'Impromptu de Versailles*, scene iv; and *Premier Placet au Roi sur la Comédie du Tartuffe* (1664).

Evidently there was a remarkable unanimity of opinion concerning the aims of comedy. How those aims were carried out in practice will be considered later ; [1] at present it is necessary only to add that they did not remain merely theoretic ideals but became firmly established conventions, understood by the contemporary public and supported by it. Hence what surprised the audience that attended the first night of *Love's Last Shift* was not that the comedy had a moral purpose, but that it evoked tearful sympathy for its characters.

The drama of sensibility, which includes sentimental comedy and domestic tragedy, was from its birth a protest against the orthodox view of life, and against those literary conventions which had served that view. It implied that human nature, when not, as in some cases, already perfect, was perfectible by an appeal to the emotions. It refused to assume that virtuous persons must be sought in a romantic realm apart from the everyday world. It wished to show that beings who were good at heart were found in the ordinary walks of life. It so represented their conduct as to arouse admiration for their virtues and pity for their sufferings. In sentimental comedy, it showed them contending against distresses but finally rewarded by morally deserved happiness. In domestic tragedy, it showed them overwhelmed by catastrophes for which they were morally not responsible. [2] A new ethics had arisen, and new forms of literature were thereby demanded.

[1] Cf. chap. iv, below.

[2] This definition of sentimental comedy and domestic tragedy differs from those current, among which may be mentioned the following: A. W. Ward, *History of Dramatic Literature*, III, 495; A. W. Ward, Introduction to Lillo's *London Merchant* (1906), pp. xxii–xxiii; Gustave Larroumet, *Marivaux* (1882), pp. 300–301; Gustave Lanson, *La Chaussée* (2d ed. 1903), pp. 1, 179; and De Witt C. Croissant, *Studies in Colley Cibber* (1912), p. 30.

CHAPTER II

THE SENTIMENTAL MISINTERPRETATION OF
PLAUTUS AND TERENCE

Such was the respect of eighteenth-century critics for Greek
and Latin literature that the defenders of the drama of sensibility sought to justify its existence by classical precedents. In
the case of domestic tragedy, they found this impossible ; for,
even in Euripides, classical tragedy was too obviously far removed from common life. For sentimental comedy, however,
they ventured to seek classical exemplars in certain plays by
Plautus and by Terence. Where seventeenth-century critics,
whom their successors considered hard-hearted, had seen nothing but the comic, Richard Steele — after English sentimental
comedy had flourished about fifteen years — was pleased to find
sensibility. His suggestion was a welcome one, and by the
middle of the eighteenth century it was supported by many
English, French, and German critics. Three plays by Plautus
— *Captivi*, *Stichus*, and *Trinummus*, — and three by Terence —
Andria, *Hecyra*, and *Adelphi*, — were regarded as prototypes
of sentimental comedy.

Lessing, the most notable German writer of dramas of sensibility, said of both *Captivi* and *Trinummus* : " They contain
scenes which cannot help bringing tears to him who possesses
a tender heart." [1] A tender heart is too often acquired at the
cost of a sense of humor, only the lack of which should enable

---

[1] G. E. Lessing, "Abhandlungen von dem weinerlichen oder rührenden
Lustspiele" in *Theatralische Bibliothek* (1754), *Werke*, ed. Lachmann-Muncker
(1890), VI, 50.

one to weep in reading *Captivi*. This famous comedy deals
with the fortunes of Hegio of Ætolia and his two sons, the
younger of whom is stolen in infancy, and under the name of
Tyndarus becomes a slave in Elis. Ætolia and Elis are at war.
Shortly before the opening of the play, the elder son, Philopolemus, is made a prisoner by the Eleans. In the hope of re-
leasing him, Hegio buys Elean captives. Among them chance
to be Tyndarus and his master Philocrates. By agreement, the
slave changes places with the master; and Hegio sends the
latter on parole to Elis to arrange the liberation of his captive
son. Hegio is unaware of the trick played upon him, knowing
neither that Tyndarus is the slave, nor that Tyndarus is his lost
son; but, it should be observed, the prologue has informed the
audience of the true facts. When Tyndarus is discovered to
have impersonated his master, the wrathful Hegio throws him
into chains. Finally Philocrates returns with the liberated Philopolemus, and Tyndarus is recognized as the lost son. Regarded
as a whole, the play is obviously a comedy of errors.

Because Tyndarus lies to enable his master to go home, and
because he remains imperturbable under Hegio's threats, he
is termed, by a German critic under Lessing's influence, "an
heroic figure" who nobly suffers martyrdom; and his last words
on being dragged away to chains are regarded as "the utterance of a heart conscious of no guilt." [1] There is, however,
nothing affecting in Tyndarus' readiness to help out the trick
which Philocrates plays upon Hegio. So far is Plautus from
sentimentally idealizing the relationship of the master and the
slave that he takes evident pains to make the farewell scene
between them amusing, — as it must have been to an audience
aware of the real situation. In the presence of Hegio, the supposed master (Tyndarus) addresses his supposed slave (Philocrates) in these condescending terms:

[1] Karl von Reinhardstoettner, *Plautus* (1886), pp. 328–330.

We have never quarreled together; you have never committed a fault; I have nothing to complain of in you; in the midst of so many misfortunes you have conducted yourself well towards your master. . . . When my father learns how well you have acted, he will not be so cruel as not to give you your freedom.

To this clever hint, the supposed slave replies:

Very true, I am glad you remember these things. But you are worthy of my devotion; and if I were to recount all the kindness you have shown me, I should not find one day sufficient. Why, if you were my slave, you could not have shown me more consideration.

Hegio, fooled into believing these words sincere, exclaims in an ecstacy of admiration:

Ye gods, what generous hearts they have! They move me to tears. What cordiality they display in friendship! What touching praises does the slave bestow upon the master![1]

The scenes of Tyndarus' discovery and discomfiture are written in the same comic vein. In them Tyndarus displays, not "heroism," but delightfully amusing impudence. He nearly succeeds in making Hegio believe that the person who identifies him is afflicted with madness; and when he is finally trapped, his exclamations are those of a saucy rascal who is being handled none too gently by the slaves that are dragging him off,—

Vis haec quidem, herclest, et trahi et trudi simul.[2]

It is his own trickery that leads him into predicaments, and his distresses are not pathetic but comic. When it is finally revealed that he is the son of Hegio, we have no moving scene of reunion; the occasion passes off with a trifling jest. Tyndarus is brought forth from the darkness of his prison, Hegio greets him as his son, and Tyndarus rejoins: "What? You my father? I your son? Oh, I see; you mean you have brought me to light!" The meeting between Hegio and his other son,

---

[1] Act II, scene iii.   [2] Act III, scene v.

Philopolemus, furnished again an opportunity for an affecting scene; but Plautus does not allow it to take place in view of the audience, and when Hegio seems inclined to talk about it, Philopolemus promptly checks him, saying: " I have heard enough of your afflictions; you reminded me of them down at the harbor."[1] From first to last, serious scenes and idealized characters are deliberately avoided.

Plautus' *Stichus*, which has been called "certainly a serious comedy or 'drame,'"[2] deals with the experiences of the two married daughters of Antipho, who have been left at their father's home while their husbands are seeking fortunes abroad. Three years have passed; and, according to law, they may be married to other husbands. The main action is concerned with their father's attempts to induce them to marry again. They are obstinate in refusal; and presently, to the general satisfaction, their husbands return home wealthy. Their faithfulness is nowhere presented in a pathetic light. The only scene which might be considered sentimental is that in which the daughters are told by Antipho that he wants them to take new husbands.[3] But in this it is made clear that they know he will not force them to do so; and they obtain a delay from him, not by means of tearful supplications, but by clever replies to his assumed anger. An opportunity for a scene of pathetic devotion would not have been missed in this fashion by a writer of sentimental comedy.

Trinummus, like *Captivi* and *Stichus*, presents characters whose imperfections are not the extravagantly ridiculous follies of plebeians, but the amusing foibles of people of respectable station in life. Charmides has gone on a journey, and has confided to his friend Callicles the charge of his affairs, as well as the knowledge that there is a treasure hidden in his house.

---

[1] Act V, scene i.   [2] G. Lanson, *La Chaussée* (1903), p. 2.
[3] Act I, scene ii.

Ignorant of this secret, the merry and extravagant son of Charmides, Lesbonicus, sells the house, — which Callicles, to protect
the treasure, buys. A youth named Lysiteles desires to marry
Lesbonicus' sister, and loves her so greatly that he will take
her without a dowry; but Lesbonicus, regarding such a marriage as disgraceful to the family honor, will not consent.
Thereupon Callicles secretly sends Lesbonicus money for his
sister's dowry, charging the messenger to say that it comes from
the absent father. The messenger is intercepted by the returning Charmides, who takes the money, learns the state of affairs,
and arranges the marriage of his daughter to Lysiteles. When
these events are disclosed to Lesbonicus, he agrees to cease
his spendthrift career.

Throughout *Trinummus* the emphasis is laid on the amusing nature of the situations that the various misunderstandings
create. Those things which sentimental comedy would elaborate, — the faithfulness of Callicles to the interests of Charmides, the refusal of Lesbonicus to let his sister marry in a
manner beneath her dignity, and his final decision to give up
his extravagances, — are treated, not as lovely illustrations of
virtuous conduct, but as matters of no great consequence; nor
are they ever represented as being caused by an appeal to
the feelings. In the final scene, for example, when Lesbonicus meets his father, there is no pathetic repentance and
forgiveness. His marriage to Callicles' daughter is not looked
upon as either the means or the reward of his promised change
of conduct; it is disposed of gaily. On being offered the girl's
hand he nonchalantly says: " I 'll marry her, father, — and
another girl too if you wish." [1] In the drama of sensibility
the comic spirit is not allowed to play lightly with such situations, as may be seen in an eighteenth-century adaptation of
Trinummus, Destouches' *Le Trésor Caché* (1745).

[1] Act V, scene iii.

In Destouches' play, a sentimental comedy, the love affair of Lesbonicus [1] is treated in a serious manner. In the presence of Callicles' daughter he deplores his prodigality, and by his sorrow arouses her sympathy and love.[2] Accordingly, when Charmides returns and angrily refuses to forgive his son, she declares her willingness to marry the scapegrace even if he be disinherited; for, she says, "his goodness of heart is sufficient assurance that he will for my sake conduct himself well." Lesbonicus himself mournfully confesses his errors, and Charmides is so deeply moved that he forgives him. "Too long," he declares, "have I done violence to the impulses of my heart; now I can no longer contain them." [3] The sentimentalizing of the relationship between father and son appears in many other passages, but these are sufficient to illustrate the contrast. The very scenes which render *Le Trésor Caché* a sentimental comedy are absent in *Trinummus*. With what seems to be deliberate intention, such scenes were avoided in the comedies of Plautus.

Terence, more frequently than Plautus, was in the eighteenth century said to be the inspirer of modern sentimental comedy. Though this assertion was never vigorously combatted, it did not pass unchallenged. Christophe Fagan, himself an experimenter in sentimental comedy, admitted that the work of Terence was of a different type since it did not "display the lovable and the perfect." [4] Chassiron, a notable opponent of the drama of sensibility, granted that there were one or two pathetic scenes in Terence, but these, he maintained, were merely episodic, whereas in contemporary dramatists such scenes had become dominant; and he firmly denied that sentimental comedy was sanctioned by the practice of the ancients.[5]

---

[1] To prevent confusion, I retain Plautus' names for the characters.
[2] Act IV, scene iii.   [3] Act V, scene vii.
[4] C. B. Fagan, Preface of *L'Amitié Rivale* (1736), *Œuvres* (1760), I, 210.
[5] Chassiron, *Réflexions sur le Comique Larmoyant* (1749).

Alexis Piron, who was qualified to distinguish between sentimental comedy and true comedy inasmuch as he had written
in each of those styles, said : " The masters of literature have,
to be sure, allowed Chremes to be angry and to inveigh, —

> Interdum iratus tumido delitigat ore, —

but they have not permitted him to despair or to weep."[1] Oliver
Goldsmith, though believing that Terence had made the nearest
approaches to the sentimental, asserted that he " always judi-
ciously stops short before he comes to the downright pathetic."[2]

By far the majority of the critics, however, maintained the
opposite opinion. It is a significant fact that though the doctrine of Terence's sentimentality was most extensively preached
in France, it arose in England. The first writer on sentimental
comedy to interpret Terence in this manner was Richard Steele.
In *The Spectator*, No. 502, he wrote as follows :

> I drew this morning conclusions of their [the Romans'] eminence
> in what I think great, to wit, in having worthy sentiments, from
> reading a comedy of Terence. The play was *The Self-Tormentor*. It
> is from the beginning to the end a perfect picture of human life, but
> I did not observe in the whole one passage that could raise a laugh.
> How well-disposed must that people be who could be entertained with
> satisfaction by so sober and polite mirth ! In the first scene of the
> comedy, when one of the old men accuses the other of impertinence
> for interposing in his affairs, he answers: " I am a man, and cannot
> help feeling any sorrow that can arrive at man." It is said this sen-
> tence was received with an universal applause.

In a postscript to No. 521, he added :

> There are in the play of *The Self-Tormentor* of Terence, which is
> allowed a most excellent comedy, several incidents which would draw
> tears from any man of sense, and not one which would move his
> laughter.

---

[1] A. Piron, Preface of *Les Fils Ingrats* (1758 ?), *Œuvres*, ed. Rigoley de
Juvigny (1776), I, 15.

[2] Goldsmith, "An Essay on the Theatre," *Westminster Magazine* (1772),
I, 4. Reprinted in Goldsmith, *The Good Natured Man*, ed. Austin Dobson
(1903), pp. 125–130.

Nothing could better illustrate the manner in which the real nature of Terence's plays was distorted in eighteenth-century criticism than Steele's translation of the famous line,

Homo sum: humani nihil a me alienum puto.

Instead of literally interpreting this utterance as meaning that to a man nothing whatever in human nature can lack interest, the man of feeling must needs consider it as declaring specifically that the sorrows of man arouse human sympathy; and presently we have Colman, in a mood similar to Steele's, translating the verse:

> I am a man; and all calamities
> That touch humanity, come home to me.

The maxim, detached from its context, may indeed serve as a serious and noble sentiment; and as such it was quoted by Cicero and Seneca.[1] But when it is used to express the general spirit of *Heautontimorumenos*, violence is done to truth. As a matter of fact, the line was originally intended to be amusing.[2] It is the lame apology made by Chremes, that persistent meddler in the affairs of his neighbors, when he is replying to the sarcastic inquiry how he happens to have so much time to bestow upon other people's business. In the course of the play, furthermore, the inquisitiveness of Chremes is represented, not as bringing him the gratitude of his fellows, but as leading him into comic predicaments.

In *Heautontimorumenos*, Steele had seized upon an inept illustration of his doctrine concerning Terence, nor was he in that particular often followed by subsequent critics; but the doctrine in its general bearings met with approval in England, and especially in France. Steele's remarks gave rise to the first passage of French criticism in which Terence was brought

---

[1] Cicero, *De Legibus*, I, xii; *De Finibus*, iii, 19. Seneca, Epistle 95.
[2] The tradition to the contrary rests on St. Augustine, Epistle 51.

into connection with sentimental comedy. Having been quoted and defended in *The Universal Spectator*,[1] they were thence translated by the Abbé Prévost, who in *Le Pour et Contre* periodically acquainted Frenchmen with English literary matters. "It concerns," he added, "the partisans of the new method of comedy to make use of the arms which I herewith furnish them for their defense."[2] The notion was widely spread by Marmontel's article on Comedy in *L'Encyclopédie*, which declared that sentimental comedy was no new thing, and found it "hard to understand how this error can have subsisted a moment among a people accustomed to representations of *Andria*, at which one weeps from the first act." Grimm remarked: "La Chaussée is no more the inventor of this class of play than I am, for it was known to the ancients"; and Bougainville maintained before the Academy that "it was known to the author of *Andria*, and perhaps we owe it to the reformer of Greek comedy." Diderot, seeking support for the drama of sensibility, said: "I call attention to the beautiful passages in Terence, and I ask in what style of comedy his scenes between fathers and lovers are written?" Even the aged Voltaire, at a time when he had become bitterly hostile to the new comedy, granted that there were one or two pathetic scenes in Terence. Under the influence of French criticism, similar opinions arose in Germany: Gellert considered his own sentimental plays justified by the example of Terence, and Lessing agreed with him.[3] *Eunuchus*, *Phormio*, and (except by Steele) *Heautontimorumenos*, were, however, regarded as

---

[1] No. 339. Cf. *The Lay Monastery*, No. 54. *The Universal Spectator* attributed the remarks to Addison. Cf. *The Gentleman's Magazine* (1735), V, 186.

[2] *Le Pour et Contre* (1737), XII, 148.

[3] *L'Encyclopédie* (1753), III, 668. F. M. Grimm, *Correspondance Littéraire*, 1 April, 1754. Bougainville, in La Chaussée's *Œuvres* (1777), I, xv. Diderot, *Œuvres* (1875), VII, 311. Voltaire, *Œuvres* (1878), XVII, 420. Lessing, *Werke* (1890), VI, 32–33.

comedies of intrigue. The sentimental comedies were supposed
to be *Adelphi*, *Hecyra*, and *Andria*.

The last of these has been called a sentimental comedy more
frequently than any other Roman play. In it Simo tries to put
an end to a suspected love-affair between his son Pamphilus
and Glycerium, the alleged sister of an Andrian courtesan.
To break off this apparently imprudent entanglement, Simo
directs that a wedding feast be prepared, and purposes to order
his son to marry within two hours the daughter of his friend
Chremes. His resolve might well lead to a serious conflict;
but in the very first scene Terence informs his audience that
Simo has not gained the consent of Chremes to the match,
that the wedding preparations are a pretense, and that Pamphilus stands in no immediate danger of having to marry.
Consequently, when Pamphilus enters, worried by the thought
of being forced to give up Glycerium, he appears no genuinely
pathetic figure but simply the amusing victim of his father's
trick.[1] Again and again in *Andria*, the complicated intrigue
of which it is here unnecessary to follow, Terence thus renders
the perplexities of his personages ridiculous. When the lover
of Chremes' daughter thinks he has a rival in Pamphilus, his
despair amuses an audience which knows better.[2] When the
rascally Davus seems to be betraying the interests of Glycerium,
and thereby arousing the fears of her maid, all in the theatre are
aware that the clever slave is really aiding her cause.[3] Throughout, the persons in the play are laboring under misunderstandings which the spectator knows to be absurd.

In *Andria* life is regarded as an amusing game, victory in
which is determined partly by superior gifts for intrigue, and
partly by the incalculable accidents of fortune. It is not the
possession of virtues that confers success. Pamphilus defeats

---

[1] Act I, scenes i and vi.   [2] Act II, scene i; Act IV, scene v.

[3] Act IV, scenes iv–vii.

his father's efforts to prevent his union with Glycerium; but in doing so he finally relies, not upon an appeal to paternal affection, but upon the fact that Glycerium proves to be a long-lost daughter of Chremes and thus eligible for marriage. Compare with Terence's attitude towards the situation that of Steele in his sentimental comedy, *The Conscious Lovers*, which is based on *Andria*. Here the recognition of Glycerium by Chremes [1] is regarded, not as the fortuitous ending of a course of plots and counter-plots, but as the just reward for the purity and constancy of the lovers. Against the objections of their elders, Steele's lovers contend with no arts of deception; on the contrary, in a strongly pathetic scene [2] (absent from the original) their candor and conscientiousness is glorified, and they are blessed in the approving words: "Your happiness is owing to your constancy and merit." Precisely those qualities of characterization and action which make *The Conscious Lovers* sentimental are changes and additions by Steele, and are not found in the true comedy of Terence.

When Diderot sought in classical comedy a precedent for the drama of sensibility, he believed that he had found it in *Hecyra*. His *Réflexions sur Térence* ascribed the failure of *Hecyra* to the following causes:

> The poet had banished the comic personages from it. Purposing to introduce a taste for comedy entirely grave and serious, he did not understand that this kind of dramatic composition will not admit of a feeble scene, and that force of action and dialogue must everywhere take the place of gayety in the subordinate characters. [3]

In his famous *Entretiens sur Le Fils Naturel* he wrote:

> Terence has composed a play of which this is the subject. A young man marries. Scarcely is he married, when business calls him into another country. He departs. He returns. He believes that he sees

---

[1] Steele names these characters Indiana and Mr. Sealand.
[2] Act V, scene iii.   [3] *Œuvres*, V, 230–231.

in his wife unmistakable proofs of infidelity. He is in despair. He wants to send her back to her parents. Judge of the state of the father, the mother, and the daughter! There is, to be sure, also one Davus, a comic personage. What has the poet done with him? He has kept him off the stage during the first four acts, and not summoned him except to enliven the dénouement a little.

I ask to what type this play belongs. Is it a comedy? There is not a word of laughter. A tragedy? Terror and pity are not excited by it. Nevertheless it has interest. And without ridiculous matters to arouse laughter, without dangers to make one tremble, there will be interest in every dramatic composition of which the subject is important, in which the poet imitates the tone of our serious concerns, and in which the action is advanced by means of perplexity and embarrassment . . . I shall call this kind of play ' le genre sérieux.' [1]

Is this interpretation of *Hecyra* true as a whole; if not, has it any support in details?

Diderot's outline of *Hecyra* describes the play as Diderot himself would have written it rather than as Terence actually did. The principal character, Pamphilus, a youth enamoured with the courtesan Bacchis, has been forced to marry Philumena; but, hoping that his wife will leave him, has never consummated the marriage. Just as he is growing tired of Bacchis, and turning his affections towards Philumena, he has to go on a journey. He leaves his wife in charge of his mother, Sostrata. During his absence, Philumena, for reasons unintelligible to her father-in-law, returns to her family. Attempts to fix the blame for her departure result in amusing scenes of recrimination: Laches, father of Pamphilus, scolds Sostrata for disrupting the family by her irritable disposition; and Phidippus, father of Philumena, eagerly protests that it is not he who is at fault.

When Pamphilus arrives home, he discovers the secret cause: his wife has been ravished by an unknown, two months before her marriage, and is about to become a mother. Though he is not expected to retain her, her mother Myrrhina begs him to

---

[1] *Œuvres*, VI, 135.

keep the secret, and he consents to do so. His attempts to
conceal the real state of affairs (known, as usual, to the audience) from Laches, Sostrata, and Phidippus lead to the comic
situations which ensue. His excuse for not bringing home
Philumena is the alleged antipathy between his wife and his
mother, — an explanation which again brings down the wrath
of Laches upon the perplexed Sostrata. Then Phidippus discovers his daughter's condition, and Myrrhina defends herself
from his anger by assuring him that the child is legitimate.
Phidippus, with a proud grandfatherly air, announces the birth
of the child. All congratulate the unhappy Pamphilus, who is
of course expected to receive the news with joy. When he
still protests against receiving his wife, both grandfathers are
indignant. They hit upon the notion that his real reason must
be his infatuation with the courtesan Bacchis.

Bacchis is thereupon summoned. She informs Laches that
her relations with Phidippus have ceased, and consents to assure
Philumena of that fact. Thereby she becomes the means of
unraveling the mystery; for she wears a ring, formerly given
to her by Phidippus, and now recognized as one torn from
Philumena by the ravisher. Thus it transpires that the father
of Philumena's child is none other than Phidippus himself. Of
course he is now willing to rejoin her; but, it should be noted,
he does not explain the entire truth either to her father or to
his parents, who remain to the end the unwitting victims of
trickery. Without adducing additional evidences of the comic
spirit in this play, such as the doings of the slave Parmenon,
it is clear that Terence has conducted the plot as a whole in a
truly comic manner.

Though there is no eighteenth-century version of *Hecyra*
suitable for comparison with it,[1] the manner in which a senti-

---

[1] Henry Brooke's *The Charitable Association* (1778) does not follow *Hecyra*,
its source, closely enough.

mental dramatist would treat this story may fairly be set forth
on the analogy of transmutations like *The Conscious Lovers*.
The opportunities for idealizing some of the characters, and
rendering some of the scenes pathetic, would have been improved. The innocence of Philumena would have been shown
in a sympathetic light; the tearful appeal to Pamphilus would
have resulted not only in his safeguarding her secret, but also
in his pitying her wronged innocence; and the final discovery
would be an instance of poetical justice, — a reward for his
faith in her. His parents, instead of being ignorant of Philumena's misfortune and eager to unite her with him, would have
known the truth about her condition, would have opposed his
forgiving her, and would have consented to the reunion only
when their own hearts had been softened by the unhappiness
of the lovers. In some such fashion Diderot himself would
have written the play, in order that it might conform to his
critical principles. By his remarks on *Hecyra* he put himself
into the curious position of approving a comedy that gaily sports
with domestic relations which he deemed too sacred to become
the playthings of the Comic Muse.

Though *Hecyra* in its general spirit, main action, and chief
personages is a true comedy, it contains two passages[1] which
might indeed seem pathetic to a man of sensibility. The situation of Pamphilus, wearying of his rapacious mistress and turning
his thoughts toward his neglected wife,[2] would stir in him an
emotion which was constantly appealed to in such plays as *The
Careless Husband*. This episode has, however, no decisive influence on the main course of the action; and it is described
by a low comedy character, a garrulous slave quite unfit to call

---

[1] A. F. Villemain, *Cours de Littérature Française, Dix-huitième Siècle* (1858),
I, 295, suggests a third, — Act I, scene ii. But Sostrata's offer to withdraw
to the country, made in ignorance of the true situation, puts her son into a
ridiculous plight. [2] Act I, scene ii.

forth pathetic feelings. More interesting is the passage in which Pamphilus recounts his discovery of Philumena's condition, and his promise to her pleading mother not to betray her secret.[1] Had Terence continued in that mood, had he made this episode an important incident, had he glorified it as a deed of virtue bringing the just reward of happiness, he would have written a sentimental comedy. But as a matter of fact it is purely episodic; and, instead of being interpreted as the conduct of a hero, it is shown to be that of a soft-hearted fool, leading him into absurd predicaments. Neither the situation between the husband and the wife, nor that between the parents and the children, is ultimately settled by an appeal to the feelings.

Not even an inconsequential departure from the comic mood is found in *Adelphi*. It is the original of the many plays which depict the different consequences of too rigorous and too indulgent systems of education. Demea has reared one of his sons under strict discipline, but has given his other son, Æschinus, into the adoption of his complaisant brother Micio. The latter, a Roman Rousseau, expects that freedom will induce his ward "to do right following his own impulses." At first the strict Demea is made a laughing-stock: the escapades of his son show him that tyranny may foster license. At that point the sentimentalist, departing from the comic mood, would proceed to idealize the liberal system. But Terence does not let the doting Micio escape so easily. Demea, perceiving that Micio's kindly temper has cheaply made him popular, himself begins to act as a dispenser of joys. He preaches benevolence, and insists that Micio shall marry the indigent Sostrata, — aged though she is. Micio, already sufficiently perplexed by the necessity of living up to his creed, is further desired to put his sentiments into practice by giving away his estate. Finally Demea advises him to free a rascally slave on the ironic ground

[1] Act III, scene ii.

that "he has taught the boys such noble lessons." With un-
concealed glee Demea explains to Micio his reasons for making
such demands, namely,

> Ut id ostenderem, quod te isti facilem et festivum putant,
> Id non fieri ex vera vita, neque adeo ex aequo et bono,
> Sed ex adsentando, indulgendo et largiendo, Micio.[1]

The serious moral truth, that exaggerated kindliness is as great
a folly as exaggerated severity, is thus driven home by delightfully comic means.

Genuine though sporadic instances of sentimental comedy before 1696 may, as we shall presently see, be found in French
and in English drama of the sixteenth and seventeenth centuries; but these were not of classical inspiration. When Roman
comedies were adapted by dramatists of the seventeenth century,
such adaptations (for example, those of *Andria* by Molière and
by Shadwell[2]) remained comic. It was not until 1710, — four-
teen years after sentimental comedy had begun its uninterrupted
career, — that the theory of sentimentalism in Roman comedy
was invented; and it was not until after 1721 that plays of
Terence and Plautus were made over into such sentimental
works as *The Conscious Lovers* (1722) and *Le Trésor Caché*
(1745). No author was ever made a sentimentalist by reading
Roman comedies; but when one who was already of that disposition criticized them or reworked them, his temperament
affected the result. In other cases, when the sense of humor
was not weakened by sensibility, the plays of Plautus and
Terence sustained, even in the eighteenth century, the spirit
of true comedy.[3]

---

[1] Act V, scene ix.
[2] *L'Ecole des Maris* and *The Squire of Alsatia*.
[3] An attempt to show that among the lost plays of antiquity there were
comedies more sentimental than those of Terence, was made by Richard
Cumberland in his dedication of *The Choleric Man* (1774).

CHAPTER III

EARLY APPROACHES TO THE DRAMA OF SENSIBILITY

The heyday of sentimentalism was the eighteenth century, and some have attempted to ascribe its appearance solely to the social conditions of that period. But the desire to think well of mankind is too constant and powerful a yearning of the human heart not to find occasional expression in the literature of any nation and any age. It is therefore not surprising to find in the drama of the sixteenth and early seventeenth centuries plays which, however distinct in their style and their picture of manners from those of a later period, approach in spirit closely to the eighteenth-century dramas of sensibility. The early dramatists of England and of France, independently of each other, now and then treated domestic themes in a sentimental manner, and, despite differences of national character, produced plays of strikingly similar sort.

In France and in England the morality was the parent of sentimental comedy. The first extant French play of the latter type was *La Moralité de l'Enfant Prodigue*, published in 1535, but doubtless written much earlier. The anonymous author, following rather inexactly the parable of St. Luke, represents the prodigal son beginning his course of dissipation, and the father mourning therefor. The elder son urges him to cast adrift the prodigal, who has stolen money to make good his gambling debts, but the father out of pity refuses. The prodigal, having again lost his money, is thrown out of a brothel, and goes to herd swine. His master suspects his real position, learns the truth from him, and induces him to return home. On the way,

the repentant youth meets L'Ami de Bonnefoy, who promises
to make the father forgive all his son's faults. With tears of
joy, he is received by his father, who does not neglect to point
him out to the spectators as an example of repentant folly.
The story, it is interesting to observe, has ceased to be a sacred
parable : it is no longer an allegory teaching the infinitude of
divine compassion ; it has become a pathetic tale of everyday life, idealizing human mercy.

A dramatization of a non-biblical story is *La Moralité d'une
Pauvre Villageoise*.[1] Herein a nameless lord tries to seduce
the country maid Esglantine, daughter of his tenant Grouxmoulu. After she has with virtuous indignation rejected his
offer of money, he orders his servant to seize her by force ;
but Grouxmoulu strikes the man with an axe, and drives him
away. Then the lord himself goes to the hut, and amid the
jeers of his man beats Grouxmoulu with his sword. Esglantine
begs that she be allowed to talk for a moment with Grouxmoulu
alone ; they withdraw, and she begs her father to cut off her
head to save her from dishonor. The lord is listening, is seized
with pity, and just as Grouxmoulu raises his hand to kill Esglantine, he tears open the door, arrests the blow, and addresses the
maiden :

> O vénérable créature
> Sur toutes bonnes la régente,
> Je renonce à ma folle cure ;
> Pardonnez-moi, pucelle gente.
> Levez-vous, sur tost excellente,
> En vertu la source et fontaine,
> De chastété la fleur regnante,
> Et en vous d'odeur souveraine.
>
> .   .   .   .
>
> Mais votre constance certaine
> M'en faict avoir compassion.

---

[1] Dated 1536. It was revived in 1580. Cf. Parfaict Frères, *Histoire du
Théatre Français* (1745), III, 145–150 ; and Emile Faguet, *La Tragédie Française
au Seizième Siècle* (1883), pp. 367–368.

He crowns her with a garland, makes the father an overseer,
and frees them both from villenage. The theme, — none other
than that of Pamela, — was to become a favorite in eighteenth-
century literature, the only difference being that sixteenth-
century social conditions made the marriage of a lord to a
poor village maiden almost unthinkable.

L'Enfant Ingrat (1540) is termed, not a morality, but a
"history." [1] It begins cheerfully : A father and a mother are
congratulating each other on the apparent worthiness of their
son, for whose career they are saving money. They apprentice
him to a merchant, but soon the spoiled youth leaves his em-
ployment. Richly dressed, and attended by one of his master's
servants, he comes to the castle of a lord, makes a good impression there, is invited to remain, and is offered the lord's
daughter in marriage. He promptly accepts the offer, and
guarantees that his parents will transfer all their property to
him, — a promise which they gladly enable him to keep. The
wedding is celebrated with festive music and an interlude.

Presently his parents, finding themselves in need, come to
his house asking aid. He offers them nothing except a piece
of brown bread, and insults them when they protest. A second
time his father begs relief, but is ignominiously driven away.
The weeping parents heap maledictions on the ingrate, and
the father solemnly curses him. The divine punishment is
immediate : as the son is cutting open a pie, a frog leaps out
and covers his face. In terror he seeks relief from the curé,
from the bishop, finally from the Pope himself. The Pope,
convinced of his repentance, absolves him ; and the frog dis-
appears. The son returns home, falls at his parents' feet, and
receives their forgiveness. Especially in its grotesque element,
L'Enfant Ingrat appears a dramatization of a "conte dévot."
It is a more ambitious attempt than the preceding sentimental

[1] Cf. Parfaict, *Histoire*, III, 153–162.

comedies, having a greater number of characters and more variety of incident. Though still medieval in its supernatural features, it is free from the fetters of allegory, and aims to serve a moral purpose by portraying actual personages in pathetic situations.

The fantastic has not yet entirely disappeared from sentimental comedy in Louis Le Jars' *Lucelle* (1576),[1] but this is on the whole the best of the early French examples of the type. It is the romance of a poor young man, — again a theme that was to be employed in the eighteenth century.[2] Lucelle, a banker's daughter, is desired by her father to marry the Baron de Saint-Amour, but secretly she has fallen in love with her father's clerk Ascagne. Since the latter's humble position does not allow him to take the initiative, she must make the advances. This she does in a scene that is written with a delicacy of feeling singular in its age. The pathetic — and somewhat grotesque — situations thereupon begin. The lovers are discovered together. The father forces the youth to drink from a cup of poison, and bears his lifeless body before Lucelle, who laments grievously — and drinks the rest of the poison. But her devotion receives its due : the poison, it transpires, is only a sleeping draught, and the clerk is the son of a nobleman. The play, unlike its forerunners, is written in prose, which, Le Jars argued, gave a more natural effect to drama of ordinary life. Le Jars was thus advancing towards the sentimental comedy of the future, when the influence of classicism inhibited, for a century and a half, further progress in that direction.

Contemporary with the early French sentimental comedies were three plays that dealt with bourgeois characters but that

---

[1] It was versified by Du Hamel, and thus performed in 1604. Cf. Parfaict, *Histoire*, III, 377–379; and Faguet, *Tragédie*, pp. 373–381.

[2] For example, in Marivaux' *Les Fausses Confidences*. Cf. chap. x, below.

ended unhappily. These are, in a sense, domestic tragedies ;
but two of them differ in an essential respect, to be presently
pointed out, from the typical eighteenth-century dramas of
that kind. Nevertheless, since these tragedies present persons
not of exalted social rank, they anticipate at least one striking
characteristic of the future drama of sensibility, and on that
account demand attention.

The first of these "domestic tragedies" was, like the earliest
sentimental comedy, patterned upon the moralities. *La Moralité
de l'Enfant de Perdition* (1540),[1] the personages in which are
"le bourgeois," "la bourgeoise," "le fils du bourgeois," and
four highwaymen, is the story of a prodigal whose repentance
comes too late. In his condition and fate he resembles George
Barnwell, but his character stands in black contrast to that of
the well-intentioned London apprentice. Despising the appeals
of his lamenting father, he deliberately addicts himself to evil
courses, joins a band of highwaymen, and plots with them the
robbery and murder of his parent. In sight of the audience,
the father is hanged by this unnatural son ; and, to conceal the
crime, the mother is also murdered. In conclusion the highwaymen win the son's share of the booty, and leave him prey
to a remorse so terrible that he goes insane. This crude production seems to have been played more than half a century ;
it was reprinted as late as 1608.

Jean Bretog's *L'Amour d'un Serviteur envers sa Maistresse*
(1551),[2] like the Elizabethan *A Warning for Fair Women*,
retains allegorical characters like those in the moralities. They
are, in the French play, not confined to an induction or dumb
show but move among the human beings. Venus urges the

---

[1] Published at Lyon (1608). Reprinted in *Recueil de Livrets Singuliers* by
M. de Montaran (1829–1830).

[2] Lyon (1571); reprinted by G. Duplessis, Chartres (1831). Cf. Lanson,
La Chaussée, pp. 2–3; and Faguet, *Tragédie*, p. 369.

servant to seduce his mistress, Chastity vainly tries to inspire him with purity, and Jealousy incites the husband. In other respects the play, which professes to be based on an actual occurrence, aims to represent the temptation, fall, and discovery of the faithless wife as realistically as possible. The action moves very slowly, owing to Bretog's praiseworthy but unrealized desire to give psychological depth to his personages. At the end the wife is weeping bitterly; the husband dies of grief; and the servant, after a lengthy sermon on his crime, is led away to death, the spectators of his execution expressing their moral observations upon his conduct.

What is alleged to be a true story, and what is certainly a repulsive one, is dramatized in Claude Rouillet's *Philanire*,[1] originally (1556) published in Latin, but in 1560 performed in a French translation. "Some years ago," says Rouillet, "a lady of Piedmont obtained from the provost of the region a promise that her husband, then imprisoned on account of a brawl and about to be condemned to death, should be sent back to her, provided she would one night admit the provost to her chamber. That having been done, her husband was the next day sent back to her — but dead. She, lamenting, went to the governor, who, to secure her honor, compelled the provost to marry her, and thereafter had his head cut off, so that the lady remained bereft of two husbands." In the earlier portion of his play, Rouillet succeeded in sympathetically portraying Philanire, whose emotions as she realizes the price she must pay for her husband's release, and takes farewell of her children, are expressed in a natural and touching manner. When her second husband, the villainous provost, is executed, her lamentations appear, however, equally sincere, and the pathos of the style is lost in the monstrosity of the characterization.

---

[1] *Claudii Roilleti Belnensis Varia Poemata* (1556). *Philanire, femme d'Hippolyte* (1563 and 1577). Cf. Parfaict, III, 342; Faguet, pp. 369–371.

Philanire, despite its grotesqueness, which is owing to its source, represents a distinct advance over earlier domestic tragedies. Its merits are due to the classical learning of Rouillet, who tried to wring a Senecan terror from his domestic theme, brought in a chorus to lend its voice at the moment of greatest lamentation, and (what is more important) succeeded in individualizing his characters and conducting his plot with some skill. With less offensive subjects, French domestic tragedy might soon have developed really admirable work; but that very classical influence which worked beneficially upon *Philanire* operated to oppose further experimentation in this type of drama. Just as the goal was in sight, advance was prohibited. Against the victorious doctrines of the Pléiade, attempts to treat bourgeois life tragically could not prevail; and for almost two centuries (1560–1741) France produced no domestic tragedy.

The differences between the sentimental comedies of the sixteenth century and those of the eighteenth are obvious and superficial; the distinctions between most of the so-called "domestic tragedies" of the early period and those of the later, are profound. The "domestic tragedies" of sixteenth-century France and Elizabethan England resemble those of the future in that they show the fatal end of middle-class persons. But these persons, unlike those in sentimental comedy, are, as a rule, not amiable. Rouillet's heroine, Philanire, is in this respect quite exceptional; for it is evident that, however unconvincing she may seem to us, he regarded her as a model of noble conduct. The other authors of "domestic tragedy" in his time exhibited a different conception of human nature, one not at all characteristic of the drama of sensibility. They regarded their personages not as virtuous beings forced into disaster by circumstances beyond their control, but as miserable sinners who paid the just penalty for their crimes. In short, they were not sentimentalists.

That the ethical standards of Elizabethan "domestic tragedy" exhibit a decided contrast to those of sentimental drama may be shown by a comparison of *Arden of Feversham* (1591) and *A Woman Killed with Kindness* (1607), the most distinguished examples of their kind,[1] with the eighteenth-century domestic tragedies based upon them. *Arden of Feversham* is the most impressively somber among the French and English domestic dramas of its period. Though our sympathetic hopes are again and again raised by Arden's escape from death, we feel from the beginning that he will not elude the inexorable hatred to which he falls at last a victim. Several persons are concerned in his murder, but his wife Alice is the relentless force which drives them onward. Her crime is, indeed, motivated by her illicit passion for Mosbie, but it is never excused. From the outset, when, after hypocritical words of love to her husband, she reveals in soliloquy her yearning for his death, until the end, when she drives the dagger into his heart with the triumphant "Take this for hindering Mosbie's love and mine!" we are left in no doubt as to her full responsibility for the crime. She is unmistakably what Arden calls her, —

> Rooted in her wickedness,
> Perverse and stubborn, not to be reclaimed;
> Good counsel is to her as rain to weeds,
> And reprehension makes her vice to grow
> As Hydra's head that plenished by decay.[2]

---

[1] The group of plays which are commonly regarded as direct forerunners of eighteenth-century domestic tragedies includes the following: *A Warning for Fair Women, Arden of Feversham, Two Tragedies in One, A Woman Killed with Kindness, The Miseries of Enforced Marriage, A Yorkshire Tragedy, The Witch of Edmonton, The English Traveler, The Late Lancashire Witches,* and *The Vow Breaker.* Cf. J. A. Symonds, *Shakspere's Predecessors* (1884), chap. xi; H. W. Singer, *Das bürgerliche Trauerspiel in England* (1891); A. W. Ward, Introduction to Heywood's *A Woman Killed with Kindness* (1897), *History of English Dramatic Literature* (2d ed. 1899), II, 228 ff. and III, 493 ff., and Introduction to Lillo's *The London Merchant* (1906); and F. E. Schelling, *Elizabethan Drama* (1910), chap. vii.   [2] Act III, scene i.

In George Lillo's *Arden of Feversham* (1759), what a reformation has her character undergone! She is still, to be sure,
the cause of Arden's murder, and most of the incidents of the
play are the same; but the interpretation of her personality is
totally dissimilar. Mosbie had, according to Lillo, been the
love of her youth, and she had been married to Arden against
her will. It is not she, but Mosbie, who conceives the plan of
murdering Arden, a plan which is at first repellant to her gentle
nature. When her lover's urgings have persuaded her to attempt
Arden's life, and she has stolen, dagger in hand, to his bed-
side, pity for him disarms her, and she stands "irresolute and
drowned in tears." She refuses to continue her relations with
Mosbie, and her anguish of conscience is described as extreme:

> Her lovely, downcast eyes,
> That used to gladden each beholder's heart,
> Now wash the flinty bosom of the earth;
> Her troubled breast heaves with incessant sighs.[1]

Her remorse arouses the compassion of Arden; and, in a scene
of ecstatic happiness, she is reconciled to him, saying:

> The wand'ring fires that have so long misled me,
> Are now extinguished, and my heart is Arden's.
> The flowery path of innocence and peace
> Shines bright before, and I shall stray no longer.[2]

When Mosbie persists in seeking Arden's death, she does all
in her power to save her husband; and his murder drives her
insane. Of such is the kingdom of sensibility.

Thomas Heywood was of a much gentler temper than the
author of the Elizabethan *Arden of Feversham*, and does not
portray Mrs. Frankford, the central character in *A Woman
Killed with Kindness*, with such uncompromising rigor as his
predecessor visited upon Alice. She is, in her offense against

---

[1] Act IV, scene ii.   [2] Act IV, scene ii.

her husband, not eager and persistent: her infidelity to him
soon "clogs her soul" with disquietude, her deep repentance
reduces her to "the wofull'st wretch on earth, a woman made
of tears," and her contrition enables her to die "honest at
heart."[1] But Heywood makes it perfectly clear that neither
she nor her husband considers that she has "lived honest."
Blessed with children and a loving and generous husband, she
had every reason to preserve her marriage vow inviolate; yet
she listened without hesitation to the "enchanting tongue" of
her seducer. Frankford, though the mildest of men, calls her
a strumpet, and she herself recognizes that the term is just.
He shows "kindness" in exiling instead of slaying her, not
because he sees anything to exonerate her conduct, but because
the protracted bitterness of a lingering exile is a more fitting
penalty for her crime than instant death. And the pity which
he afterwards feels for her when her end is approaching, the
forgiveness he grants her, is not sympathy for an unfortunate
innocent but pardon for a repentant sinner.[2] It is precisely the
kind of pity that passes the understanding of the sentimentalist.
It conflicts with his disbelief in wilful sin. His notion of pity
is sympathy for a person who could not help his error; the
orthodox idea of pity is compassion towards one who knows
and owns his guilt.

A true sentimentalist was Benjamin Victor, who in 1776
published *The Fatal Error*, a three-act adaptation in stilted
prose of *A Woman Killed with Kindness*. In Heywood's play,
he tells us, he saw "several fine strokes of nature, on matri-
monial distress, brought in by female infidelity." "But," he
adds, "where the seducer brings the wife to consent, who is
happily situated with a young fond accomplished husband, it is
hardly possible to render her an object of pity." He thought

[1] Act IV, scene ii; Act V, scenes iii, v.
[2] Act IV, scene v; Act V, scene v.

to improve the original by "founding the husband's forgiveness on humanity," — that is, on sentimentalism. Accordingly his Mrs. Frankford, unlike Heywood's, "repulses with a proper indignation" the advances of her lover, and never consents to her undoing, which is brought about by her maid treacherously admitting the lover to her one night when her husband's absence has left her unprotected. She is thus the innocent victim of a ravisher, and her "fatal error" lies in not informing her husband at the first opportunity. That error, furthermore, proceeds from her maternal affection; she keeps silent for the "dear sakes" of her children.[1] Such was the process of exculpation that was necessary to convert Elizabethan "domestic tragedies" into dramas of sensibility.

Much closer approaches to such dramas are found in early comedy. In English comedy, as in French, manifestations of sentimentalism appear in sixteenth-century plays that are outgrowths of the moralities, in interludes like *The History of Jacob and Esau,* and in dramatic variations of the Prodigal Son theme; for example, *Acolastus, The Nice Wanton, Misogynus, The Disobedient Child,* and *The Glasse of Government.*[2] These were unknown at the beginning of the eighteenth century; but any instances of sentimentalism in the fully developed comedy of about 1600 to 1642 might well have been transmitted to the future. Among the hundreds of Elizabethan comedies, however, comparatively few that deal with contemporary English life present idealized characters and pathetic scenes. Such characters and scenes were as a rule set in distant times or places, — in an enchanted isle, an Italian city, or a forest of Arden. The sentimental portrayal of life was usually made

---

[1] Benjamin Victor, *The Fatal Error,* in his *Original Letters, Dramatic Pieces, and Poems* (1776), II, 81 ff. See especially pp. 81, 99, 102, 132, 134, 139–140.

[2] Cf. Charles M. Gayley, *Representative English Comedies,* Vol. I (1903), especially pp. lxx, lxxii, lxxiv, lxxx.

by means of romantic comedy. But this artistic practice was
not yet enforced by canons of criticism, and departures from
it were more frequent than in the contemporary comedy of
France.[1]

Heywood's *The Fair Maid of the West*, the history of the
fair Besse and her lover Spencer, has some serious passages;
but as the chief scenes are laid at the outlandish court of King
Mullisheg of Fez, it is worth mentioning here chiefly as an
illustration of the tendency of any work resembling a sentimental comedy to pass into a romantic setting. Among comedies
that are wholly confined to English life, some introduce a few
scenes of pathos, without allowing these to dominate the plot
or drive home the moral of the play. Thus in Middleton's
Michaelmas Term (1604) three scenes are in strange contrast
to the general spirit of this amusing comedy. "The country
wench's father" laments the disappearance of his daughter,
searches for her in the disreputable quarters of London, and
finds her a bold wanton. These episodes are sad; they lead,
however, to no reconciliation between father and daughter, nor
to repentance on the part of the seducer.[2] Middleton and
Rowley's *A Fair Quarrel* (1616) contains a tragic scene, in
which a mother defames herself to keep her son from taking
up arms in defense of her honor.[3] But the duel takes place:
Steele would have made the mother succeed in preventing it
by her pathetic appeal. In Cowley's *The Guardian* (1633), a
forged letter leads Truman to believe that his beloved Lucia is

---

[1] No special study of approaches to sentimental comedy in the drama prior
to 1642 has yet been published. Hazlitt calls *The Merry Devil of Edmonton*
"perhaps the first example of sentimental comedy we have." But this play,
in which "love, thwarted, turns itself to thousand wiles," is a true comedy
of intrigue. Cf. William Hazlitt, *Lectures on the Dramatic Literature of the
Age of Elizabeth* (1821), p. 221; and Robert Dodsley, *Old English Plays*, ed.
W. C. Hazlitt, X (1875), 202.

[2] Act II, scene ii; Act III, scene i; Act IV, scene ii.

[3] Act II, scene i.

faithless, and his grief is voiced at considerable length; but the dénouement, in which the lovers are united by means of a trick, is in no way dependent upon his temporary distress.[1]

Less insignificant are the pathetic passages in Heywood's *The Wise Woman of Hogsdon* (1604). It is in the main a comedy of intrigue; but Luce, the deserted mistress of Chartley, at moments arouses compassion. She makes the scapegrace lover her husband, however, not by tearfully begging him to do justice, but by cheating him into marrying her under a mistaken impression as to her identity. Heywood and Rowley's *Fortune by Land and Sea* (1607) is termed a "tragi-comedy."[2] In it Philip Harding has, against his father's will, married Susan Forest. They are treated with indignity, and forced to become servants in his father's house. The most pathetic scene is that in which the impoverished Old Forest begs the wealthy Old Harding to be more merciful to the lovers.[3] The younger brothers of Philip expect to be his heirs; but Old Harding dies intestate, and Philip thus comes into his own. By forgiving his unnatural brothers, he shows himself worthy of his good fortune.

Beaumont and Fletcher's *The Coxcomb* (1609) is noteworthy as containing the pathetic figure of Viola, who seems to have strayed, so to speak, from one of her creators' romantic comedies into this play of contemporary life. About to elope with her lover, she slips from her home at midnight, and with joyful anticipations stands waiting for him in the dark street. He reels drunkenly by, does not recognize the shrinking girl, and insults her with ribald jests as she flees into the night. Subsequently,

---

[1] Act III, scene iii; Act IV, scenes i and viii.

[2] Apparently because it contains a death, Dr. H. W. Singer (*Das bürgerliche Trauerspiel*, 1891) calls it a domestic tragedy, — an inapplicable term, for the person who dies is not the chief character, nor is his death (Act IV, scene i) meant to arouse either pity or terror.

[3] Act III, scene iii.

when he has come to his sober senses, he frantically seeks his
beloved, finds the broken-hearted Viola in the outskirts of the
city, and after expressing his sincere penitence obtains her forgiveness. Again, in Fletcher's *Monsieur Thomas* (1610?) there
are scenes unusual in realistic comedy. The story, though taken
from Bandello and retaining foreign names, is transferred to
English life. The elderly Valentine is about to marry his beloved ward Cellide. At the last moment he discovers that
Francis, a youth of whom he is very fond, secretly loves the
girl, and is in the deepest sorrow at the prospect of losing her.
He sacrifices his own affection to the younger man's passion,
and resigns Cellide to Francis. In each of these two plays, one
part of the double plot is a merry comedy of manners, and the
other is serious in tone.

Still more incongruous with its surroundings is the subplot
of Middleton's *A Mad World, my Masters* (1606). A physician, significantly named Penitent Brothel, seduces the citizen's
wife, Mistress Harebrain. Remorse seizes him. " Enter out of
his study Penitent Brothel, a book in his hand," saying :

> Ha? read that place again — " Adultery
> Draws the divorce 'twixt heaven and the soul."
> Accursed man, that stand'st divorced from heaven!
> Thou wretched unthrift, that hast played away
> Thy eternal portion at a minute's game;
> To please the flesh hast blotted out thy name!
> .   .   .   .
> Within these three days the next meeting's fixed;
> If I meet then, hell and my soul be mixed!
> .   .   .   .
> Sin's hate is the best gift that sin bestows:
> I 'll ne'er embrace her more; never, bear witness, never!

He resists temptation by " a succubus in the shape of Mistress
Harebrain "; and on seeing his paramour again renounces his
wickedness, and gravely admonishes her to reform, saying :

Live honest, and live happy; keep thy vows;
She 's part a virgin whom but one man knows.
Embrace thy husband, and beside him none;
Having but one heart, give it but to one.

Mistress Harebrain

I vow it on my knees, with tears true-bred;
No man shall ever wrong my husband's bed![1]

Nathaniel Field professed to intend his *Amends for Ladies* (1611) as a reparation for satirical remarks against women. Based partly upon Cervantes' *Il Curioso Impertinente,* the play deals with a Lady Perfect, whose husband is so morbidly suspicious that he instigates his friend Subtle to attempt her virtue. She repeatedly rejects Subtle.

Lady Perfect

For 't is not in thy power, wert thou the sweet'st
Of nature's children and the happiest,
To conquer me, nor in mine own to yield;
And thus it is with every pious wife.
Thy daily railing at my absent husband
Makes me endure thee worse; for let him do
The most preposterous, ill-relishing things,
To me they seem good, since my husband does 'em. . . .

Subtle

Zounds! I have wronged you, mistress; on my knees
I ask your pardon, and will nevermore
Attempt your purity. . . .

The Husband

Madam, wife,
Upon my knees, with weeping eyes, heaved hands,
I ask thy pardon; oh, sweet virtuous creature![2]

In both *A Mad World, my Masters* and *Amends for Ladies,* it should be noted, the serious passages form but small portions of the plays.

---

[1] Act IV, scenes i and iv.   [2] Act V, scene i.

There are moments of pathos in Chapman, Jonson, and Marston's *Eastward Hoe!* (1605). It is the story of "a prodigal child reclaimed." The idle apprentice Quicksilver is imprisoned on the charge of having embezzled from his master Touchstone. The doggerel in which he confesses his sins was probably intended to be amusing; yet his sincere repentance leads to a dénouement that can hardly be considered purely comic.

Quicksilver

Farewell, Cheapside; farewell sweet trade
Of goldsmiths all, that never shall fade;
Farewell, dear fellow prentices all,
And be you warned by my fall.

. . . .

So shall you thrive by little and little,
Scape Tyburn, Counters, and the Spittle.

Touchstone

And scape them shalt thou, my penitent and dear Francis!

Quicksilver

Master! . . .

Touchstone

I can no longer forbear to do your humility right. Arise, and let me honor your repentance with the hearty and joyful embraces of a father and friend's love. Quicksilver, thou hast eat into my breast, Quicksilver, with the drops of thy sorrow, and killed the desperate opinion I had of thy reclaim.[1]

In this scene it needs but little to metamorphose Touchstone and Quicksilver into the Thorowgood and George Barnwell of the eighteenth century. Yet even here obvious efforts are made to sustain the comic spirit; and the rest of the play is consistently a comedy of manners.

Like *Amends for Ladies*, Shirley's *The Example* (1634) shows the triumph of a virtuous wife. Debts have compelled

---

[1] Act V, scene v.

Sir Walter Peregrine to go to the wars. In his absence, Lord
Fitzavarice, a rich libertine, attempts to seduce Lady Peregrine.
He even threatens to kill her if she will not yield. Her firm
refusals, her distress at being exposed to such insults, arouse
his pity, and he craves forgiveness:

> Can there be a hope
> After so great a wrong to find a mercy?
> You must be more than woman, and you are so.
> It was the error of my soul that drew
> The heavy mist upon my eyes; they now
> See and admire your innocence. . . .

Lady Peregrine

If this be earnest, 't is a heavenly language.

Lord Fitzavarice

I feel a holy flame disperse rich heat
About me; the corruption of my blood
Is fallen away; and of that virtue which
A devil in me would have betrayed, I rise
A servant and admirer; live, oh live,
Thou best of wives, and practise still new wonders
Upon the heart of lust-transformed men,
Until time boast the example of thy faith
Hath purged the world, and taught us how to count
Our hours by thy miracles. . . .

Lady Peregrine

This is a noble change, and speaks his nature
Not barren when good seeds are trusted with it.

Subsequently he sends her, in acknowledgment of her goodness, a cancellation of all her husband's debts. Sir Walter,
returning, looks upon the gift as an evidence of infidelity;
but receives new proofs of Fitzavarice's honor and sincerity,
and is finally reunited in friendship with him.[1] A bourgeois

---

[1] Act III, scene i; Act V, scene ii.

counterpart of this story is the subplot of Dekker's *The Shoe-maker's Holiday* (ca. 1597), where the virtuous conduct of the shoemaker's wife so impresses her wealthy pursuer that he generously rescues her husband and herself from poverty.

A still larger element of seriousness enters into Robert Tailor's *The Hog hath lost his Pearl* (1613), which is interesting also because it was written for London apprentices to act. One half of it is boisterously comic; the other is from beginning to end pathetic. Maria is waiting at the chamber window for her lover Carracus, with whom she has agreed to elope. His friend Albert, who is to aid in their escape, arrives first, and cannot resist the temptation which the dark night offers him: he climbs into the window, is received by the unwitting maiden as her husband, and makes his exit, — promising to return immediately. Carracus arrives, carries off Maria, and marries her. Albert, seized with remorse for his betrayal of friendship and love, withdraws to a hermitage. A month later, by means of a ring left in the chamber, the wrong is discovered; the husband goes mad, and the wife wanders about distracted, seeking death by starvation. Both come upon the hermitage. Albert succors the fainting Maria, restores Carracus to reason, and implores them to pardon his crime. In gratitude for his aid, they forgive him.[1]

Equally unmistakable approaches to sentimental comedy are found in four of the Elizabethan plays that deal with a husband who maltreats his virtuous and patient wife but who finally reforms. In *How a Man may choose a Good Wife from a Bad* (1602), Master Arthur, having fallen in love with a courtesan, tries to rid himself of his wife by giving her what he supposes to be poison, but what is really a sleeping draught. After she has been carried to the tomb, he marries the courtesan. His

[1] Dodsley's *Old English Plays*, ed. W. C. Hazlitt, XI, 423 ff., especially pp. 439, 443, 456, 460, 474, 483.

"bad wife," to whom he confides his crime, makes him miserable, and will not conceal his secret. Fleeing from justice, he meets a charitable woman, who relieves his wants, and in whom he fails to recognize his virtuous wife. To this sympathetic stranger he explains that he is mourning for a friend who poisoned a good wife and is now bitterly remorseful.

Young Arthur

Why weep you, mistress? If you had the heart
Of her whom you resemble in your face, —
But she is dead, and for her death
The sponge of either eye
Shall weep red tears till every vein is dry.

Mrs. Arthur

Why weep you, friend? Your rainy drops pray keep;
Repentance wipes away the drops of sin.

.   .   .   .

Yet say one like her, far more chaste than fair,
Bids him be of good comfort, not despair.
Her soul's appeased with his repentant tears,
Wishing he may survive her many years.

Arthur is arrested, and about to be condemned to death, when his forgiving wife appears, and brings their sufferings to a happy conclusion.[1]

The second of the plays in this group, *The Fair Maid of Bristow* (1602), so much resembles the first as to make description superfluous.[2] The third is *The London Prodigal* (1603), in which Flowerdale deserts his wife, Luce, owing to her loss of a dowry, becomes a thieving vagabond, and is suspected of having murdered his bride. She has, however, disguised herself as a Dutch maid-servant, and reveals her identity when he is in danger of imprisonment.

[1] Act V, scenes ii and iii.
[2] In the introduction to his edition (1902) of *The Fair Maid of Bristow*, Dr. A. H. Quinn makes a special study of these "neglected wife" plays.

Luce

O Master Flowerdale, if too much grief
Have not stopped up the organs of your voice,
Then speak to her that is thy faithful wife!
Or doth contempt of me thus tie thy tongue?
Turn not away; I am no Aethiop,
No wanton Cressid, nor a changing Helen,
But rather one made wretched by thy loss.
What, turn'st thou still from me? O then
I guess thee wofull'st among hapless men.

Flowerdale

I am indeed, wife, wonder among wives!
Thy chastity and virtue hath infused
Another soul in me, red with defame,
For in my blushing cheeks is seen my shame.[1]

The last of these plays, George Wilkins' *The Miseries of Enforced Marriage* (1605), which will be presently considered in
relation to the Restoration play based upon it,[2] combines sentimental comedy not only with comedy of manners but also with
"domestic tragedy." This combination, with the comic element excluded, — an exclusion which of course deepens the
emotional effect of the drama as a whole, — appears in Heywood's *A Woman Killed with Kindness* (1603), the subplot of
which shows the virtuous Susan Mountford refusing, even to
save her brother and herself from destitution, to accept the
illicit advances of Sir Francis Acton:

I spurn his gold!
My honor never shall for gain be sold.

Sir Francis, touched with admiration, finally makes her his wife.[3]

In some respects the nearest approach in this period to
sentimental comedy, in the strict sense of the term, is Rowley's

---

[1] Act V, scene ii.
[2] Mrs. Behn's *The Town Fop*; see chap. iv, below.
[3] Act III, scene iii; Act V, scene i.

A New Wonder: A Woman never Vexed (1631). Based
upon the careers of two wealthy and public-spirited London
merchants, Stephen Foster and Walter Bruin, it is intimately
related to the daily life and business of the commercial class.
The serious portion of the play deals with Old Foster, his
brother Stephen, and his son Robert. Stephen has been a
shiftless and unsuccessful merchant. Twice his older brother
has released him from a debtors' prison ; now he refuses to do
so a third time, and forbids Robert to associate with the bankrupt. But Robert is of a tender-hearted nature : he releases
his uncle, and is thereupon disowned by his father. Stephen
is fortunate enough to gain the love of the " woman never
vexed," a wealthy widow. He marries her, reforms, and dili-
gently increases her property. He is raised to the dignity of
an alderman, and rebuilds Ludgate. Robert he welcomes to
his home, takes into his business, and looks upon as his heir.

Old Foster in the meantime has invested all his capital in
one trading venture. When his ships are wrecked, he is in his
turn thrown into debtors' prison. To his astonishment Robert,
defying the supposed orders of Stephen, comes to visit him,
and relieves his wants. It transpires that Stephen has desired
this outcome, and in the end the family of Foster is happily
reunited. Several of the scenes, especially that in Ludgate
between Robert and his father, are affecting. Though there
is nothing in the language or manners that is not contemporary, the action is laid in a former age. On that account,
A New Wonder does not conform to the type of sentimental
comedy as closely as the principal plot of *The Miseries of Enforced Marriage* or the subplot of *A Woman Killed with
Kindness*. On the other hand, the comic element is in
Rowley's play not so destructive of the total impression as
it is in Wilkins', and the serious element is much more conspicuous than the subplot of Heywood's. Without instancing

other clear or dubious cases, it is evident that Elizabethan comedy not infrequently bordered so closely on sentimental comedy as to produce a similar artistic and ethical effect.

The eighteenth-century dramas of sensibility were steps in an uninterrupted literary movement; they formed a large proportion of all the plays of their period; and their sentimentalism was a more or less conscious attitude towards life. The Elizabethan plays that resemble them were, on the contrary, disconnected and sporadic; they were few in number; and what seems like sentimentalism in them was probably a temporary and unconsidered mood. They were unsupported by a contemporary sentimental movement in popular taste or ethical thought. Yet these plays of domestic life showed scenes of sorrow and characters of virtue. They might well have served as sources of inspiration to the founders of the eighteenth-century drama of sensibility. Did they, as a matter of historical fact, exercise such influence?

CHAPTER IV

THE INHIBITION OF SENTIMENTALISM FROM PLAYS
OF DOMESTIC LIFE: 1660–1695

Many tragedies and comedies by Beaumont and Fletcher, Shakespeare, and Jonson, became stock plays after the Restoration, in either their original or an adapted form; and the sources of new plays were often Elizabethan. One might reasonably expect that between 1660 and 1695 a considerable portion of the Elizabethan domestic plays with sentimental tendencies would have been revived, remodelled, or used as sources. Of the seventeen comedies discussed in the previous chapter, however, twelve seem not to have thus reappeared during this period.[1] Two of the remaining five comedies were in their original form only slightly pathetic, and did not in their transformation become more so. *Monsieur Thomas* passed into D'Urfey's *Trick for Trick* (1678), with a suppression of the serious passages between Valentine and Francis. *Eastward Hoe!* became the source of Tate's *Cuckold's Haven* (1685), but the affectionate Touchstone did not remain a sympathetic figure.

Cowley's *The Guardian* reappeared as *The Cutter of Coleman Street* (1661) at the very beginning of the Restoration. The serious passages, brief in *The Guardian*, were shortened in *The Cutter*, which, after 1661, was laid aside for over forty years. Shirley's *The Example* was performed at some time

---

[1] Cf. John Downes, *Roscius Anglicanus* (1708), and John Genest, *Some Account of the English Stage* (1832), I and II. The lists given in these works are, of course, not complete.

between 1663 and 1682. Here again the serious passages were not very conspicuous, nor does the play seem to have been performed in more than one season. It can hardly be maintained that either of these revivals was significant.

The plays under discussion were recovered from oblivion in only one really noteworthy instance. Disguised under the title of *The Town Fop*, there appeared in 1676 an adaptation, by Mrs. Behn, of George Wilkins' *The Miseries of Enforced Marriage*. The Elizabethan play, though relieved by touches of low comedy, is a gloomy picture of the distressful consequences that a compulsory marriage brought upon one William Scarborough. He had most solemnly vowed eternal constancy to his beloved, Clare; and his forced marriage leads her, in order to prevent his committing what she considers adultery, to kill herself. The news of her tragic end drives Scarborough to violent hatred of his wife Katherine, which even the birth of children to them fails to soften. He joins a roistering band, wastes his money in dissipation, and ruins the prospects of his brothers and sister. When the fortunes of the family are desperate, a faithful old butler, hoping to reunite his master and mistress, brings Katherine and her children before Scarborough, only to meet with repulse and threats of murder. (In the eighteenth century, this emotional appeal would not have failed.) Not until the parson who joined them in marriage points out the cruel wickedness of his conduct, does Scarborough relent and reform. Opportunely he falls heir to an estate. He begs forgiveness of the patient Katherine, and they are reconciled amid tears of joy. A situation which logically should end in disaster, is thus forcibly brought to a happy issue.[1]

Most of the alterations which Mrs. Behn made in transforming *The Miseries* into *The Town Fop* show that she

[1] The important scenes are Act I, scene ii; Act II, scene ii; and Act V, scene ii.

thought the original overburdened with pathos. She expunged the tragic death of Clare, and broadened the comic passages. Remarkably enough, however, she retained much of the sentimental element. Her hero Bellmour (corresponding to Scarborough) and her heroine Celinda (Clare), defying the commands of his uncle, plight their troth in an impressive scene ; and when Bellmour is ordered to marry Diana (Katherine), he, weeping, protests that his " second marriage " means " adultery." But his tears are unavailing ; the forced marriage is made ; and at the wedding festival Bellmour receives this note from Celinda :

> I have took in the poison which you sent in those few fatal words, " Forgive me, my Celinda, I am married," — 't was thus you said, — and I have only life to return, " Forgive me, my sweet Bellmour, I am dead."

The statement is false ; but Bellmour, believing it true, promptly leaves Diana, who, in turn, runs off with an unknown youth, — none other than Celinda disguised as a page.

Celinda thus learns that Bellmour has really been faithful to her, but great distresses are yet to visit them. The despairing Bellmour sinks to the lowest levels of society, and, loathing himself, exclaims :

> I will not die ; that peace my sins deserve not.
> I 'll live and let my tyrant uncle see
> The sad effects of perjury and forced marriage.
> Surely the powers above envied my bliss ;
> Marrying Celinda, I had been an angel,
> So truly blest and good.   (*Weeps*)

In a moment of great excitement he rushes into Diana's house, where Celinda (whom he thinks dead) resides. Not recognizing Diana, he by mistake addresses penitent words to her ; but Celinda, who overhears them, and is at first distressed, presently realizes the situation and reveals herself. He confesses that he has not had a moment's happiness since he even nominally broke his vows, which he now renews. Diana, having providentially fallen in love with another man, is glad to have her marriage to Bellmour annulled; and Celinda thereupon becomes his wife.[1]

During the Restoration compulsory marriage was, as it always has been, a fruitful subject for comic dramatists; but it was ridiculed by representing the folly of tyrannous parents and their discomfiture through the intrigues of rebellious lovers. Under Elizabethan influence, Mrs. Behn for once ventured to show the immorality of enforced marriage by calling forth pity for its innocent victims. Her central personages, Bellmour and Celinda, retain their original nobility of character. Before his calamitous marriage, Bellmour is distinguished by purity of ideals and conduct; and even thereafter he shrinks in disgust from the surroundings in which he vainly tries to submerge his true nature. Had Mrs. Behn continued in this direction, or pointed the way to others, Restoration dramatists might have arrived at modern sentimental comedy. But her play was not an inspiring success: there is nothing to indicate that it enjoyed a long run in its first season (1676), and it seems not to have been revived, adapted, or used as the source of later works. For twenty years no one repeated the experiment. Thus *The Town Fop* merely furnishes an interesting exception to the general rule that the influence of Elizabethan sentimental plays upon the Restoration was so faint as to be insignificant.

The neglect of those plays modern sentimentalists might hastily attribute to the alleged corruption and cynicism of the entire Restoration drama. They need to be reminded that Restoration comedy, upon a misreading or a second-hand knowledge of which this contemptuous impression is usually founded, was not the whole of the drama of that period. Other

---

[1] The important scenes are Act I, scene ii; Act III, scene i; and Act IV, scene iii.

divisions thereof show unmistakably that the age was far from being insensible to the love of the beautiful and good in human nature. Audiences found no greater delight in the brilliant satire of vices and follies exhibited in comedy, than in the enthusiastic exaltation of the virtues presented in romantic drama. Playwrights who, if unintelligently judged by their comedies alone, might be thought gross materialists, wrote romantic plays instinct with idealism. Thus, to cite but one instance among scores, Dryden produced in the same year (1663) the satiric *Wild Gallant* and the poetical *Rival Ladies*. In the former we have a silly tailor and his jealous wife, a shy and stupid country squire, some knavish bounders who live by their wits, a lover who does not hesitate to supply his necessities by fraud, a young lady of fashion who steals money from her father, and another who sums up the thoughtless gayety of her kind in the words, "These little mischiefs are meat and drink to me!" In *The Rival Ladies*, on the other hand, though humor is not banished, we have youths that are virtuous and brave, and maidens that are modest amid happiness and constant amid distresses, — beings who know

> The pride
> Of noble minds, which is to give, not take.

Still higher idealizations appear in the pastoral plays, and, above all, in the heroic drama, the heroes and heroines of which are so noble in their love and honor that they are (sometimes by the same critics who call the age immoral because of its comedy) condemned as too extravagantly virtuous.

The romantic dramas, the pastoral, and the heroic, whatever their artistic weaknesses, thus gratified abundantly the yearning toward moral excellence. With a regularity even more marked than among the Elizabethans, the summits of virtue were not revealed in the light of common day. Actions and characters very similar to those of the Elizabethan sentimental plays appeared after 1660; but they are (except in the few cases discussed above) removed to a romantic environment. Otway's *The Orphan* (1680) is an analogue of *The Hog hath lost his Pearl*. Otway's Polydore and Monimia, however, though they undergo the same trials as Tailor's Albert and Maria,[1] are not persons of middle-class life and manners; they move on higher levels and speak in a poetical style. The result is a sharp difference of moral as well as artistic effect, — a difference even more conspicuous on the stage than in the closet. For the pathetic characters, Otway, with incomparably superior art, successfully created an imaginary world; Tailor had tried to represent them in the real one.[2]

Among the tragedies of 1660–1695, it is difficult to find an instance of perfect characters exhibited in an environment that is not in some manner raised above ordinary life. The nearest approach to such a work appeared towards the close of that period, in Thomas Southerne's *The Fatal Marriage* (1694). Its central figure is the pathetic Isabella. Her marriage with Biron led his father, Count Baldwin, to disown him in favor of his younger brother Carlos, the villain of the drama. Biron goes to the wars, and at the time when the tragedy begins, has been absent seven years. Isabella, who, on the authority of Carlos, believes him to have perished, has sunk into poverty. As a last resort, she appears with her little boy before Count Baldwin, and implores him to provide at least for his grandson; but she cannot move the implacable old man. Unable to pay her debts, and on the point of being seized by officers of the law, she is rescued by one Villeroy, a man of admirable character, who has long loved her, and who begs to

---

[1] Chap. iii, above.

[2] The similarity of *The Orphan* to domestic tragedy is often mentioned; for example, in A. H. Thorndike's *Tragedy* (1908), p. 272.

be permitted to discharge her debts in the capacity of a life-
long friend. She is deeply distressed by being under such obligations, and is urged by the scheming Carlos to marry Villeroy
and thus secure the future of her son. Thus harrassed, she
says to Villeroy:

> I have a soul that's thoroughly sensible
> Of your great worth, and busy to contrive,
> If possible, to make you a return —
>
> *Villeroy*
> Oh, easily possible!
> *Isabella*
> It cannot be your way; my pleasures are
> Buried and cold in my dead husband's grave;
> And I should wrong the truth, myself, and you,
> To say that I can ever love again. . . .
> . . . [But what I can] I give you all, —
> My hand, — and would I had a heart to give.

At the urgent desire of Villeroy, they are married without delay,
and establish themselves in Isabella's former apartments. The
next morning, important affairs call Villeroy away.

That night, Biron returns: he had not been killed, but merely
made a prisoner. He proceeds to his house, and without announcing his name, sends up a ring to Isabella, requesting to
see her. Recognizing the jewel as her first husband's, she
trembles with fear, but imagines that it must be one of Biron's
surviving friends who brings it. He enters; "she shrieks, and
falls into a swoon." She revives, to find herself in his arms,
and to hear his passionate words of love.

> *Isabella*
> Where have I been? why do you keep him from me?
> I know his voice: my life upon the wing
> Hears the soft lure that brings me back again . . .
> My true loved husband, do I hold you fast,
> Never to part again?

Biron retires, expecting his wife to join him presently.

Isabella

> I 'll but say my prayers and follow you. —
> My prayers! No, I must ne'er pray again. . . .
> I promised him to follow, — him!
> Is he without a name? Biron, my husband;
> To follow him to bed, — my husband, ha!
> What then is Villeroy? . . .
> O Biron! hadst thou come but one day sooner,
> I would have followed thee through beggary,
> Through all the chances of this weary life,
> Wandered the many ways of wretchedness
> With thee, to find a hospitable grave,
> For that's the only bed that's left me now.

Biron returns, and she distractedly exclaims:

> Oh, if ever I was dear to you,
> As sometimes you have thought me, on my knees . . .
> I beg you, beg, to think me innocent. . . .
> The rugged hand of fate has got between
> Our meeting hearts, and thrusts them from their joys. . . .
> Can I bear that? Bear to be cursed and torn
> And thrown out from thy family and name,
> Like a disease? Can I bear this from thee?
> I never can; no, all things have their end;
> When I am dead, forgive and pity me!

Finally, after prolonged agonies, Biron is killed by ruffians in the employ of Carlos, and Isabella dies insane.[1]

What is emphasized in conspicuous scenes of the play is Isabella's irresponsibility for the calamities that fall upon her. Had such been Southerne's attitude toward her throughout, there would be little to differentiate his work from typical domestic tragedy. It should, however, not escape notice that the miseries of Isabella are at times thought of as justly incurred. At the outset much is made of the circumstance that when she

[1] Act II, scene ii; Act IV, scene iii; Act V, scene iv.

married Biron she broke her vows as a nun, and Count Baldwin ascribes to this impiety not only her distresses but the loss of his son. And though the action is not, as in regular contemporary tragedy, involved with state affairs, it does not move amid English domestic life. Nominally at least, it is laid in a Catholic country; and there is something exotic in the atmosphere of the whole work. It is therefore, strictly speaking, a romantic drama adjacent to the domestic drama of sensibility, but not governed by precisely the same artistic and ethical principles that rule the latter.

The main tendency of tragedy was, of course, towards the classical. The heroic play and romantic drama were regarded as inferior genres, which were not so profound interpretations of life as true tragedy. From the latter the bourgeois was excluded, and — what is equally important — the perfect character. Even the gentle Otway, who a hundred years later would doubtless have written dramas of sensibility, did not, in his most famous tragedy, *Venice Preserved* (1682) present a Jaffier without vacillation or a Belvidera without frailty. The more masculine hands of Dryden and Lee formed tragic characters that, though endowed with noble qualities, perished beneath their passions or through some weakness of their souls. Such a character is Dryden's Antony in *All for Love* (1677), and — to take for illustration a normal example of less exceptional artistic brilliance — the hero of Nathaniel Lee's *Mithridates* (1678).

Mithridates is a lofty and forceful personality, whose prowess is such that he may gain eternal fame by successfully opposing the designs of imperial Rome. Just when he needs to devote the whole strength of his soul and mind to the defense of his kingdom, however, he allows an illicit passion to distract him. At one time he is strong enough to conquer it, and says:

> 'T is done; the conquest is at last obtained,
> And manly virtue lords it o'er my passion.

It shall be so. Away, thou feeble god,
I banish thee my bosom; hence, I say,
Be gone, or I will tear the strings that hold thee,
And stab thee in thy heart. The wars come on;
By Heaven, I 'll drown thy laughing deity
In blood, and drive thee with my brandished sword
To Rome; I will, yes, to the Capitol;
There to resume thy godhead once again,
And vaunt thy majesty without control;
But never reign in Mithridates' soul.

Archilaus

O wonderful effect of highest virtue!
O conquest which deserves more triumphs than
A hundred victories in battle gained![1]

Presently, however, the infatuation of Mithridates again enslaves him, and estranges him from those — including his son Ziphares — who would have supported him on the path of duty to the goal of victory. His defeat by the Romans concludes the tragedy; it is, however, not her legions that destroy him, but his own passions. He is summoned to the decisive battle with the words:

Arm, arm, great Mithridates; the big war
Comes with vast leaps, bounding o'er all the east,
Which crouches to the torrent; Pompey comes,
Pompey the Great, saluted Emperor. . . .
Pompey, Rome's darling, and Fame's eldest son,
Proclaims with Mithridates mortal war.

Realizing that he has brought his ruin upon himself, he replies, — striking his bosom:

Were all well here, what force, what Roman arms,
What general marching at the head of millions,
Could daunt the bold, the forward Mithridates?
But here, Pharnaces, in my guilty bosom,
The fatal foe does undermine me quite:

[1] Act II, scene i.

> Black legions are my thoughts; not Pompey, but
> Ziphares comes, with all his wrongs for arms,
> Like the lieutenant of the gods, against me.
> Semandra too, like bleeding victory,
> Stands on his side, and cries out, kill, kill, kill
> That cursed parricide, that ravisher!
> Oh, heaven sustain me, or I shall go mad;
> My ugly guilt flies in my conscious face,
> And I am vanquished, slain with bosom war.[1]

The *Mithridate* (1673) of Racine, though exhibiting all the traits in which French classical tragedy differs from English, rests upon the same ethical conception; and in it likewise the great scene is one in which the royal hero recognizes and laments his tragic weakness.[2]

The drama of seventeenth-century France, which was in so many ways influential upon England, inhibited sentimentalism in plays of domestic life. The French, even more thoroughly than the English, discouraged the revival of the early sentimental experiments; and such tendencies as had appeared in Le Jars' *Lucelle* and the other pathetic plays discussed in the previous chapter were in the first third of the seventeenth century absorbed by the romantic drama of playwrights like Hardy and Schelandre.[3]

Corneille, in his " examen " of *Don Sanche d'Aragon* (1650), alluded to the introduction of middle-class people in tragedy; but the allusion was casual, and is not to be regarded as a pronouncement of revolutionary character or effect.[4] Corneille's

---

[1] Act IV, scene i.   [2] Act IV, scenes iv–v.

[3] Alexandre Hardy's *Scédasse* (1604), as well as Jean de Schelandre's *Tyr et Sidon* (1608) and *Frégonde* (1621), have been considered anticipations of the domestic drama of sensibility. Their scenes are placed respectively in Sparta, the Orient, and Spain. Cf. E. Rigal, *Alexandre Hardy* (1889), p. 283; and F.-A. Aulard, *Les Théories dramatiques de Jean de Schelandre* (1883), p. 10.

[4] M. Kawczynski, in his *Moralische Zeitschriften* (1880), pp. 167 ff., opines that Steele was influenced by Corneille's statement that the comic is not essential in comedy. But Corneille was writing of romantic comedy.

real thesis was that noble personages might be introduced in romantic comedies, such as *Don Sanche*. He reasons analogically: what is, according to Aristotle, true of tragedy is, he declares, likewise true of comedy, — namely, that the determining quality of the genre is the nature of the action, not the rank of the personages. Speaking of calamities, he says:

> I do not see why these things can happen only to princes, and why a humbler rank is protected from such misfortunes. . . . I will even go farther. Tragedy must call forth pity and terror. . . . If it is true that the latter emotion is called forth in us by its representation only when we see the sufferings of our fellowmen, and when their misfortunes cause us to fear similar things, is it not also true that terror may be more strongly excited by the sight of disasters happening to persons of our own rank, whom we resemble in every particular?

After these lines, he resumes his main argument: "If you do not deny that one might write a tragedy dealing with middle-class persons, provided such misfortunes were not beneath its dignity, allow me to draw the conclusion *a simili* that we may write a comedy concerning illustrious persons." [1] The "domestic tragedy" here imagined is not sentimental, nor is it mentioned as something which Corneille has written, means to write, or desires others to write; it is incidentally touched upon as something permissible. The suggestion was, moreover, never acted upon by seventeenth-century dramatists.

Really significant was Corneille's ideal of comedy. In 1629 he produced the epoch-making *Mélite*. It ridiculed the jealousy of a lover; and, as its author justly says, "called forth laughter without such ridiculous personages as clownish servants, parasites, captains, physicians, etc., . . . producing its effects by the lively humor of people of a superior rank than those we see in Plautus or Terence." Unlike the low comedy that had held the stage, it appealed, not to what the French aptly call "le

---

[1] Pierre Corneille, *Œuvres*, ed. Marty-Laveaux (1862), V, 407.

rire en dehors," but to "le rire en dedans." Yet it was never pathetic.[1] The Comic Muse of Corneille might well say what the lively Cloris says in *Mélite* :

> S'il attend que je pleure, il attendra longtemps!

The high comedy of Molière, notably *Le Misanthrope* (1666), has suffered the same misinterpretation as that of Terence. Alceste, according to the sentimental opinion of a German critic,[2] "arouses within us an infinite melancholy and sadness." To his creator and contemporaries, Alceste was "that ridiculous man" who absurdly revolted against conventionalities ; and Boileau commended *Le Misanthrope* in the line which immediately precedes the significant verses,

> Le comique, ennemi des soupirs et des pleurs,
> N'admet point en ces vers de tragiques douleurs.[3]

In the first half of the eighteenth century, the work of Molière continued to be recognized as purely comic : when Riccoboni wished to bring out the novelty of La Chaussée's sentimental drama, he contrasted it with *Le Misanthrope* ; and Voltaire said that sentimental comedies ought not to be condemned though they were not in the style of Molière.[4] By the middle

---

[1] For a contrary opinion, see A. W. Ward, Introduction to George Lillo's *The London Merchant* (1906), p. xxiv, where the allusion is presumably to *Mélite*. The confusion between high comedy and sentimental comedy is often met with in criticism.

[2] W. Wetz, *Die Anfänge der ernsten bürgerlichen Dichtung des achtzehnten Jahrhunderts* (1885), I, 76. F. M. Warren, in *French Classical Drama and the Comédie Larmoyante, Studies in Honor of A. Marshall Elliott* (1911), I, 183, considers the Valère-Élise love-affair in Molière's *L'Avare* an anticipation of sentimental comedy. The action is conducted in a comic manner.

[3] *L'Art poétique*, III, 401–402. Cf. E. Despois, Introduction to *Le Misanthrope*, Molière's *Œuvres*, ed. Despois et Mesnard (1880), I, 371.

[4] Riccoboni's remarks, dated 30th May, 1737, are found in La Chaussée's *Œuvres* (1777), V, 198–201. Voltaire, *Conseils à un Journaliste* (1744), *Œuvres*, XXII, 247 ; cf. XLVI, 265. In *Questions sur l'Encyclopédie* (1770), XVII, 420, he speaks cursorily of a few pathetic scenes in Molière.

of the century, *Le Misanthrope* came to be read after a new fashion. Fontenelle, among others, declared that it was almost entirely sentimental in tone;[1] but the modern misreading of *Le Misanthrope* is chiefly due to the influential opinions of Jean Jacques Rousseau.

This arch-sentimentalist, in his famous *Lettre sur les Spectacles* (1758), attacked all comedy because it was based upon what he considered a vicious inclination, the love of ridicule. He would not pardon "the ridicule of virtue which Molière has shown in *Le Misanthrope*." To prove this charge, Rousseau is forced to postulate two Alcestes. In discussing the Alceste of Molière, he is conservative and correct: he calls him "a ridiculous personage," and reproachfully says that Molière made him the prey of the comic spirit. The other Alceste, whom he speaks of as the real one, and whom, it is to be suspected, he identified with himself, is "an honorable, sincere, estimable, truly good man."[2] His numberless disciples went further. In reading *Le Misanthrope*, they substituted for the Alceste of Molière the Alceste of Rousseau, — with the result that to this day, wherever the sentimental school dominates criticism, the play is regarded as tragic. It has been preposterously called "the French Hamlet." The late Mr. Richard Mansfield used to act Alceste as if that character's ridiculous inability to adapt himself to his environment were a noble independence of mind; and our audiences would admiringly applaud the outbursts at which those of Louis XIV laughed.

In Alceste, Molière satirizes hypersensitive regard for virtue in the abstract, the assumption that men are either wholly good or wholly bad, tirades against the conventions of social life, and attacks on the need of compromise in worldly affairs, — tendencies, in short, which the sentimental dramatists were to

[1] *Œuvres*, VII (1766), p. xxxiii.
[2] *Lettre sur les Spectacles*, ed. L. Brunel (1896), pp. 54–57, 64, etc.

represent admiringly. The character of that exquisitely ridiculous prude Arsinoé stands in sharp contrast to the sentimental
heroines of the future : her reproving words to Célimène, heard
with amusement in the time of Louis XIV, caricature by anticipation, as it were, those virtuous admonitions which elicited
sympathetic regard in the days of Louis XV. The change in
public taste may be described in the unintentionally prophetic
remark of Célimène :

> Il est une saison pour la galanterie,
> Il en est une aussi propre à la pruderie.

The reign of the prudes was not to begin in the days of Molière.
During the half century following his death, the divisions of the
drama remained distinct, and popular taste tolerated no intrusion
of pathos into comedy.[1]

The illustrious example of Corneille and Molière doubtless
confirmed English comic dramatists in their almost unbroken
habit of avoiding the pathetic. To the exception already mentioned, Mrs. Behn's *The Town Fop*, only one other needs to be
added, — one not derived from an Elizabethan source. Sir
George Etherege intermingled with the witty prose scenes of
The Comical Revenge (1664) a poetical subplot which borrows
from the heroic drama not only its couplets but also something
of its ideals of conduct. In it Aurelia is secretly in love with
Colonel Bruce, but since he is engaged to her sister Graciana,
she loyally aids his wooing. A rival suitor, Lord Beaufort, fights
a duel with the Colonel, and in exemplary generosity spares
his life. The Colonel, knowing that Graciana, though she loves
Beaufort, will not dishonorably break her engagement, wounds
himself in an attempt at suicide. The sisters are thus grievously
distressed before Bruce becomes aware of Aurelia's love for him,

---

[1] Edme Boursault's *La Princesse de Clèves* (1678), Michel Baron's *L'Andri-
enne* (1703), and J. G. de Campistron's *Le Jaloux désabusé* (1709), have been
called sentimental comedies, — in my opinion, erroneously.

and relieves the situation by his recovery and by his marriage to her. Love and honor are the ruling motives in this emotional drama, and the characters are such as sensibility rejoices to behold. Etherege did not, however, continue in this vein; he found the satirical portions of his play especially admired, and confined himself thereafter to true comedy of manners.

In the talented hands of Etherege, Wycherley, Shadwell, and Congreve, the plots of comedies were artfully designed to conduct foolish or vicious persons to a logical catastrophe which showed the ridiculous consequences of their folly or vice. In Wycherley's *The Country Wife* (1673), Pinchwife proceeds on the principle that " he 's a fool that marries, but he 's a greater that does not marry a fool." " Good wives," he believes, " should be kept ignorant " ; and he marries Margery thinking " because she 's ugly, she 's the likelier to be my own, and being ill-bred, she 'll hate conversation." When he goes out, he locks her into her room, with the lying threat that he has a spy in the street ; and he forbids anyone to inform her of the pleasures of city life. The methods that he trusts are shown to cause the results they were intended to prevent : Margery's ignorance makes her welcome pleasures that are vulgar ; her curiosity, unnaturally stimulated, leads her into adventures, and her lack of refinement, into vice.[1] Wholly dissimilar from Pinchwife is Manly in Wycherley's *The Plain Dealer* (1674 ?), but his story is conducted on the same principles. Manly scorns the politeness of social intercourse, and is sure that all courtesy is flattery and all kindness a sham. He will tell the naked truth to everyone, and will trust none, — except the fair Olivia whom he is to marry, and his friend Vernish. He finds that Olivia is faithless, and Vernish dishonest, and that it is those whom he despised for their gentleness who are his true friends.

[1] William Wycherley, *The Country Wife*, ed. *Mermaid Series*, especially pp. 261–263, 265, 284, 292, 315, 319.

The method of Congreve's plots is similar. In *The Old Bachelor* (1693), Heartwell boasts that he is not susceptible to woman's charms. He falls in love, however; tries to avoid ridicule by keeping the affair secret; and is consequently almost made the victim of a disreputable female. Maskwell, in *The Double Dealer* (1693), trusts to his skill in intrigue to win a fortune and a wife; but the elaborate snares he lays for others destroy himself. Such typical instances suffice to show that the plots of Restoration comedies were not planned to provide opportunities for scenes of virtuous conduct or pathetic emotion.

They allowed, nevertheless, a considerable variety of appeal. Merriment and ridicule, though their main effects, were not their only ones. "Interdum tamen," as Horace had granted, "et vocem Comœdia tollit," — and then it excited disdain. The virile work of Wycherley, a spirit akin to Juvenal and Swift, was especially charged with an indignant irony that was too bitter to be playful; and Congreve inflicted upon the principal characters of *The Double Dealer* a derision that was full of contempt. So dark grew at times its picture of life that true comedy seemed to border upon tragedy, — not, of course, as sentimental comedy was to do, by eliciting pity, but by arousing an emotion compounded of terror and scorn.

The range of characters, from those that were distinctly odious to those that were but slightly foolish or affected, was wide enough. There were degrees in folly: the ill-bred country squire was more absurd than the courtier, though the latter had affectations which made him a coxcomb; and the tradesman's wife, who hankered after fashionable dissipation, was more ridiculous than the society girl, though she on her part was vain and capricious and mischief-loving. So subtle were the touches of satire applied to some characters that a strong sense of humor was needed to recognize them, and in a few cases such strokes were entirely absent. The admission of characters of the latter class was a liberty which serious moralists came to regard as licentious. A particularly shining mark for their attacks was Horner, in Wycherley's *The Country Wife*. He was, they complained, successful in illicit amours, and escaped without censure. To Wycherley, however, Horner's successes were a necessary means to the satiric ends of the play, — to the thorough exposure of Mrs. Fidget and Mrs. Squeamish, women who were at heart unchaste but who were scrupulously careful of their reputation, and the hollowness of whose virtue could not have been fully demonstrated except under the circumstances which Horner created. These women, as well as Pinchwife and Margery, comprised the principal objects of his satire, and were duly punished; but it was a practical impossibility to visit poetical justice upon every character of the play. So extreme a requirement Dryden had protested against in the preface to *The Mock Astrologer* (1671), saying that he knew "no such law to have been constantly observed in comedy, either by the ancient or modern poets."

The distinction between characters that preoccupy the dramatist's attention and characters that are merely serviceable to his main purpose accounts for the occasional appearance in these comedies of figures that are amiable. Fidelia, in *The Plain Dealer*, who is reminiscent of Shakespeare's Viola, at times resembles a romantic or sentimental heroine. Her love for Manly, and its apparent hopelessness, engage our sympathy. To Wycherley, however, she seems to have been chiefly a means to make Manly's infatuation with the unworthy Olivia appear all the more contemptible because of his blindness to the true devotion at his side. Fidelia herself, moreover, does not wholly escape the satirist. She disguised herself as a page and entered the service of Manly in order to find a way to his heart; thereby she places herself under the hateful necessity of aiding his courtship of Olivia, — a predicament that seemed to the robust sense of humor in those days an amusing one. It may be added that no sentimental heroine of the eighteenth century would have been allowed to impair her self-esteem by engaging in so gross a deception as that which Fidelia carries out at Manly's behest.[1]

To a degree far less than is the case with the very unusual character of Fidelia, other persons in Restoration comedy at times exhibit good qualities; but these are as a rule unimportant in comparison with their follies and affectations. Such characters may be momentarily grave, but their general temper is merry. So Alithea, in *The Country Wife*, refuses to jilt her fiancé Sparkish on the honorable principle that " his confidence in my truth obliges me to be faithful to him "; but she breaks off the match when she finds that he can be made foolishly jealous, and for the most part she is engaged in a merry combat of wit with another lover.[2] So Angelica, in Congreve's *Love for Love* (1695), finally accepts Valentine because he does a generous deed; but such is not her dominant mood. Until that final moment, she and Valentine are intriguing, not only against her father, but against one another. She loves him; but when he feigns madness in order to gain his ends, and she discovers the deception, she exclaims: " If I don't play trick for trick, may I never taste the pleasure of revenge! "[3] Those are the traits and moods that Congreve sought after; anything out of harmony with them is casual and insignificant.

Sir Edward Belfond, in Thomas Shadwell's *Squire of Alsatia* (1688), is less ridiculed than his original, Micio in Terence's *Adelphi*; indeed Shadwell describes him as one who " lives

---

[1] *The Plain Dealer:* Act I, scene i; Act III, scene i; Act IV, scene ii; Act V, scene iv.

[2] *The Country Wife:* Act IV, scene i; Act V, scene iii.

[3] *Love for Love:* Act IV, scene i; Act V, scene ii.

with ease and pleasure, reasonably and virtuously, — a man of
great humanity and gentleness and compassion towards mankind, well read in good books, possessed with all gentleman-like
qualities." This raises the expectation that Sir Edward is one
of those patterns of moral excellence whose precepts edify the
youths of sentimental comedy: but his code is not high enough;
it is too worldly. He protests to his tyrannous brother, Sir
William, that his nephew "does no ungentleman-like things."
Says he:

> Prithee, consider youth a little. What if he does wench a little, and
> now and then is somewhat extravagant in wine; where's the great
> crime? All young fellows that have mettle in them will do the first;
> and if they have wit and good humor in them, in this drinking coun-
> try, they will sometimes be forced upon the latter; and he must be a
> very dull phlegmatical lump whom wine will not elevate to some
> extravagance now and then.

> *Sir William*
> Will you distract me? What, are drinking and whoring no faults?

Sir William's blunt reply on this occasion upholds the higher
ideal, but he is on the whole a brutal person, and Shadwell
gives Sir Edward distinctly the preference. Yet they differ
only in the degree of their imperfection: Sir Edward is a
gentleman, but surely no immaculate saint and sage. Though
his liberal system of education is shown superior to Sir William's despotic one, it has not the wholly elevating effect that
he hoped for; and he makes a scandalous discovery at his
nephew's apartments which is comically disconcerting.[1]

Sir Edward's nephew is "reformed" at the end of the play,
when, after having sowed a large crop of wild oats, he assures
his fiancée, Isabella, that he has "abandoned all the thoughts
of vice and folly" for her, and presents himself "a sacrifice

[1] *The Squire of Alsatia:* Dramatis Personae; Act I, scene i; Act II,
scene i.

without a blemish." He thus seems to foreshadow the reformed prodigals of sentimental comedy, but he has been much too deliberately wicked to bear comparison with them. His vices were not the thoughtless aberrations of a heart inclined to virtue. They were the free indulgence of passionate desires; and he himself, having no sentimental delusions on that point, owns that such passions "make a young fellow a knave." He jeers at his cast-off mistress Termagant, even when she weeps and speaks of her child; and though he says that it is "with some convulsions" that he abandons the young girl he seduced, he does, as a matter of fact, desert her for Isabella. He "reforms" chiefly because of the ridiculously embarrassing situations his previous course of life placed him in, forswearing it as "foolish, restless, and anxious." And he wins Isabella, not by repentance that arouses her pity, but by ingenious and somewhat unscrupulous stratagems.[1] In short, the passages in *The Squire of Alsatia* which appear to approach sentimental comedy, are really illustrations of the flexibility of the prevailing comic methods.

Those vacillations of the comic needle which, in view of the future course of comedy, appear interesting to us would to the Restoration dramatists themselves have seemed negligible. What engrossed their attention was the discovery and revelation of absurdities. The boldness of their satire allowed nothing to escape, — from the seven deadly sins of hoary antiquity to the numberless fashionable affectations of their own day. The Gallicized coxcomb, the vulgar squire, the hypocritical alderman, gave excellent sport; and the gouty Cavalier was as fair game as the sleek Puritan.[2] What disturbs modern readers is that women were not spared. The veils of their affectations

---

[1] *The Squire of Alsatia:* Act II, scene i; Act IV, scene i; Act V, scene i.

[2] In Crowne's popular *Sir Courtly Nice* (1685) we have Cavalier and Puritan satirized side by side.

were torn away, and there appeared the faults that Congreve
enumerates, — "pride, folly, wantonness, inconstancy, covetous-
ness, dissimulation, malice, and ignorance." [1] The assumption,
which the drama of sensibility was to make common, that
woman was the passive victim of man, would have seemed to
these playwrights false; the contrary supposition, so gaily manifested in Mr. Shaw's *Man and Superman*, is more nearly in
harmony with their judgment. Says Congreve's Lucy:

> Man was by nature woman's cully made;
> We never are but by ourselves betrayed.[2]

If the course of love did not run smooth, it was because it was
a struggle of sex against sex, as well as of youth against age.

Courtship, like everything else in life, appeared in its merry
or foolish aspects. Its serious and ennobling possibilities, comedy
left to tragedy and romantic drama. Shadwell, in the prologue
to *The Sullen Lovers* (1668), boasted that he presented

> No kind romantic lovers in his play
> To sigh and whine out passion, such as may
> Charm waiting-women with heroic chime,
> And still resolve to live and die in rhyme.

"Love in jest," says one of his characters, "is but just toler-
able; but serious love is duller than a rhyming play." [3] When
one of Congreve's lovers begins to grow sentimental, his mistress protests: "Nay, come; I find we are growing serious,
and then we are in great danger of being dull." [4] In sentimental comedy, on the other hand, as lovers grew serious, they
grew interesting.

The departures from the dominant practice amount, as we
have seen, to little. Very early in the period a sentimental

---

[1] *Love for Love*, Act I, scene ii.

[2] *The Old Bachelor*, Act III, scene i. Cf. John Palmer, *The Comedy of
Manners* (1913), pp. 77–78.

[3] *Bury Fair*, Act IV, scene ii.   [4] *The Old Bachelor*, Act II, scene ii.

comedy was written by Etherege; in 1676, under Elizabethan influence, another was produced by Mrs. Behn; and throughout the Restoration, Wycherley, Shadwell, and Congreve felt somewhat less restrained than their French contemporaries from deviating into anything that seemed a momentary approach to a pathetic scene or an exemplary character. In view of the freedom from convention which characterizes English literature in general, Restoration comedy appears a remarkable instance of obedience to rule. Its compliance is explicable partly on the literary ground that classical authority, which demanded unity of tone within each genre, was strong; but quite as much on the ethical ground that the distrust of ordinary human nature was a deep-seated conviction. Such being the orthodox theory and practice, the appearance in 1696 of sentimental comedy was, in the true sense of a much abused term, revolutionary.

CHAPTER V

THE RISE OF SENTIMENTAL COMEDY: 1696–1704

Much of Colley Cibber's *Love's Last Shift*, with the production of which, in January, 1696, the rise of sentimental comedy begins, was written in the manner of Restoration comedy.[1] Several of its characters, notably the famous coxcomb Sir Novelty Fashion, were variations of familiar satiric types. The general theme, a wife's discovery of her husband's faithlessness, was commonplace. With a bold departure from convention, however, this situation was motivated and resolved on principles repugnant to the comic spirit. In true comedy, the theme would have been treated, as it was, for example, in Shirley's *The Gamester* or Dorimond's *L'Amant de sa Femme*, as an amusing struggle between the waywardness of the husband and the ingenuity of the wife. Thus in Dorimond's play the husband falls in love with a masked lady, and offers her a valuable ring; she accepts it, presently unmasks, and turns out to be his wife. He, though much astonished, does not lose his merry wit; but impudently avers that it was her irresistible personality which, even under her disguise, has won his heart, and that therefore he had not been really unfaithful at all. There is no idealization of character, no pathos, nothing but the tone of gallantry.

Amanda, the heroine of *Love's Last Shift*, is "a woman of strict virtue." Deserted by her husband, she has been saved from poverty through a large inheritance; but her wealth does

---

[1] The comic portions of the play were in part borrowed from Carlile's *The Fortune Hunters* (1689).

not make her happy. We see her at first, dressed in deep mourning, in conversation with ladies who are reproaching her for not dismissing the memory of so bad a husband.

Hillaria

Why d'ye persist in such a hopeless grief?

Amanda

Because 'tis hopeless. For, if he be alive, he is dead to me. His dead affections, not virtue itself can e'er retrieve. Would I were with him, though in his grave!

Hillaria

... The grave! Young widows use to have warmer wishes. But methinks the death of a rich old uncle should be a cordial to your sorrows.

Amanda

That adds to them. ... He was as tender to me as the nearest; he was a father to me ...

Hillaria

The greatest reason I think you have to grieve is that you are not sure your husband's dead; for, were that confirmed, then indeed there were hopes that one poison might drive out another: you might marry again.

Amanda

All the comfort of my life is that I can tell my conscience I have been true to virtue.[1]

Loveless, the husband, returns to England penniless. His friend Worthy lends him a guinea; but, fearing that he will bring nothing but trouble to Amanda, confirms him in his belief that she is dead. Worthy hastens to Amanda, informs her of the situation, and bids her hope for a good outcome; for the escapades of Loveless, he declares, do not mark an incurably evil disposition but "proceed from an affectation of being fashionably vicious." To regain the prodigal, however, she

---

[1] Act I, scene iii, in Colley Cibber's *Works* (1760), I, 21-22.

must resort to "a stratagem that will either make him ashamed of his folly or in love with your virtue." A plan which the wife in Shirley's *The Gamester* entered upon with zest arouses the moral scruples of the unhappy Amanda. "Why," she moans, "if I court and conquer him as a mistress, am I not accessory to violating the bonds of marriage?" Only because there seems no other way to "reclaim the man I 'm bound by Heaven to love, and expose the folly of a roving mind," does she consent to have Loveless summoned to her by a message declaring that a fair stranger has fallen in love with him.

When Loveless appears and, not recognizing her after eight years' absence, is entranced by her beauty and gentleness, Amanda is torn by conflicting emotions, — the joy of knowing that his heart is hers, the sorrow of hearing his licentious ardor, and the agony of realizing that she must entertain him as his mistress if she is to make his better self feel that happy love and faithful virtue are compatible. The next morning, supported by her faith that "there are charms in virtue stronger and more pleasing far than hateful vice can boast of," and picturing to Loveless the miseries that infidelity inflicts upon virtue, she "awakens his soul," and with deep emotion approaches the ordeal of recognition.

Amanda

Arm your mind with gentle pity first, or I am lost forever.

Loveless

I am all pity, all faith, expectation, and confused amazement; be kind, be quick, and ease my wonder.

Amanda

Look on me well; revive your dead remembrance; and oh, for pity's sake (*kneels*) hate me not for loving long and faithfully! Forgive this innocent attempt of a despairing passion, and I shall die in quiet.

Loveless (amazed)

Hah! speak on!

Amanda

It will not be — the word's too weighty for my faltering tongue, and my soul sinks beneath the fatal burden. Oh! (*falls to the ground*).

Loveless

Ha! she faints! Look up, fair creature; behold a heart that bleeds for your distress, and fain would share the weight of your oppressive sorrows. Oh, thou hast raised a thought within me that shocks my soul.

Amanda (*rising*)

'T is done. — The conflict's past, and Heaven bids me speak undaunted. Know then, even all the boasted raptures of your last night's love you found in your Amanda's arms! — I am your wife . . . forever blessed or miserable as your next breath shall sentence me. . . .

Loveless

Oh, I am confounded with my guilt, and tremble to behold thee. . . . I have wronged you . . . basely wronged you . . .

Amanda

One kind, one pitying look, cancels those wrongs forever . . .

Loveless

Oh, seal my pardon with thy trembling lips, while with this tender grasp of fond reviving love I seize my bliss, and stifle all thy wrongs forever (*embraces her*).

Amanda

No more; I'll wash away their memory in tears of flowing joy.

Loveless

Oh, thou hast roused me from my deepest lethargy of vice. . . . Thus let me kneel and pay my thanks to her whose conquering virtue has at last subdued me. Here will I fix, thus prostrate, sigh my shame, and wash my crimes in never ceasing tears of penitence.[1]

Such was the epoch-making scene at which, according to credible eighteenth-century tradition, "the audience shed honest tears." [2]

---

[1] Act V, scene ii, pp. 79-80.
[2] Thomas Davies, *Dramatic Miscellanies* (1784), III, 412. Davies, it should be said, is not invariably to be trusted. Cf. Genest, VI, 13.

Loveless swears that henceforth he will for Amanda's sake "labor, dig, beg, or starve"; she joyfully informs him of her wealth, and, confident of his reform, places it at his disposal. Their reconciliation is celebrated in a masque glorifying conjugal love. "'Twas generously designed," says Loveless in conclusion, "and all my life to come shall show how I approve the moral." [1] What is noteworthy in the play, however, is not the moralizing, but the sentimentality, — the characterization of Loveless as good at heart; above all, that of Amanda with her moral scrupulosity and the power of her virtue to triumph through an appeal to pity. These characters, transferred from the exotic environment of romance to everyday London life, were created in precisely the mood that was to dominate the whole course of the drama of sensibility. *Love's Last Shift*, though artistically no masterpiece, occupies historically the same leading position that *The Tatler* holds among moral periodicals, and *Pamela* among sentimental novels.

When Cibber wrote *Love's Last Shift*, he was only twenty-four years of age. He had not been influenced (perhaps we should say he had not been hampered) by that conservative and classical spirit which a university education bred in most of his immediate predecessors. His schooling, obtained at a provincial academy, had ceased when he was fifteen. After two years of military life, he became a hanger-on of the London theatres, and in 1690 he was engaged as an actor at the Theatre Royal. His university was the theatre, his tutors were the public, and the lesson he mastered was quick adaptation to the changing tastes of audiences. His ability to foresee and straightway gratify their moods, an ability which was later to make him a highly successful manager, now made him the first dramatist to meet the demand for a sentimental representation of

[1] Colley Cibber, *Love's Last Shift*, in *Works* (1760), I, especially pp. 23–28, 42, 63–68, 78–80, 90–91.

contemporary life. His play was an immediate success, and it held the stage for at least sixty years.[1]

Immediately after the appearance of sentimental comedy, its conception of human nature was attacked by John Vanbrugh's *The Relapse* (December, 1696), in which Loveless and Amanda were represented from the comic point of view. Vanbrugh would have been a thoroughly consistent upholder of the traditional standard if he had not introduced in his play an episode in which a lover of Amanda, repulsed by her, speaks in a seriously penitent strain;[2] but the passage is brief, and does not defeat the author's purpose, which was to cast a doubt upon the perfection of Amanda and upon the perfectibility of Loveless. The latter, tempted by a coquette, relapses into infidelity; Amanda, being too proud of her virtue, falls in danger of losing it.

Their characters as he saw them, Vanbrugh analyzed in his *Vindication of the Relapse*, of which the following passages strikingly show the orthodox insistence on the moral weaknesses of mankind:

> [Loveless is] proud to think on what a rock his reformation is built. . . . But Berinthia is there to chastise his presumption. . . . She's beautiful in her person, gay in her temper, coquet in her behavior, and warm in her desires. In a word, the battery is so near, there's no standing the shot; constancy's beaten down, the breach is made, resolution gives ground, and the town's taken. This I designed for a natural instance of the frailty of mankind, even in his most fixed determinations; and for a mark upon the defect of the most steady resolve, without that necessary guard of keeping out of temptation. . . .
>
> [Amanda is] a woman whose virtue is raised upon the utmost strength of foundation: religion, modesty, and love defend it. It

---

[1] On Cibber cf. DeWitt C. Croissant, *Studies in the Work of Colley Cibber*, reprinted from *The Bulletin of the University of Kansas, Humanistic Studies*, I, No. 1 (1912).

[2] Act V, scene iv. It should be noted, however, that immediately after his penitent mood the lover remarks, "How long this influence may last, Heaven knows."

looks so sacred one would think no mortal durst approach it, and seems so fixed one would believe no engine could shake it ; yet loosen one stone, the weather works in, and the structure moulders apace to decay. She discovers her husband's return to his inconstancy. The unsteadiness of his love gives her a contempt of his person, and what lessens her opinion declines her inclination. As her passion for him is abated, that against him's enflamed; and as her anger increases, her reason's confused, her judgment in disorder, her religion un-hinged, and that fence being broken, she lies widely exposed. Worthy's too sensible of the advantage to let slip the occasion; he has intelligence of the vacancy and puts in for the place.

Poor Amanda's persuaded he's only to be her friend, and that all he asks is to be admitted as a comforter in her afflictions. But when people are sick, they are so fond of a cordial that when they get it to their nose they are apt to take too much on 't. She finds in his com-pany such a relief to her pain, she desires the physician may be always in her sight. She grows pleased with his person, as well as his advice, yet she's sure he can never put her virtue in danger. But she might have remembered her husband was once of the same opinion, and have taken warning from him, as the audience, I intended, should do from 'em both.[1]

Thus at the very outset of the long conflict between true comedy and sentimental, their antagonistic views of human nature were evidenced. Both genres had their moral aim. Vanbrugh strove to reach his by exhibiting characters from which the audience should " take warning " ; Cibber, by exhibiting characters which the audience should emulate.

Vanbrugh again supported the traditional ideal of comedy in *The Provoked Wife* (1697). Clearer in plot and simpler in style than the plays of Congreve, it was a most effective exposure of a foolish marriage. The contrast between Cibber's Amanda and Vanbrugh's Lady Brute, whose husband lives up to his name, is complete. The wrongs of Lady Brute proceed from her own folly, and she meets them with little patience and few moral scruples. She married her husband, who is wealthy, out of

---

[1] *A Short Vindication of The Relapse, etc.* (1698), pp. 65–71.

vanity and ambition, thinks to revenge herself for his brutality by encouraging a gallant, and is by this expedient repeatedly thrown into comic distresses. Sir John Brute, a cowardly bully, who thought that to marry her was to own her as a slave, believes at the end of the play that he has lost not only her but also what he calls his honor (meaning his monopoly).

The struggle between the comic and the sentimental had barely begun when Jeremy Collier, with his *A Short View of the Immorality and Profaneness of the English Stage* (March, 1698), delivered an attack which threw both ranks into confusion, and which has made it difficult to this day to discern the early stages of the real campaign. It is commonly thought that Collier encouraged the sentimental dramatists.[1] As a matter of fact, this nonjuring high churchman, the spiritual brother of Northbrooke and Prynne, looked upon all dramatists as the favorite children of Satan; and his ultimate desire was the abolition of the theatre. In his blind hatred for the contemporary stage, however, he admitted that the drama of the past was not quite so diabolical a thing as that of his own day. When he gave grudging admiration to any comedies whatever, he gave it to those of Plautus, Terence, Ben Jonson, Corneille, and Molière.[2] His critical standards, like his theological, were strongly conservative;[3] and "the sense of antiquity upon this argument" was always law to him. His definition of the end of comedy, — "the exposure of knavery and making lewdness ridiculous,"[4] — was precisely that of the Restoration dramatists.

---

[1] This is stated or implied in nearly every history of eighteenth-century literature, as well as in special studies of the drama. Cf., for example, Alexandre Beljame, *Le Public et les Hommes de Lettres en Angleterre au Dix-huitième Siècle*, (1881), pp. 258 ff.; and G. A. Aitken, *The Life of Richard Steele* (1889), I, 71 ff., both works of exceptionally high scholarship.

[2] *A Short View of the Immorality and Profaneness of the English Stage* (1698), 3d ed., pp. 15–24, 51–55, 86, 123, 126, 146–147.

[3] He supports the three unities, pp. 228–229.

[4] Pp. 156–157. Cf. pp. 148–155.

But the Restoration comedies, in his opinion, did not answer that end. He declared that the chief persons of the plays were held up to admiration (which was untrue), that they were wanton (which was undeniable), and that poetical justice should have been meted out to all characters (a doctrine to which, as we have seen,[1] Dryden had demurred). From this position, — which in the main supported the theory of the comic dramatists, yet wholly condemned their practice, — he was but delivering with greater energy an attack which Restoration comedies had always endured.[2] His immediate predecessor, Sir Richard Blackmore, a City physician who believed that epics (like those composed by himself) were the truly moral literature, had briefly assailed the comedies in 1695 ;[3] and, just like Collier, had advised the dramatists to "abandon their profession and take up some honest lawful calling," while at the same time recognizing that "the business of comedy was to render vice ridiculous." Both the cit and the zealot lacked a sense of humor, and were incapable of recognizing satire that was subtle.

Collier insisted not only upon complete poetical justice but also upon decorum. He commanded the Comic Muse to shut her ears to the profanity of common conversation, and close her eyes when a fool or rogue appeared among clergymen. These two restrictions he frightened her into obeying henceforth rather strictly. He also forbade her, though theoretically she was to expose the vices of mankind, to be so unladylike as to betray her knowledge that carnality was a prevailing one. It

---

[1] Chap. iv, above. Cf. Collier, pp. 148 ff.

[2] Among the writings which show that the morality of comedy was constantly attacked after 1660, are: Cowley's Preface to *The Cutter of Coleman Street* (1663); Flecknoe's *Short Discourse of the English Stage* (1664); Shadwell's Preface to *The Sullen Lovers* (1668); Dryden's Preface to *The Mock Astrologer* (1671); Wycherley's *The Plain Dealer* (1676), II, i; Ravenscroft's Prologue to *Dame Dobson* (1684); Mrs. Behn's Preface to *The Lucky Chance* (1687); Congreve's Preface to *The Double Dealer* (1694); and James Wright's *Country Conversations* (1694).   [3] Preface to *Prince Arthur.*

has been thought that this prohibition was likewise effective, especially as to sentimental comedy. There is indeed a kind of affinity between purism, with its desire to represent the world as immaculate in speech, and sentimentalism, with its desire to represent it as lovely in thought and deed; but, as a matter of historic fact, purism did not appear in English comedy until much later than sentimentalism. Comedy might well have grown modest in utterance without becoming sentimental in spirit: in France, a puristic movement, beginning about 1630, led to the true comedy of Corneille and Molière.[1] In England it was not until about 1770 that anything strongly resembling what moderns call "the conspiracy of silence" began. The comedies of Cibber, Vanbrugh, Mrs. Centlivre, Hoadly, and the other playwrights of the first half of the century, were full of outspoken allusions to the sexual. Farquhar, who began his work after Collier's reputed " reform," wrote more gratuitous lubricity than Congreve; and Fielding introduced in *The Universal Gallant* (1735) as indecorous a situation as Wycherley had in *The Country Wife*. The sentimental comedies did not in this respect notably differ from contemporary satiric ones; indeed Richard Steele himself confessed the seeming impossibility of writing plays without salaciousness.[2]

Sentimentalism displeased Collier even more than bold satire. He had no appreciative word of welcome for *Love's Last Shift*, but condemned it because it "swears at length and is scandalously smutty and profane."[3] The romantic treatment of love which the sentimentalist admired, Collier condemned as follows:

---

[1] E. N. S. Thompson, *The Controversy between the Puritans and the Stage* (1903), p. 264.

[2] *The Spectator*, No. 51.

[3] *A Defense of the Short View* (1699), pp. i–ii. In the *Short View*, p. 154, he approves *The London Prodigal* (cf. chap. iii, above), not because it appeals on behalf of virtue in distress (such an idea never comes within his horizon), but because it does not improperly reward folly.

> This subject [love] is generally treated home, and in the most
> tender and passionate manner imaginable: . . . the incidents make
> way, and the plot turns upon 't. . . . This is a cunning way enough
> of stealing upon the blind side, and practising upon the weakness of
> human nature. . . . As for the general strains of courtship, there can
> be nothing more profane and extravagant. The hero's mistress is no
> less than his deity. She disposes of his reason, prescribes his motions,
> and commands his interest. What sovereign respect, what religious
> address, what idolizing raptures, are we pestered with![1]

The brief serious episode in *The Relapse* was no less offensive
to him than the comedy as a whole. Of the "virtuous Amanda,"
he sneeringly remarks : "she has nothing to do but to stand
a shock of courtship, and carry off her virtue." Against the
sudden reformation of her tempter, he protests : "his passion
is metamorphosed in the turn of a hand; he is reformed into
a Platonic admirer, and goes off as like a town-spark as you
would wish."[2] This very incident, the only one that approaches
the sentimental, Vanbrugh found himself obliged to defend ;
and he expressed his astonishment that Collier did not approve
a representation of virtuous conduct, saying :

> I almost fancy when he and I are fast asleep in our graves, those
> who shall read what we both have produced will be apt to conclude
> there 's a mistake in the tradition about the authors; and that 't was
> the reforming divine writ the play, and the scandalous poet the
> remarks upon 't.[3]

There is indeed "a mistake in the tradition" about Collier.
His influence was, to be sure, great and beneficent in reminding
dramatists of all schools that their aims should be moral. Had
his work called forth a race of satiric but mealy-mouthed Ben
Jonsons, they might have placated his hostility to the stage ;
but for two generations his plea for decorum was granted to

---

[1] *Short View*, pp. 281–283.   [2] Pp. 79, 209–210, 227.
[3] John Vanbrugh, *A Vindication of the Relapse* (1698), pp. 78–79. Cf.
pp. 61–78.

only a small extent. He never advocated the reformation of
humanity by a comedy which should appeal to its feelings for
virtue in distress, and the sentimentalists who were to indulge
that hope would have seemed to him a contemptible band of
whining fools.

Between 1698 and 1702, the most important new comedies
were Congreve's *The Way of the World* (1700) and the early
plays of Farquhar. Congreve, in the prologue of his comedy,
glancing at Collier, said to his audience :

> Satire, he thinks, you ought not to expect,
> For so reformed a town who dares correct?

This was characteristically ironic, for satire permeates his play.
The famous love-affair of Mirabell and Millamant is as antagonistic to the sentimental style of courtship as possible. Mirabell
frankly owns that Millamant has faults and follies, and is fascinated not in spite of them but by them.[1] He himself is no
hero, and deceives her aunt with a pretense of love in order
to gain opportunities to woo Millamant. The obstacles he meets
are not only Millamant's coquetry, which gives rise to the most
brilliant repartee in English comedy, but also the designs that
his own duplicity has stimulated in her aunt. Others, who see
something to gain in the defeat of his hopes, likewise intrigue
against him. Such is to Congreve " the way of the world," —
a battle of wits, now merry, now ridiculous, wherein even love
partakes of egotism and affectation. Had he continued his great
career, true comedy would not have declined because of a failure
to understand its principles or an inability to apply them.

Farquhar,[2] whose style is sprightlier than Vanbrugh's, and
whose plots, though less well built, are livelier, had artistic gifts

[1] Act I, scene ii.

[2] Cf. William Archer, Introduction to Farquhar's plays in the *Mermaid Series*
(1902) ; John Palmer, *The Comedy of Manners* (1913), chap. vii ; and Louis A.
Strauss, Introduction to Farquhar's plays in the *Belles Lettres Series* (1914).

which might have enabled him to support the highest traditions in comedy. He was acquainted with that tradition, and could in his brilliant but shallow *Essay on Comedy* chat about "schooling mankind into better manners" being "the *utile*," "the primary design of comedy";[1] yet he was ever ready to sacrifice the ethical to the entertaining. His observation of life was as superficial as quick, and he was too much a creature of moods to cultivate singleness of purpose. The standards of comedy were, as we have seen, flexible; but he bent them so far that at times he distorted them. His first three plays, — *Love and a Bottle* (1698), *The Constant Couple* (1699), and *Sir Harry Wildair* (1701), — admitted characters that came near being lovable, and situations that hovered on the verge of the emotional, with a freedom that transcended the most liberal practices of his predecessors. These plays were nevertheless, in general intention and effect, true comedies, their frequent vacillations toward the sentimental being invariably checked.

Farquhar's young gentlemen are too sincerely eloquent and passionate lovers to be the rakes of Restoration comedy, and are too joyously abandoned to dissipation to be the exculpated prodigals of sentimental comedy. Their creator loved them without diminishing or wholly excusing their offenses. In *Love and a Bottle*, Leanthe apostrophises one of them:

> Wild as winds, and unconfined as air! Yet I may reclaim him. His follies are weakly founded, upon the principles of honor, where the very foundation helps to undermine the structure. How charming would virtue look in him, whose behavior can add a grace to the unseemliness of vice![2]

Yet neither she nor the other young ladies in these three plays, reclaim such youths by a touching appeal to "the principles of honor." Leanthe wins her scapegrace by a stratagem of no little

---

[1] *Essay on Comedy* (1702), ed. L. A. Strauss, p. 21.
[2] Act III, scene i.

impropriety.[1] The modest Angelica in *The Constant Couple* is rendered very unhappy by Sir Harry Wildair's profligacy; but the notable scene between them, which might easily have been made sentimental, is kept comic (and very far from " genteel ") by the drunken Sir Harry's mistaken belief that she is a lady of pleasure and that her virtuous protestations are mock-heroics. He is quite unabashed by her innocence, and finally marries her not out of pity or respect but out of reluctance to fight a duel.[2]

In the same play, Lady Lurewell and Colonel Standard, lovers who were separated for many years, find each other again and are joyfully reunited, — a theme of inexhaustible interest to sentimentalists, who interpreted such reunions as a reward for the virtue of the characters. That is not, however, Farquhar's conception. Colonel Standard has distinctly attractive qualities, but he does not even pretend that his proposals to Lady Lurewell (before the recognition) are honorable. He and Lady Lurewell are " constant " to one another's memories only in the somewhat esoteric sense that neither will engage in love-affairs with the intention of matrimony. Lady Lurewell,[3] though she weeps when thinking of the lover of her youth, is during most of the play spitefully occupied in entrapping and plaguing all the suitors she can attract. In these instances and many similar ones, Farquhar with some effort saves himself from a surrender to the sentimental mood; but so often he nearly submits to it that these three comedies suffer a lamentable impairment in unity of tone and in consistency of ethical principle.[4]

---

[1] Act V, scenes i, iii.   [2] Act V, scene i.

[3] Like Madam Fickle in D'Urfey's comedy of that title, from which Farquhar borrowed much of his play.

[4] Dr. L. A. Strauss, p. xxxix, sees sentimental tendencies in Farquhar's *The Inconstant* (1702), based on Fletcher's *The Wild-Goose Chase*. The scene is Paris; and Oriana, like Leanthe in *Love and a Bottle*, wins her lover by a trick.

Such being Farquhar's tendency, it is not surprising that he was the first to follow Cibber in writing sentimental comedy. In *The Twin Rivals* (1702) he bestowed upon the appropriately named Constance a fidelity which was not dubious like Lady Lurewell's but as true as that of Cibber's Amanda. During the long absence of Constance's fiancé Wouldbe, his rascally twin brother tries, by intrigues which occupy the greater portion of the play, to gain both her and the estate of Wouldbe. All his machinations are in vain against her faithful love. She is led to believe Wouldbe dead, and mourns him in the following words, which he, concealed, overhears :

> I have ... no pomp of black and darkened rooms, no formal month for visits on my bed; I am content with the slight mourning of a broken heart, and all my form is tears. ... [*Gazing on his portrait*] With this I 'll sigh, with this converse, gaze on his image, till I grow blind with weeping. . .
>
> *Wouldbe* [*rushing forward*]
>
> Here let me worship that perfection whose virtue might attract the listening angels, and make 'em smile to see such purity, so like themselves in human shape ! [1]

Before their troubles are at an end, there is another tearful scene, in which Wouldbe, having been thrown into prison, is visited and consoled by Constance. To the sympathetically drawn portrait of these lovers, Farquhar added that of the generous merchant Fairbank, a kind-hearted citizen who, on relieving Wouldbe from poverty, is justly praised by him as follows :

> Gramercy, citizen ! surely if Justice were an herald she would give this tradesman a nobler coat of arms than my brother.[2]

Even more sentimentally treated than the story of Wouldbe and Constance is that of Richmore and Clelia. She is his

---

[1] Act III, scene iii.   [2] Act III, scene ii.

forsaken mistress. In Restoration comedy she might have inveigled him into marriage by tricks of comic effect.[1] But Richmore is induced to atone for his conduct by an appeal to his feelings. The man upon whom he tries to pass off Clelia discovers her plight, takes pity on her, and determines to see justice done. After sparing Richmore's life in a duel, he nobly pleads for the wronged girl. Richmore, exclaiming "your virtue warms my breast and melts it into tenderness," is moved to repentance and agrees to marry Clelia.[2] This reformation Farquhar, with characteristic flightiness, sneered at in his preface, remarking that Richmore "was no sooner off the stage but he changed his mind, and the poor lady is still *in statu quo*"; in the play itself, however, the sentimental tone of the episode is sustained to the end. The preface admitted that though "the persons are too mean for the heroic," *The Twin Rivals* had "sentiments too grave for diversion." This departure from the rules Farquhar defended on the ground that "exposing vice is the business of the drama." The real issue, — whether comedy should not confine itself to exposing vice by ridicule, — he evaded.[3]

The second writer to follow Cibber was an actor in the same company with him, Richard Estcourt.[4] The title of his sentimental comedy, *The Fair Example* (10 April, 1703), is a significant one, as is also this line of the prologue: "Some mirth, some pity, would our action move." The "fair example"

---

[1] Such tricks, usually unsuccessful, as those of Madam Fickle in D'Urfey's play of that title (1676), Mrs. Loveit in Etherege's *Man of Mode* (1676), Corina in Betterton's *Revenge* (1680), Mrs. Termagant in Shadwell's *Squire of Alsatia* (1688) (wherein the disposal of Lucia by false representations also furnishes a contrast to the above treatment), Silvia in Congreve's *Old Bachelor* (1693), Belira in Mrs. Manley's *Lost Lover* (1696), etc.

[2] Act V, scene iii.

[3] Farquhar alludes to Collier both in this preface and apparently also in that to his true comedy, *The Constant Couple*.

[4] Cf. *The Spectator*, Nos. 358 and 468.

is set by Lucia. Her heart had been formerly won by Spring-love; but he, being too poor to make her his wife, has had to see her married to an elderly and jealous husband. He there-upon tries to seduce Lucia, whose husband treats her so un-kindly that she might almost be excused for infidelity to him. But though "her heart bleeds with tenderness and pity," she remains true to her vows. She does not circumvent her lover by means of comic intrigues; she repulses his repeated advances by firm refusals and exhortations to virtue.[1] Inspired by her exemplary conduct, Springlove renounces his immoral passion. Estcourt had not sufficient stylistic power to express this sacri-fice of love on the altar of duty with the poignancy it demanded; yet he deserves to be remembered as one of the three dram-atists who preceded Richard Steele in the writing of senti-mental comedies.

The development of Steele as a dramatist resembles that of Farquhar, and was influenced by it. He too wrote his first play, *The Funeral* (1701), in the comic style, but admitted some passages out of harmony with its dominant tone. Too often the faithful servant Trusty "indulges himself in telling fond tales that melt him and interrupt his story."[2] His master, Lord Brumpton, finds it difficult to steel his heart against his unworthy wife.[3] Young Lord Hardy solemnly protests that a woman's beauty is less to be praised than her "friendship, piety, house-hold cares, maternal tenderness."[4] His beloved, Lady Sharlot, rapturously acclaims the purity of his affection.[5] But none of these sentimental touches is the main impulse of the action. What is emphasized in the courtship of Lady Sharlot and Lord

---

[1] Act II, scene i; Act IV, scene ii; Act V, scene i. Contrast Mrs. Ford and Mrs. Page in *The Merry Wives of Windsor*, which was being played at this time (Genest, II, 307).

[2] *The Funeral*, Act IV, scene ii; in *Mermaid Series*, pp. 65–67.

[3] Act V, scene iv, pp. 91–92.

[4] Act II, scene i, p. 30.   [5] Act V, scene iv, p. 87.

Hardy is the humorous bashfulness of his wooing, and her ingenious elopement in a coffin. Her sister's love-affair is likewise conducted in the traditional way: after her "vanity of being pursued by sighs" has been overcome by the raillery of her lover, they elope in ridiculous disguises. The principal character of the play, Lady Brumpton, a heartless hypocrite who mistakenly thinks her husband dead and thereupon, though secretly glad, goes into pretentious mourning, is not sentimentally forgiven, nor does she repent. After her schemes for the future have been frustrated by Trusty, and Lord Brumpton's eyes have been opened to her perfidy, she is dismissed with contempt. Some farcical scenes dealing with undertakers, the merry comedy of intrigue in which the lovers figure, and especially the scornful satire against hypocrisy, — these are the essential elements of the play. All else is of significance only as pointing to the author's future.

Steele's first sentimental comedy is *The Lying Lover* (2 December, 1703).[1] In its preface he confessed that pathetic scenes were perhaps "an injury to the rules of comedy," but he had observed that they were "frequently applauded on the stage."[2] The time had come, it seemed to him, to attack debauchery, not with ridicule, but by causing the public "to tremble with horror" at its grievous consequences. To excite mirth was a lower achievement than "with pity to chastise delight." Laughter was the despicable issue of pride and scorn, and left us discontented; pity was of divine origin, and "made us ourselves both more approve and know."[3] Society should banish "all entertainment which does not proceed from simplicity of

---

[1] It has long been maintained that with this play the history of sentimental comedy begins. Cf. A. W. Ward, *History of English Dramatic Literature* (1899), III, 495; and M. E. Hare, *Steele and the Sentimental Comedy*, in *Oxford Miscellany* (1909), p. 9.

[2] It should be noted that Steele makes no pretensions to be the founder of sentimental comedy.   [3] Epilogue.

mind, good-nature, friendship, and honor." [1] In view of these grave sentiments, it is surprising that the first four acts of *The Lying Lover*, like those of *Love's Last Shift*, were mainly comic. In them Steele followed the methods of his source, Corneille's *Le Menteur*, which exposed the folly of a liar by placing him in ridiculous predicaments. So Steele's Young Bookwit, through persistent lying to gain the ladies' favor, gets into amusing scrapes, flirts outrageously with his friend Lovemore's fiancée Penelope, and fights a duel with the jealous lover. Not until then do the serious events begin.

Since Lovemore is believed to have been killed, Young Bookwit is thrown into prison. In his distress, his better self is aroused : he deplores, not his own desperate situation, but the death of his friend. Too late he realizes that the so-called honor which demands duelling is a euphemism for revenge. His weeping father tries to comfort him.

> *Young Bookwit*
>
> Oh, best of fathers! Let me not see your tears;
> Don't double my afflictions by your woe.
> There's consolation when a friend laments us,
> But when a parent grieves the anguish is
> Too native, too much our own, to be called pity.[2]

Penelope too is distressed by Lovemore's supposed death, laments her foolish flirtation, and mourns "one whose love I know too late." At Young Bookwit's trial, his friend Latine tries to save him by alleging that he, and not the prisoner, struck the fatal blow. Thereupon Lovemore, who was not even wounded, and who, disguised, has observed the penitence of Young Bookwit and the generosity of Latine, reveals himself, exclaiming, "Let me grasp you both, who in an age as

[1] Dedication.

[2] Act V, scene iii, pp. 179–180. Steele's verse and his prose are not always distinguishable.

degenerate as this have such transcendent virtue ! " [1]   Need
one add that all ends happily ?

Says Thackeray in one of his American lectures :

> Steele was the founder of sentimental writing in English, and how
> the land has been since occupied, and what hundreds of us have laid
> out gardens and built up tenements on Steele's ground! Before his
> time readers or hearers were never called upon to cry except at a
> tragedy. . . . He took away comedy from behind the fine lady's al-
> cove, or the screen where the libertine was watching her. He ended
> all that wretched business of wives jeering at their husbands ; of rakes
> laughing wives, and husbands too, to scorn. That miserable, rouged,
> tawdry, sparkling, hollow-hearted comedy of the Restoration fled be-
> fore him, and, like the wicked spirit of the fairy-books, shrank, as
> Steele let the daylight in, and shrieked, and shuddered, and vanished. [2]

That is prettily said, but it is not history. Steele neither exorcised Restoration comedy, which held the stage decades after
his death ; nor did he found sentimental comedy. Cibber and
Farquhar set him the example of arousing a moral emotion by
a pathetic appeal, and they created the types of character upon
which most of the personages in *The Lying Lover* are modelled.
Old Bookwit, the pathetic father, is in this play Steele's only
wholly new contribution to the personnel of the drama of sensibility. His attack upon duelling was also novel. The rest of
the play is not remarkable for either originality of conception
or superior skill in execution.

Of the four sentimental comedies so far produced (1696–
1703), the first had won a lasting success, but the others came
very near being failures. [3] The progress of the genre was thus
doubtful, when Cibber came to its rescue with *The Careless*

---

[1] Act V, scene iii, pp. 181–183.

[2] W. M. Thackeray, *Charity and Humour*.

[3] *The Fair Example* may have run seven or eight nights (Genest, II, 270–
272). *The Twin Rivals* and *The Lying Lover* ran six. Both Farquhar and
Steele acknowledged them unsuccessful. Cf. Farquhar in *Belles Lettres Series*,
p. ix ; and Steele in *Mermaid Series*, pp. xviii–xix and 98.

Husband (7 December, 1704), and established, in the face of declining fortunes, its permanent popularity. The serious passages of the play are at least as extensive as in any previous work of its kind, and from first to last it is dominated by its sentimental heroine, Lady Easy. Though she feels her "careless husband" to be good at heart, she suffers under his waywardness. She knows that she has reason to be jealous of his relations with her maid, Mrs. Edging, and with the fashionable Lady Graveairs. But she conceals from him her knowledge of his conduct, and strives to win him by affectionate patience. When the impudent Mrs. Edging tries to arouse her jealousy of Lady Graveairs, she reproves her. Even when Sir Charles Easy himself tries to discover whether his wife suspects him, she is not moved to reproach him.[1]

A crowning act of love and forbearance brings Lady Easy her deserved reward. At the climax of the play, she comes upon "Sir Charles without his periwig, and Mrs. Edging by him, both asleep in two easy chairs." At the sight of this bold infidelity, she "starts, and trembles, sometime unable to speak," and then exclaims :

> Protect me, Virtue, Patience, Reason!
> Teach me to bear this killing sight, or let
> Me think my dreaming senses are deceived!
> For sure a sight like this might raise the arm
> Of duty, even to the breast of love! At least
> I 'll throw this vizor of my patience off,
> Now wake him in his guilt,
> And barefaced front him with my wrongs;
> I 'll talk to him till he blushes, nay till he —
> Frowns on me perhaps — and then
> I 'm lost again. — The ease of a few tears
> Is all that 's left to me ;
> And duty too forbids me to insult
> When I have vowed obedience. Perhaps

---

[1] Act I, scene i; Act II, scene i.

The fault 's in me, and nature has not formed
Me with the thousand little requisites
That warm the heart to love.
Somewhere there is a fault,
But Heaven best knows what both of us deserve. —
    Ha! bare-headed, and in so sound a sleep!
Who knows while thus exposed to th' unwholesome air
But Heaven offended may overtake his crime,
And in some languishing distemper leave him
A severe example of its violated laws, —
Forbid it mercy, and forbid it love:
This may prevent it.
    [*Takes a steenkirk off her neck and lays it gently on his head.*][1]

When Sir Charles awakes, and observes what his wife has done, "a crowd of recollected circumstances" throng upon his remorseful soul, and assure him that her forbearance of his errors was not due to her being unaware of them. He hastens to her, humbles himself, confesses all, and begs to be forgiven. She weeps with joy: at last the recognition of virtue has reformed him.[2]

A curious circumstance concerning *The Careless Husband* throws a strong light upon the relation of sentimental comedy to the real life of the time. The original of Lady Easy was the wife of Cibber's friend, Colonel Henry Brett.[3] The actual Mrs. Brett will, however, hardly bear comparison with her literary portrait. Her first husband, the Earl of Macclesfield, she deserted. Thereafter she had two illegitimate children, with one of whom the poet Richard Savage claimed identity. She finally

---

[1] Act V, scene iv.

[2] Act V, scene v. DeW. C. Croissant, *Studies in Cibber*, p. 50, remarks that the reformation of Sir Charles Easy is felt to be more permanent than that of Loveless in *Love's Last Shift*. I think Cibber intended Loveless to be as thoroughly reformed; it was Vanbrugh's *Relapse* which questioned the possibility.

[3] James Boswell, *Life of Dr. Johnson*, ed. George Birkbeck Hill (1891), I, 201, note 1.

became the wife of Colonel Brett, whose handsome looks had led her to rescue him, then a stranger to her, from the hands of bailiffs. Her daughter was the first English mistress of George I.[1] The transformation of the notorious Mrs. Brett into the exemplary Lady Easy strikingly illustrates that the sentimental dramatist aimed not at a truthful but at a flattering picture of life.

Love's Last Shift, The Twin Rivals, The Fair Example, The Lying Lover, and *The Careless Husband* are of remarkable historical interest because they were in their day the only works, — not merely in the drama, but in all literature, — that interpreted ordinary life sentimentally. Tendencies toward sentimentalism may, to be sure, be seen in Rowe's tragedies; the hero of his *Tamerlane* (1702) is a faultless pacificist who stands in striking contrast to Lee's Mithridates, and *The Fair Penitent* (1703) calls itself "a melancholy tale of private woes";[2] but Rowe did not break the rule that forbade the pathetic representation of contemporary domestic life. The masterpieces of 1696–1704 were (besides the previously mentioned true comedies by Vanbrugh and Congreve) Dryden's translation of Virgil, Defoe's *Shortest Way with the Dissenters* and *Hymn to the Pillory*, and Swift's *Battle of the Books* and *Tale of a Tub*. It was to the classical and the satiric that the highest literary abilities of the time were devoted. Artistically *The Provoked Wife* and *The Way of the World* are far superior to the five sentimental comedies. In the latter themselves the pathetic passages are written with noticeably less ease than are the comic. To make ordinary personages speak in a sentimental way was an aim contrary to the accepted views of life and the regular methods of literature. It meant almost the learning of a new language; and in the first attempts the style was halting and inexpressive, if not grotesque.

---

[1] *Dictionary of National Biography*, art. "Henry Brett."
[2] Cf. A. H. Thorndike, *Tragedy* (1908), pp. 283–287.

Though Cibber, Farquhar, and Steele knew that their senti-mental comedies represented a revolt against authority, they did not themselves clearly comprehend the fundamental impulse of that revolt. Vanbrugh had seen and attacked it, but they paid no attention to him. They talked vaguely about the morality of their plays ; they said nothing about their sentimentality. They indulged this mood, not because they had reflected upon it, not because they thought it the supremest state of the human spirit, but merely by chance or out of caprice. Not one of them confined himself to writing sentimental comedies, or excluded the comic therefrom. At its rise, the drama of sen-sibility was without the support of clearly conceived ethical and literary principles.

Though they worked somewhat blindly, the founders of the school accomplished between 1696 and 1704 work of lasting im-portance. They destroyed forever the tradition that the pathetic must be excluded from comedy, and that virtuous characters must be confined to romantic drama. They created several characters which were in the future to be copied, with slight variations, again and again, — the sorely-tried but loyal wife, the maiden faithful to her absent lover, the pitiable forsaken mistress finally restored to respect, the repentant young prodi-gal, the nobly generous friend, and the wayward but reclaimable husband. They made these characters utter virtuous sentiments that uplifted the hearts of their audiences with admiration, and they placed them in emotional situations that evoked the tribute of tears. They opened the doors of a new world, which pro-fessed to be an image of the real one, but in which pity and love and virtue dwelt supreme.

CHAPTER VI

THE DRAMA OF SENSIBILITY, THE MORAL ESSAY, AND SENTIMENTAL PHILOSOPHY: 1704–1709

After successfully invading comedy, sentimentalism appeared in domestic tragedy. The first eighteenth-century play of that type is an anonymous work, *The Rival Brothers* (1704).[1] In purpose and in characterization, it is indistinguishable from sentimental comedy; what differentiates it is the dénouement. The action of the tragedy, which (again as in sentimental comedy) is written partly in prose and partly in blank verse, takes place at a country house. Two brothers are in love with the same maiden. The elder wins her heart, and marries her secretly. He tells his bride that, to prevent discovery by her father, who sleeps in an adjoining room, he will come at night to her chamber door, knock softly thrice, and silently enter. The younger brother overhears the agreement, which he imagines to mean a seduction. Intending to save the maiden's honor, and compel her to marry him, he takes the bridegroom's place. The next morning he is horrified to discover that instead of preventing a wrong, he has betrayed his brother's wife. All three seek relief in death.

Here is again the theme which Otway, in *The Orphan* (1680), had elevated by a romantic style and setting; and for which the author of *The Hog hath lost his Pearl* (1613) had provided, in spite of the apparently irremediable calamity, a conclusion that was not unhappy.[2] The Elizabethan dramatist

[1] Genest, II, 311; H. W. Singer, *Das bürgerliche Trauerspiel*, pp. 80–83.
[2] Chaps. iii and iv, above.

showed the betrayer fully conscious of the enormity of his deed, and the distress the logical result of sinful passion. In the eighteenth-century play, on the contrary, the catastrophe is the accidental consequence of a virtuous intention. The younger brother means to right what he thinks a wrong; it is the mere fatality of his overhearing only one half of his brother's secret that brings misery and death to three innocent people. Fate looms large in this branch of the drama of sensibility. The running title of *The Rival Brothers* is *The Fatal Secret*, and the word " fatal " is harped upon in succeeding domestic tragedies. Without fate as the determining power, consistent sentimentalists could not have written tragedy at all; for their personages, who were too virtuous to deserve a miserable end, could be brought thereto only by accident. The writers of domestic tragedy, like the poets in Pandemonium that Milton scorned,

> complain that Fate
> Free Virtue should enthral to force or chance.

That note, first struck by the author of *The Rival Brothers*, gave the key to all his successors. His attempt was, however, premature, and the play was a failure. The public, ready to receive sympathetically scenes of temporary distress, still insisted upon a happy ending.

The popularity of sentimental comedy between 1705 and 1709 is evidenced by the fact that of the eight comedies produced during those years with distinct success, four were of the new type. The other four, fashioned in the older manner, were Vanbrugh's *Confederacy* (1705). Farquhar's *The Recruiting Officer* (1706), Cibber's *The Double Gallant* (1707), and Mrs. Centlivre's *The Busy-Body* (1709). With the exception of Farquhar's play, these were influenced by the French comic tradition as well as by the English; for they borrowed directly or indirectly from plays by Dancourt, Corneille, and Molière.

Vanbrugh continued to be the most unwavering supporter of the orthodox standard. His *Confederacy*, in which two rich citizens' wives try to ape the dissipation of the fashionable set, ends with the comic exposure of all concerned ; nobody is "reformed," and the satiric purpose is never abandoned. Farquhar, temporarily discouraged by the failure of *The Twin Rivals* from pursuing the sentimental way, returned to the humorous manner of his earliest plays. *The Recruiting Officer* involves two pairs of lovers in absurd misunderstandings, and presents the amusing aspects of army enlistments in a country town. Its satire, unlike Vanbrugh's, is always good-natured. The characters in Cibber's *The Double Gallant* are less engaging than Farquhar's ;[1] and the twofold purpose of the play is to show the comic predicaments into which duplicity throws a lover, and to "cure" by ridicule a woman who affects to be a valetudinarian. Its extraordinary success shows that Cibber could write at least as acceptably in the comic style as in the sentimental. Mrs. Centlivre's *The Busy-Body* is an ingeniously constructed comedy of intrigue, in which bourgeois fathers are outwitted by their daughters' lovers, and the well-known Marplot disturbs the plans of those he tries to aid. In these various efforts, — whether predominantly satiric, humorous, or farcical, — the comic tradition did not as yet show alarming signs of a decline.

Three of the four sentimental comedies of 1705–1709 do not manifest that further development of the characteristic quality of the type which the hearty welcome accorded to the emotional scenes of *The Careless Husband* might lead one to expect. Mrs. Centlivre, most of whose plays are comic, made a moderately successful, but not a bold, experiment in the sentimental with *The Gamester* (22 February, 1705). Its source was Regnard's *Le Joueur*, a true comedy, in which Valère, after

---

[1] Clerimont's offering his undefended breast to his rival's sword (Act V, scene ii) is a generous act of little consequence.

losing his beloved Angelica through his inability to refrain from hazarding her gift at the gaming table, remains to the end the slave of his ruling passion, consoling himself with the hope that

> quelque jour
> Le jeu m'acquittera des pertes de l'amour.

Mrs. Centlivre, while retaining much of the French play, modified sentimentally the character of Valère and the dénouement. The instant after her Valere loses Angelica's gift, he is stricken with remorse, and vows never to gamble again ;[1] and when Angelica breaks her engagement with him, and his father disinherits him, his contrition is sincere. Resolving to go abroad, he asks Angelica not to dismiss him without a word of pardon, saying :

> My being disinherited weighs not a hair, compared with what I 've lost in losing you, whom my soul prefers before all wealth, friends, or family. . . . Thus on my knees I beg you not to hate my memory, nor suffer the follies which I have now cashiered forever from my breast (but oh, too late !) to drive my name as distant as my body from you. Sometimes vouchsafe to think on lost Valere !

Angelica, who is touched by his humility, and whose heart " beats as if the strings were breaking," thereupon relents, and marries him, fully confident that he has reformed forever.[2] There is sentimentalism likewise in the subplot of *The Gamester*, in which Angelica's sister, a widow fascinated by fashionable follies, but one " in whose soul honor is centered," is reclaimed by her lover, who generously protects her reputation though her conduct might well have incited him to betray it.[3] These serious passages, though they determine the outcome of

[1] Close of Act IV.

[2] Close of Act V. In Mrs. Centlivre's *Dramatic Works* (1872), I, 191–192, Cf. Fritz Grober, *Das Verhältnis von Susannah Centlivre's " The Gamester" zu Regnards " Le Joueur"* (1900).

[3] Act V, scene ii; *Works* (1872), p. 185.

both plots, are brief; and, despite their author's sex, were not written with greater tenderness of feeling than similar scenes in previous plays. It was probably the merry intrigues of Valere and Angelica, which Mrs. Centlivre skillfully adapted from *Le Joueur*, that chiefly served to win the appreciation of her audiences. In *The Basset Table* (1705), where a female gamester is reformed by an amusing stratagem, and in subsequent plays, she avoided the sentimental.

Steele's *The Tender Husband* (23 April, 1705) was dedicated to Addison as "no improper memorial of an inviolable friendship." Addison wrote the prologue; and, to an extent which cannot be ascertained, collaborated in the play itself. "When it was last acted," says Steele, "there were so many applauded strokes in it which I had from the same hand [Addison's], that I thought very meanly of myself that I have never publicly acknowledged them." [1]

The closing lines of *The Tender Husband* sum up its double theme :

> You 've seen th' extremes of the domestic life,
> A son too much confined, too free a wife ;
> By generous bonds you either should restrain,
> And only on their inclinations gain ;
> Wives, to obey, must love ; children, revere ;
> While only slaves are governed by their fear.

The two parts of the play are disproportionate ; and it is the smaller part, concerned with "too free a wife," that is sentimental. In it Steele plainly shows the influence of Cibber, for it is a reversal of the main situation in *The Careless Husband*.[2] Mrs. Clerimont, in visiting Italy and France, has become possessed with some of the fashionable follies of those countries, including an affectation of indifference to her husband, and a fondness for dangerous flirtations. To regain her love,

---

[1] *The Spectator*, No. 555.
[2] A. W. Ward, *English Dramatic Literature* (1899), III, 495–496.

Clerimont induces his former mistress to assume male attire, play the gallant to his wife, and lure her into a compromising situation. At that juncture, he issues from concealment, discourses about the risk which she has run, and urges the claims of conjugal love. Mrs. Clerimont " kneels, weeps, and is convinced." [1] In this there is little that is original, or even progressive ; the sentimental scenes, in comparison with those of Cibber, are neither long nor intense. Perhaps it was the failure of *The Lying Lover* that discouraged Steele from advancing farther in the new path.

The moral of the other, and by far greater, portion of *The Tender Husband* is that children should be " restrained by generous bonds," and " gained only through their inclinations." Here was a doctrine well suited to the methods of sentimental comedy, but Steele did not inculcate it by portraying fond parents and naturally devoted children. After the manner of Restoration comedy, he satirized the would-be romantic Biddy Tipkin, her bumpkin lover Humphry, and the latter's despotic father, Squire Gubbin. In the scenes enlivened by these characters, Steele displayed a comic power elsewhere unsurpassed by him. *The Tender Husband* is the most enjoyable, if not the best, of his plays. So far as the development of sentimental drama is concerned, however, it marks a backward step, its author having failed to seize a good opportunity to enlarge the scope of the genre.[2]

[1] Act I, scene i ; Act V, scene i. With this treatment of the theme may be contrasted the comic method of Vanbrugh's *The Confederacy*, which was produced five months later (30 October, 1705).

[2] In framing an acceptable definition of sentimental comedy, *The Tender Husband* should not be overlooked. It shows how large may be the proportion of comic scenes in a play that, by common consent of all writers on the subject, is a sentimental comedy.

It may be noted in passing that in 1706 there was published *The Roving Husband Reclaimed*, " a comedy written by a club of ladies, in vindication of virtuous plays " (British Museum Catalogue).

Hesitant resort to sentimentalism is observable in Farquhar's *The Beaux' Stratagem* (8 March, 1707).[1] There are slight sentimental touches in the love-affair between Archer and Mrs. Sullen. She suffers under a boorish and hateful husband, and weeps when she contrasts her misery with the happiness of others.[2] The violent wooing of her bold lover provides a very emotional scene.[3] But these are merely such inconsequential aberrations as are found in Farquhar's true comedies. The emotional scene is interrupted by a farcical burglary, and the divorce of Mrs. Sullen takes place in the gayest possible manner. It is the other plot of *The Beaux' Stratagem* that Farquhar motivated and concluded sentimentally.

This begins, to be sure, merrily enough : Aimwell, a gentleman of broken fortunes, seeks to entrap the wealthy Dorinda into marriage by pretending to be a lord. Feigning to fall dangerously ill at her gates, he gains admission to her house. Dorinda is enchanted with the idea of becoming Lady Aimwell ; and after he has rescued the household from burglary, the success of his scheme seems assured. Touched by the evident sincerity of her love, however, his sense of honor is aroused.

Aimwell

(*Aside*) Such goodness who could injure! I find myself unequal to the task of villain; she has gained my soul and made it honest like her own. I cannot, cannot hurt her. . . . (*To Dorinda*) Madam, behold your lover and your proselyte, and judge of my passion by my conversion! I 'm all a lie, nor dare I give a fiction to your arms; I 'm all counterfeit except my passion. . . . I am no lord, but a poor, needy man, come with a mean, a scandalous design to prey upon your fortune. But the beauties of your mind and person have so won me from myself that, like a trusty servant, I prefer the interest of my mistress to my own. . . .

---

[1] This play is usually not considered a sentimental comedy.
[2] Act III, scene iii; Act IV, scene i; ed. *Belles Lettres Series*, pp. 273–274, 295.   [3] Act V, scene ii, pp. 312–313.

Dorinda

Matchless honesty! Once I was proud, sir, of your wealth and title, but now am prouder that you want it; now I can show my love was justly levelled, and had no aim but love.[1]

Aimwell and Dorinda are thus raised above the unscrupulous lovers in most of Farquhar's plays, and attain the moral level of Wouldbe and Constance in his *The Twin Rivals*. *The Beaux Stratagem*, like Mrs. Centlivre's *The Gamester* and Steele's *The Tender Husband*, — which it far surpasses in delightful originality of action and briskness of dialogue, — is a sentimental comedy, but one which marks no progress in the essential characteristics of the type.

The real advance during this period (1705–1709) was made by Colley Cibber in *The Lady's Last Stake* (13 December, 1707). Again he met with success: the play remained through the first half of the century a favorite, and was performed as late as 1786. In it there are, as usual, comic scenes and characters; but the general trend and the dénouement of both plots are exceptionally serious. The plot to which the sub-title, *The Wife's Resentment*, applies, was intended, as Cibber announced in his prologue, to refute those critics of *The Careless Husband* who had judged its patient heroine a poor-spirited creature. The corresponding character in the new play is, like Lady Easy, unhappy in marriage. Originally estranged by a mere trifle, she and her husband have grown, first indifferent, then hostile. She observes that he is becoming a libertine, but scorning what she terms the "groveling virtue" of Lady Easy,[2] she does not try to regain him by loving devotion. She irritates him with jealous surveillance, and causes him obstinately to persist in his course of gallantry. Suspecting that he is going to a rendezvous in Hyde Park, she pursues him thither in a hackney-coach;

---

[1] Act V, scene iv, pp. 324–325.
[2] Act IV, scene i; Cibber's *Works* (1777), II, 253.

but, the traces of it having been cut, he escapes, and she is left discomfited, "fairly overset in the middle of a swingeing shower,"[1] a situation which, in a true comedy satirizing a jealous wife, would have been the appropriate dénouement.

In this case, however, the conjugal differences, which are from the beginning not regarded as due to irremediable faults of human nature, are sentimentally adjusted. Just as the pair are about to agree upon a separation by mutual consent, a peacemaker is found in Sir Friendly Moral. He penetrates to the insignificant root of the trouble, and explains to Lady Wronglove the error of her resentment. "Lure him home with soft affection," he pleads; and the contrite Lady Wronglove weeps. Then, turning to the husband, the mediator says:

> Look there, and while those softening tears reproach you, think on the long-watched, restless hours she already has endured from your misdoing. . . .

Lord Wronglove

> Though perhaps my negligence of temper may have stood the frowns of love unmoved, yet I find no guard within that can support me against its tears. . . .

Lady Wronglove

> What means this soft effusion in my breast? an aching tenderness ne'er felt before!

Lord Wronglove

> I cannot bear that melting eloquence of eyes. Yet nearer, closer to my heart, and live forever there, — thus blending our dissolving souls in dumb unutterable softness. . . .

Sir Friendly Moral

> Age has not yet so drained me but when I see a tenderness in virtue's eye, my heart will soften, and its springs will flow. . . . I knew you both had virtue.[2]

The other plot of *The Lady's Last Stake* is devoted to an attack upon gambling. Its sentimental passages are much longer

---

[1] Act III, scene i, p. 240.   [2] Act V, scene i, pp. 279–281.

and more emotional than those in Mrs. Centlivre's *The Gamester*. The victim of the fever is in this instance a woman. Mrs. Centlivre had two years earlier than Cibber depicted a female gamester in *The Basset Table*, but in a comic manner. Her Lady Reveller is "reclaimed by a stratagem." A lover of Lady Reveller, in order to gain her hand, persuades a friend of his to lend her money and, on the strength of that favor, to assault her honor, whereupon he himself is gallantly to " rescue " her. The trick succeeds : Lady Reveller, suspecting nothing, and weeping with gratitude, accepts her noble deliverer, while his roguish accomplice, watching unbeknownst, says with gleeful satisfaction, " It takes as I could wish." [1]

In *The Lady's Last Stake*, a similar situation is seriously treated. Lady Gentle, who is " of impregnable virtue " and " inclined to the unfashionable folly of loving her husband," has become addicted to card-playing. She grows more and more heavily indebted to Lord George, who is planning to seduce her. He is, however, engaged in the intrigue chiefly because he desires to be thought a successful gallant; his real affections are centered upon Miss Conquest. The latter discovers his scheme; and, aided by Sir Friendly Moral, plans to prevent its execution. Lady Gentle loses to Lord George £2000, a sum quite beyond her means to pay. He urges her to play one more hand : if she wins, she is to regain all her losses ; if not, she is nevertheless to have the money, but must give him " leave to hope." In despair, she takes the chance, and loses. She is at his feet, begging for mercy, when a messenger, secretly sent by her two friends, brings the necessary £2000. Lord George then tries to force her to his will, whereupon Miss Conquest, in male disguise, enters to defend her ; there is a quarrel, a challenge, and a hurried exit on the part of Lord George and his unknown opponent.

[1] *The Basset Table*, Act V, scene i; *Works* (1872), I, 250–251.

Burning under the insult to which she has been exposed, and dreading the scandal which the anticipated duel will bring upon her name, Lady Gentle bemoans her folly :

> This vice of play that has, I fear, undone me, appeared at first a harmless, safe amusement ; but, stealing into habit, its greatest hazards grew so familiar that even the face of ruin lost its terror to me. Oh, reflection ! how I shudder at thee ! The shameful memory of what I have done this night will live with me forever. . . . Oh, wretch, wretch ! that stoodst the foremost in the rank of prudent, happy wives, art now become the branded mark of infamy and shame ! [1]

In the end, the duel is of course averted, by the discovery that the defender of Lady Gentle was none other than Miss Conquest. But Lord George is made to suffer for his inconstancy. He is falsely told that Miss Conquest, on her way to the meeting, has been fatally hurt by ruffians. He begs her to pardon him ; and his grief is so deep that she forgives his offense, and marries him.

That both plots are markedly sentimental is not the only respect in which *The Lady's Last Stake* furthered the development of the genre. An important addition to its personnel was made in Sir Friendly Moral. As his appropriate name suggests, he voices the ethical sentiments of the new comedy. Unlike the " raisonneur " of true comedy, he is not a man of the world wittily commenting on absurdities of conduct ; he is an idealist, solemnly protesting against vice and exhorting to virtue. By his acquaintances, Sir Friendly Moral is described as " a man of principle." " Give him his due," says Lord Wronglove, " with all his severity of principles he is as good humored and as well bred as if he had no principles at all." He loses no occasion for sententiousness : if a horse-trade is mentioned, he is right at hand with the remark, " What a shame it is the world should not call it by its true name, cheating, that men

---

[1] Act V, scene ii, p. 290.

of honor might not be guilty of it." To Lady Gentle he preaches against gambling, — " whose utmost pleasure is founded upon avarice and ill nature, for those are always the secret principles of deep play." Lord Wronglove he admonishes: " Troth! it grieves me to think you can abuse such happiness, and have no more ambition or regard to real honor than the wretched fine gentlemen in most of our modern comedies."[1] His faith in human nature, and his instant recognition of sensibility, are manifested when the emotional reconciliation of Lord and Lady Wronglove draws from him the admiring words, " I knew you both had virtue!" He had many successors. Sometimes such figures as he coalesce with the devoted father, the benevolent uncle, or the nobleman in disguise; but they are always recognizable as sentimental guides, philosophers, and friends, who seek nothing for themselves, but who confound villainy and smooth the path of distressed virtue. The first full-length portrait of this type was not the least of Cibber's many contributions to sentimental comedy.

The year 1709 marks the end of the period during which the sentimental interpretation of life was confined to the drama. Sentimentalism now begins to appear in two other kinds of literary work, one popular, the other academic, — the *Tatler* and *Spectator* papers of Richard Steele, and the philosophical rhapsodies of Lord Shaftesbury.

In most of the *Tatler* and *Spectator* papers, especially in Addison's, orthodox opinions on religious, ethical, and literary subjects prevail. The satiric or humorous spirit is stronger than the sentimental. Yet it was a dramatist of sensibility who founded *The Tatler*, and Steele left upon it and its successors the impress of the same spirit that characterizes his sentimental comedies. The aim of *The Tatler* and *The Spectator* was moral; but they were a *farrago*, and in them, as previously in comedy,

[1] Act III, scene i; Act V, scene i; pp. 246–249, 273.

the same aim was pursued by divergent and fundamentally inharmonious methods. Social prejudices, follies, and affectations, though usually attacked by ridicule or raillery, were often reproved in touching appeals to virtue. So, for example, neglectful husbands and wives are not only satirized, but at times seriously exhorted in tender descriptions of conjugal happiness.[1] The ideals of manhood and womanhood upheld are not infrequently those which had been personified in the heroes and heroines of sentimental comedies. "To be apt to shed tears," says Steele, "is a sign of great as well as little spirit"; and "that calm and elegant satisfaction which the vulgar call melancholy," he declares, "is the true and proper delight of men of knowledge and virtue."[2] The most important aids to the progress of sentimentalism, however, are to be found in certain dramatic criticisms and short narratives.

In his critical papers, Steele displayed a hostile attitude towards true comedy. He did not condemn the genre indiscriminately, but he misstated its aims and interpreted the boldness of its satire as reprehensible immorality. He asserted that some of its authors prostituted their artistic ability, and "gratified a loose age with a scandalous representation of what is reputable among men, not to say what is sacred."[3] He termed Ravenscroft's extraordinarily popular *The London Cuckolds* "that heap of vice and absurdity"; and Etherege's *The Man of Mode*, which still held the stage, "a perfect contradiction to good manners, good sense, and common honesty."[4] Wycherley's *The Country Wife* he censured as follows :

[1] For example, *Tatler*, Nos. 85, 149, 150, etc. Cf. the domestic narratives discussed below, pp. 111–114. Was it not Steele who said, "'Wife' is the most amiable term in human life"?

[2] *Tatler*, Nos. 68 and 89. Steele describes his own sensibility in a famous paper, No. 181.

[3] *Spectator*, No. 270.

[4] *Tatler*, No. 8; *Spectator*, No. 65.

The poet . . . insinuates that there is no defense against vice but the contempt of it. . . . The character of Horner, and the design of it, is a good representation of the age in which that comedy was written, at which time love and wenching were the business of life, and the gallant manner of pursuing women was the best recommendation at court. To which only it is to be imputed that a gentleman of Mr. Wycherley's character and sense condescends to represent the insults done to the honor of the bed without just reproof; but to have drawn a man of probity with regard to such considerations, had been a monster, and a poet had at that time discovered his want of knowing the manners of the age he lived in, by a virtuous character in his fine gentleman, as he would show his ignorance by drawing a vicious one to please the present audience.[1]

In this passage, Steele's insidious flattery of his own age helped to make acceptable his wilful or unintelligent misinterpretation of the purpose of the Restoration playwright.

The plays that were needed, according to Steele, were those " whence it is impossible to return without strong impressions of honor and humanity," — a criterion obviously discouraging to satiric comedy. Voicing the hopes of sentimental dramatists, he enthusiastically exclaims : " What may not be brought to pass by seeing generous things performed before our eyes?"[2] Comedies that satisfied his ideals were *The Lady's Last Stake*[3] and *The Careless Husband*. The latter will, he thinks, inspire a young dramatist who is writing a play described as follows :

It has in it all the reverent offices of life, such as regard to parents, husbands, and honorable lovers, preserved with the utmost care, and at the same time that agreeableness of behavior, with the intermixture of pleasing passions which arise from innocence and virtue, interspersed in such a manner as that to be charming and agreeable shall appear the natural consequence of being virtuous.[4]

The doctrine that it is peculiarly the function of literature to make virtue attractive, he dwelt upon with unction, saying :

[1] *Tatler*, No. 3. Cf. Steele's misinterpretation of Terence's *Heauton-timorumenos* (*Spectator*, No. 502), discussed in chap. ii, above.

[2] *Tatler*, No. 8.   [3] *Town Talk* (1715), No. 2.   [4] *Tatler*, No. 182.

The whole soul is insensibly betrayed into morality by bribing the fancy with beautiful and agreeable images of those very things that in the books of the philosophers appear austere, and have at the best but a kind of forbidden aspect. In a word, the poets do, as it were, strew the rough paths of virtue so full of flowers that we are not sensible of the uneasiness of them, and imagine ourselves in the midst of pleasures, and the most bewitching allurements at the time we are making a progress in the severest duties of life. . . . The grave and serious performances of such as write in the most engaging manner, by a kind of divine impulse, must be the most effectual persuasives to goodness.[1]

Such passages offered sentimental comedy stronger critical defenses than the brief recommendations heretofore somewhat casually expressed in the prologues and prefaces of Cibber, Farquhar, and Steele himself.

Sentimental comedy, however, was already flourishing. It was the other branch of the drama of sensibility that urgently needed an advocate. Of especial importance, therefore, are several of Steele's papers that advance theories in exact harmony with the methods of domestic tragedy.[2] Its essential principle, that tragedy is an accident to virtue, underlies the following reverie:

I have been looking at the fire, and in a pensive manner reflecting upon the great misfortunes and calamities incident to human life; among which there are none that touch us so sensibly as those which befall persons who eminently love and meet with fatal interruptions of their happiness when they least expect it. . . . The contemplation of distresses of this sort softens the mind of man, and makes the heart better. It extinguishes the seeds of envy and ill-will towards mankind, corrects the pride of prosperity, and beats down all that fierceness and insolence which are apt to get into the minds of the daring and fortunate. For this reason, the wise Athenians in their theatrical performances laid before the eyes of the people the greatest

---

[1] *Tatler*, No. 98.

[2] He likes plays in which "the persons are all of them laudable, and their misfortunes arise rather from unguarded virtue than propensity to vice."

afflictions which could befall human life, and insensibly polished their tempers by such representations. Among the moderns, indeed, there has arose a chimerical method of disposing the fortune of the persons represented according to what they call poetical justice, and letting none be unhappy but those who deserve it. In such cases an intelligent spectator, if he is concerned, knows he ought not to be so; and can learn nothing from such a tenderness but that he is a weak creature whose passions cannot follow the dictates of his understanding.[1]

In the last lines of that passage, Steele implicitly condemned the orthodox principle of tragic characterization. Against the other important established dogma, that a tragic action should exclusively deal with great personages, he entered this objection:

When unhappy catastrophes make up part of the history of princes and persons who act in high spheres, or are represented in the moving language and well-wrought scenes of tragedians, they do not fail of striking us with terror; but then they affect us only in a transient manner, and pass through our imaginations as incidents in which our fortunes are too humble to be concerned, or which writers form for the ostentation of their own force, or at most as things fit rather to exercise the powers of our minds than to create new habits in them. Instead of such passages, I was thinking it would be of great use (if anybody could hit it) to lay before the world such adventures as befall persons not exalted above the common level. This, methought, would better prevail upon the ordinary race of men, who are so prepossessed with outward appearances that they mistake fortune for nature, and believe nothing can relate to them that does not happen to such as live and look like themselves.[2]

These revolutionary literary theories were applied in a considerable number of narrative sketches and moral tales. " It has been a most exquisite pleasure to me," says Steele, " to frame characters of domestic life, and put those parts of it which are least observed into an agreeable view." [3] Concerning these stories, a correspondent (real or fictitious) wrote appreciatively: " I have perused your *Tatler* of this day, and have wept over it with great pleasure; I wish you would be more

<hr/>

[1] *Tatler*, No. 82.   [2] *Tatler*, No. 172.   [3] *Tatler*, No. 271.

frequent in your family pieces. For as I consider you under the notion of a great designer, I think these are not your least valuable performances." [1]

Among the tales that end unhappily, may be instanced that of the Cornish lovers, which Steele avowedly framed to illustrate the doctrine that the really tragic events are accidents to virtuous people. The lovers, celebrated for their virtues and constancy, have been married despite the inequality of their fortunes. Business affairs take the young husband across the seas. Some time thereafter, the wife is walking by the shore, and musing happily over their future, when a wave throws upon the sands the lifeless body of her husband, who has been drowned on his journey. On recognizing him, she falls down dead.[2] On their wedding day, two admirable young people are fondly discussing their courtship. The bridegroom toys with a supposedly empty pistol; it goes off, and kills her. He commits suicide.[3] In the story of Chloe and Clarinda, we again find characters "qualified with virtue and merit" who meet with undeserved fatality. Fire breaks out in a theatre; the ladies being masked, the lover of Chloe by mistake seizes Clarinda, and bears her out of the building. Discovering his error, he rushes back, and perishes with Chloe.[4] Two admirable papers dwell upon the domestic happiness of Mr. Bickerstaff's bosom friend. These "family pieces," which led Steele's correspondent to beg for more of the same kind, after tenderly describing the mutual love of the husband and the wife, end with the pathetic death of "that excellent woman."[5]

A favorite type of story, corresponding to that of Richmore and Clelia in *The Twin Rivals*, deals with the betrayal of an

---

[1] *Tatler*, No. 118, referring to the sad tale of domestic life in No. 114.

[2] *Tatler*, No. 82. Cf. Addison's story of Theodosius and Constantia, *Spectator*, No. 164.   [3] *Tatler*, No. 82.   [4] *Tatler*, No. 94.

[5] *Tatler*, Nos. 95 and 114. Cf. the famous account of the incidents following the death of Steele's father, No. 181.

innocent girl. The tale of Octavia in *The Spectator*[1] recounts her secret marriage, the subsequent destruction of the certificate, and her shameful desertion by her husband. One paper describes the misery of a country maid, betrayed, and thrown upon the town; another, the unhappiness of a luxuriously kept mistress.[2] The "history of Cælia" tells of the difficulties which the father of her lover interposed to their union, until "the beauty of her person, the fame of her virtue, and a certain irresistible charm in her whole behavior on so tender and delicate an occasion, wrought upon him." Some time after the wedding, however, she discovers that her husband is a bigamist; and her life is thus ruined.[3]

In other instances, such tales of seduction come to a happy conclusion. One of these is the story of Mr. Bickerstaff's sister, Jenny Distaff. At the age of sixteen, this virtuous girl attracts the attention of a noble lord, who, with the aid of an unscrupulous female relative, attempts to seduce her. The scene in which she rejects his advances is thus described by Jenny herself:

> He had the audaciousness to throw himself at my feet, talk of the stillness of the evening, and then ran into deifications of my person, pure flames, constant love, eternal raptures, and a thousand other phrases drawn from the images we have of heaven, which ill men use for the service of hell, were run over with uncommon vehemence. After which, he seized me in his arms: his design was too evident. In my utmost distress, I fell upon my knees. ' My lord, pity me, on my knees — on my knees in the cause of virtue, as you were lately in that of wickedness. Can you think of destroying the labour of a whole life, the purpose of a long education, for the base service of a sudden appetite, to throw one that loves you, that dotes on you, out of the company and the road of all that is virtuous and praiseworthy? Have I taken in all the instructions of piety, religion, and reason, for no other end but to be the sacrifice of lust, and abandoned to scorn? Assume yourself, my lord, and do not attempt to vitiate a temple

[1] No. 322. Cf. Addison's paper in *The Guardian*, No. 123.
[2] *Spectator*, No. 190; *Tatler*, No. 45.
[3] *Tatler*, No. 198.

sacred to innocence, honour, and religion. If I have injured you, stab this bosom, and let me die, but not be ruined by the hand I love.' The ardency of my passion made me incapable of uttering more; and I saw my lover astonished and reformed by my behaviour. . . .[1]

A more elaborate story on the same theme is one by John Hughes, which is termed "a scene of distress in private life." An eminent citizen becomes reduced in circumstances. His wife, "the best woman in the world," bears the misfortune bravely; and, to lessen their expense, their daughter Amanda is sent into the country. The lord of the manor falls in love with Amanda, and makes her dishonorable proposals. Repulsed by her, he writes to the parents, hoping that in their poverty they will induce her to become his mistress. The letter is received by the mother, who writes to Amanda to persist in rejecting "a proposal that insults our misfortunes, and would throw us to a lower degree of misery than anything which is come upon us." The lord intercepts this reply, and is "not a little moved at so true a picture of virtue in distress." He carries it to Amanda, "and when she burst into tears, he could no longer refrain from bearing a part in her sorrow." He begs forgiveness, and marries Amanda.[2]

These tales may be fairly described as dramas of sensibility cast into prose narrative form. They have the same purpose, the same sententiousness of style, similar characters, and similar — though less extended — plots. Accompanied by the critical theories that justified them, they introduced sentimental literature to a public much larger than the playhouse audiences which had heretofore known and favored it.

During the years in which sentimental emotions had found expression in the drama and in the moral essay, they were

---

[1] *Tatler*, No. 33.
[2] *Spectator*, No. 375. A counterpart to the sentimental comedies on "careless husbands" is Dr. Brome's story, *Spectator*, No. 302.

stirring the heart of a young aristocrat who was little influenced by such popular types of literature. Anthony Ashley Cooper, third Earl of Shaftesbury, whose early education was superintended by the greatest living English philosopher, John Locke, and whose schooling and travels made him one of the most cultivated gentlemen of his time, was by birth, breeding, and environment far removed from the bourgeois Cibber and Steele, and his personal character was more lofty and refined than theirs; but temperamentally he was akin to them. The same mood which impelled them, almost instinctively, to new literary practices, and, with little reflection, to new literary opinions, was in him deepened by meditation and developed into a new philosophy. Their influence was wide; his was profound. He was qualified to gain the attention of the aristocratic and the academic classes which were as yet untouched by sentimentalism. His *Enquiry concerning Virtue or Merit* and *The Moralists, a Philosophical Rhapsody* (1709-1711) had a stately elegance of style that caused them to be admired by the cultured leisure class, and presented ideas that commanded the respect of the learned.

Had Lord Shaftesbury condescended to witness the performance of a sentimental comedy, its amiable conception of humanity would have pleased him, but he knew that to the majority of thoughtful men in his time such a conception seemed fanciful. In his *The Moralists*, which, like Dryden's *Essay on Dramatic Poesy*, is a dialogue between gentlemen conversing on high themes, Philocles protests that mankind is too much an abstraction to call forth our love, and too insensible and unresponsive to maintain it.[1] His sentimental friend Theocles, voicing Shaftesbury's own ideas, admits that before such a love can be deeply founded we must be convinced that mankind is part of a larger whole which is indeed worthy of enthusiastic worship.

[1] *Characteristics of Men, Manners, Opinions, Times* (ed. 1732), II, 240-244.

At dawn, "in solemn places of retreat," viewing a beautiful landscape he reveals to Philocles this all-embracing object of admiration. It is the Spirit of Nature, the bond of the universe, the deity that sustains all things in mutual coördination, in peace and loveliness. When such sceptics as Philocles once perceive that the universal harmony is "not a mere notion of a creature's mind," they become filled "like poets and lovers" with a romantic enthusiasm which is the highest state of the soul because it is the recognition of the highest truth. Their æsthetic appreciation creates their moral beliefs. They learn that so harmonious a universe must exclude all ill, that the best of all possible worlds can contain no evil principle, and that, though the blind prejudices of our unenlightened minds delude us with the apparent existence of sin, the human heart is as beautiful and good as the great Spirit of Nature which animates it. This rhapsodic deism, which was presently to inspire many nature-poets, was to Shaftesbury the necessary basis of faith in man.[1]

Man seems indeed to ordinary observation, Shaftesbury admitted, an imperfect being.[2] The very limitations of man's power, his helplessness when quite cut off from his fellow creatures, are, however, he insisted, blessings in disguise; for they stimulate his social feelings.[3] The anti-social passions, — such as pride, envy, malice, and misanthropy, — are not natural to him, and put him at odds with himself.[4] But his benevolent and altruistic emotions are innate.[5] In exercising these, he has at once the pleasure of self-realization and the inexhaustible happiness of union with mankind. He sees them the source of all virtuous conduct, and becomes aware that "the order of the moral world equals that of the natural."[6] It too stands revealed in beauty. The same emotion that he has when he beholds the

---

[1] *Characteristics of Men, Manners, Opinions, Times* (ed. 1732), II, 245–246, 282–290, 343–433. [3] Ibid. II, 309. [5] Ibid. II, 43–44.
[2] Ibid. II, 291–292. [4] Ibid. II, 163–171. [6] Ibid. II, 294.

balanced design of the physical world arises in him when he perceives the true character of the human soul. Without any formal instruction, religious or philosophical, he immediately recognizes the fair and harmonious in conduct. " The heart cannot possibly remain neutral " ; it is " taken with any show or representation of the social passion." [1] For this emotion Shaftesbury coined a new phrase, — " the moral sense." [2] Unlike the " conscience " of orthodox theology, this was not a dread monitor checking and reproving our evil propensities, but an æsthetic feeling sympathetically encouraging our naturally good impulses.

The revolutionary aspect of Shaftesbury's doctrine appeared in his allusions to religion. He was not of a combative disposition, and did not openly break with the Established Church, but in his gentle manner he complained that it misconceived human character. He protested that aberrations from the path of virtue proceeded not from innate viciousness but " only from the force of custom and education in opposition to nature." [3] Orthodoxy had placed itself in conflict with the truth of nature when it " magnified to the utmost the corruption of man's heart." It had erroneously conceived virtue as a difficult and ascetic conquest over natural instincts, a conquest to be achieved only by obeying its discipline ; and, in its pessimistic view of this world, it had confined the rewards of virtue to a future existence.[4] Thus it had led man to mistrust himself, and to despair of a happy life. The apostles of the future, he urged, should find their keynote in the harmony of the universe. They should confidently appeal to man's moral sense. They should captivate his heart with a vision of society in which the natural was the admirable, in which sympathy and benevolence prevailed, and in which virtue rarely went unrewarded.[5]

---

[1] *Characteristics of Men, Manners, Opinions, Times* (ed. 1732), II, 284–285, 29–30, 53.   [3] Ibid. II, 45–46.
[2] Ibid. II, 53–54.   [4] Ibid. II, 256–273.   [5] Ibid. II, 275–279.

The teachings of Shaftesbury came to be held in high esteem both in England and on the Continent. " He was a virtuoso of humanity," says Herder, "who has signally influenced the best intellects of the eighteenth century." Gray caustically explained his repute on the grounds that men "love to take a new road even when that road leads nowhere," and that Shaftesbury "was reckoned a fine writer, and seemed always to mean more than he said"; but this reluctant testimony confirms the evidence of his vogue.

The spread of Shaftesbury's ideas, which, however disorganized from the point of view of strict philosophic system, were far more coherent and comprehensive than any previous sentimental notions, greatly helped to place the drama of sensibility in an advantageous position. After sentimental narratives had begun to appear in the periodicals, that kind of drama ceased to be a type of literature out of harmony with every other. And now that a philosophy consonant with it had arisen, future critics might defend it in a manner less opinionative than the lucubrations of Steele, and might make Shaftesbury its Aristotle. The sentimental dramatists themselves might well feel encouraged by Shaftesbury's message that the human heart was always "taken with any show or representation of the social passion." If the representation of benevolence conduced to the greatest pleasure and the highest morality, then their Amandas, Lady Easys, and Sir Friendly Morals were characters of a sort that they should continue to create in increasing numbers. Would they rest content with merely reproducing the same types, or would they search out the inexhaustible varieties of social virtue ? Would they create new situations for benevolence to triumph in after trial ? Their opportunity was immense ; had they sufficient sincerity of conviction and power of imagination to develop it ?

CHAPTER VII

A PERIOD OF SLIGHT PROGRESS: 1710–1728

For fifteen or twenty years after sentimentalism had appeared in the moral periodicals and in philosophy, it advanced very slowly. Shaftesbury's doctrines were recast in a form more cogent but less inspiring, by Francis Hutcheson, in his *The Original of our Ideas of Beauty and Virtue* (1725); but they were attacked more brilliantly than they were defended. The blunt and incisive cynic, Bernard de Mandeville, in *The Fable of the Bees* (1714–1723), declared that his lordship's "hunting after this *pulchrum et honestum* is not much better than a wild-goose chase"; and in a way that scandalized his age, he dwelt upon what seemed to him the bestial character of humanity. He scoffed at the notion that society could exist on any higher basis than a fighting, intriguing egotism. To him the so-called virtues were merely hypocritical names for various manifestations of pride and greed.[1] From a far loftier attitude, Shaftesbury and Hutcheson were assailed in the much admired *Sermons on Human Nature* (1726) delivered by Joseph Butler, of which it has been truly said that nowhere else can one find "a clearer picture of the constitution of human nature as it exists in fact."[2] Butler, the greatest eighteenth-century defender of orthodox ethics, protested that the "moral sense" and the

---

[1] Bernard de Mandeville, *The Fable of the Bees*. The first version of the work appeared in 1705, but the passages bearing on sentimentalism appeared in the prose commentaries added to the editions of 1714 and 1723. Cf. Leslie Stephen, *History of English Thought in the Eighteenth Century* (1902), II, 33–41.

[2] J. H. Bernard, Introduction to Butler's *Works* (1900), p. **xxiv**.

sentiment of benevolence were impulses too weak to depend upon wholly, and, insisting that our passions needed less uncertain guides than those, reasserted the ancient primacy of conscience.[1]

In the field of literature (to use the term in its narrower sense), the progress of sentimentalism was likewise retarded. Short sentimental tales appeared in the successors of *The Tatler* and *The Spectator*; and longer ones were in a few cases published independently, such as Mrs. Haywood's *Idalia* (c. 1723) and Mrs. Davys' *The Reformed Coquet* (1724).[2] But these were trivial countercurrents to the general stream. The literary masterpieces produced between 1709 and 1728 were by Pope, Swift, and Defoe. It was in those years that Pope established his dictatorship over poetry, with *The Rape of the Lock*, his translation of the *Iliad*, and *The Dunciad*, from which, of course, the sentimental spirit was excluded by the dominance of the classical, intellectual, and satiric. The greatest living prose author, Jonathan Swift, was also the greatest opponent of sentimentalism. The disinclination to love mankind, which had troubled Shaftesbury's Philocles before his enthusiastic conversion, was incarnated in Swift, who " ever hated all societies, professions, and communities," but " principally hated and detested that animal called man." To him the canting complacency which sentimental literature is apt to induce was above all odious; and he crowned his work as a satirist with *Gulliver's Travels* (1726), in which with the pitilessness of truth and the power of genius he laid bare the discrepancy between man's gigantic pretensions and dwarfish merits.

At the same time, Daniel Defoe was producing the first great series of novels (1719–1724). In all their variety of

---

[1] Joseph Butler, *Rolls Sermons*.

[2] See also *The Distressed Orphan* (3d ed., 1726). On these stories, cf. Charlotte M. Morgan, *The Novel of Manners* (1911), pp. 70, 99–100, 109–110.

scenes, incidents, and characters, these remained quite untouched by the emotionalism which had appeared in the short
stories of Steele and his imitators. The opportunities which
a sentimentalist would have seized upon, Defoe consistently
avoided. When his adventurous prodigals reform, it is because
they have learned the hard lesson of experience. The love-
affairs of his men and women are treated in an almost ludicrously matter-of-fact tone. His famous Quaker William is at
least as much imbued with worldly shrewdness as with inner
light. Robinson Crusoe records the death of the parrot who
was the companion of his solitude, and even the death of his
devoted Friday, with an absence of tenderness that was to
arouse the amazement and disgust of such a sentimentalist
as Dickens. The situations through which Defoe conducted
his characters might be far removed from everyday life; but
the characters themselves were ordinary enough, and his dry
realism invested them with no glamour of moral perfection or
emotional beauty.

Amid general literary conditions that encouraged the traditional distrust of human nature, true comedies were between
1710 and 1728 produced more numerously than sentimental
ones. In quality, however, they were inferior to those of 1696–
1709. The mainstay of the comic standard, Vanbrugh, had
after 1705 abandoned the writing of powerful plays for the
building of ponderous mansions; and the genial Farquhar had
died in 1707. The fortunes of true comedy came to be chiefly
dependent upon playwrights of lesser satiric and humorous
talents, — especially upon Colley Cibber and Mrs. Centlivre.
Cibber's *The Non-Juror* (1717), a skillful adaptation of Med-
bourne's version of Molière's *Tartuffe*,[1] was the best comedy of
the period. The coquette Maria, who delights in love-affairs

[1] Cf. Dudley H. Miles, "The Original of the Non-Juror," *Proceedings of the
Modern Language Association of America* (1914).

that have "difficulty, danger, and the dear spirit of contradiction" in them, was an admirable study in the Congrevian manner. Some passages in the curious fourth act of the play were, however, touched with a seriousness which, though it had no effect upon the outcome, temporarily disturbed the unity of comic tone. Mrs. Centlivre's *The Wonder* (1714) and *A Bold Stroke for a Wife* (1718) showed a deficiency in virile social satire, and depended too largely upon absurd situations. The collaboration of Pope with Arbuthnot and Gay in *Three Hours after Marriage* (1717) resulted in something little better than a silly farce. On the whole, the comic spirit, though apparently flourishing, had begun to grow weak.

It continued to be, nevertheless, an effective antagonist of sentimentalism. Gay's *The Beggar's Opera* (1728), an ingenious burlesque which created a furore, was intended, it is believed,[1] to ridicule, among many other things, the pathetic scenes and happy dénouements of sentimental comedies. Charles Shadwell's *The Fair Quaker of Deal* (1710) satirized a sect whose fundamental principles were sentimental; but its satire was superficial, being directed only against the outward demeanor of the Friends. The contrast between the methods of true comedy and those of sentimental appeared in this period most clearly in Taverner's *The Artful Husband* (1717) and Mrs. Centlivre's *The Artifice* (1722). Taverner's play showed a wife cured of extravagance, not by such an appeal to the moral sense as subdued Mrs. Clerimont in *The Tender Husband*, but by being deluded into the belief that she stood on the verge of financial ruin. Mrs. Centlivre's play presented a situation like that of Richmore and Clelia in *The Twin Rivals*, but in this case the forsaken girl induced her betrayer to marry her by making him think that he had been fatally poisoned. In

[1] G. H. Nettleton, *English Drama of the Restoration and Eighteenth Century* (1914), p. 192.

these two plays, as the titles suggest, the personages achieved their happiness by means of more or less dishonest artifices rather than by virtuous intentions or sacrifices.

The first of the five dramas of sensibility produced between 1710 and 1728 was written by no less a classicist than Joseph Addison. On at least one previous occasion, in *The Guardian*,[1] he had departed from his usual manner, and had composed in the sentimental vein of Steele a letter supposed to proceed from a heartbroken mother to a lord who had seduced her daughter. Now he wrote a sentimental comedy, *The Drummer, or the Haunted House* (10 March, 1716), but did not publicly acknowledge his authorship of it. After being praised by Steele in *Town Talk*,[2] it was performed anonymously, the prologue saying:

> Our author, anxious for his fame to-night,
> And bashful in his first attempt to write,
> Lies cautiously obscure and unrevealed. . . .
> The mighty critics will not blast for shame
> A raw young thing, who dares not tell his name.

In spite of its success, Addison would not own the play, and caused Steele to publish it as " by a gentleman." Tickell consequently omitted it from Addison's collected works (1721); and it was not openly accredited to its author until Steele issued a second edition (dated 1722), with a preface announcing the inwardness of the matter.[3] One may perhaps surmise that Addison's reluctance to appear responsible for the play was at least partly due to its violating the rules of true comedy.

That portion of the play which is referred to in the title of *The Drummer* was based upon a ridiculous incident of the

---

[1] No. 123.

[2] No. 9, 13 February, 1716.

[3] Cf. W. E. A. Axon, *The Literary History of " The Drummer"* (1895); G. A. Aitken, *Richard Steele* (1889), II, 91–92, 270–272; and A. W. Ward, *English Dramatic Literature* (1899), III, 439 and note.

time of the Restoration. A country mansion in Wiltshire had
for an entire year been disturbed by the nightly beating of an
invisible drum; the haunting became so notorious that the king
sent commissioners to investigate it; and finally the ghost was
discovered in the person of a practical joker.[1] In its own day
such an episode might well have given rise to a comedy satirizing rustic superstition, but Addison did not develop that possibility. He reduced the ghost-story to a subordinate position,
and chose for his main theme one already well worn, — that of
a husband who is supposed to have perished, but who returns
to his wife. The author's purpose is thus described in the
epilogue:

> He draws a widow who, of blameless carriage,
> True to her jointure, hates a second marriage.
>
> .   .   .   .
>
> Too long has marriage in this tasteless age
> With ill-bred raillery supplied the stage:
> No little scribbler is of wit so bare
> But has his fling at the poor wedded pair.
> Our author deals not in conceits so stale;
> For should th' examples of his play prevail,
> No man need blush though true to marriage-vows,
> Nor be a jest though he should love his spouse.

In its broad outlines *The Drummer* thus bears considerable
resemblance to sentimental comedies like *Love's Last Shift*
and *The Tender Husband*.[2]

There is little novelty in the plot. Sir George Truman is
supposed to have fallen in battle. His wife, who sincerely
mourns him, is besieged by suitors. One of these, Fantome,
tries to drive away his rivals, especially the fop Tinsel, by
haunting the house as the husband's ghost and by beating a

[1] *Mercurius Publicus*, 16–23 April, 1663; Pepys' Diary, 15 June, 1663;
Joseph Glanvill, *Saducismus Triumphatus* (1681).

[2] For a refutation of the statements that Addison borrowed from *Mostellaria*,
see Reinhardstoettner, *Plautus*, pp. 483–487.

drum. Truman, disguised as a magician, returns to observe the behavior of his wife, and is gratefully touched by her fidelity. After the affectations of Tinsel, and the tricks of Fantome, have been exposed, there is the usual scene of tender recognition. The comic element in *The Drummer* is even more conspicuous than in *The Tender Husband*, and the few sentimental passages are not as fervid as in some previous plays of the same kind. Steele tells us that Cibber and the other managers "were of the opinion that it was like a picture in which the strokes were not strong enough to appear at a distance." [1] Certainly Addison's temperament and habits of mind inhibited him from promoting the development of sentimentalism.

A sentimental comedy which lacks even the interest of having been written by an author eminent in other fields is Charles Johnson's *The Masquerade* (16 January, 1719). Its chief personage, Lady Frances Ombre, is a victim of the gambling mania. Her husband remains devoted to her, and by his aid she is saved from ruin and brought to repentance. The play was an obvious imitation of Cibber's *The Lady's Last Stake*, and deserved the quick oblivion that overtook it.

While sentimental comedy was temporarily in a listless condition on the conservative London stage, the Irish theatre produced an unconventional play of that type. This was Charles Shadwell's *Irish Hospitality, or Virtue Rewarded*, published at Dublin in 1720, [2] and first acted there probably a year or two earlier. It is a curious piece, with some of the simplicity, not to say crudeness, of a morality play. The comic portion is coarse, and most of the minor characters are unnatural abstractions. But these defects are outweighed by the clear-cut conception and sympathetic portrayal of the remarkable central character, Sir Patrick Worthy. This "generous tempered

---

[1] Preface to *The Drummer* (1716).
[2] Charles Shadwell, *Works*, Vol. I (1720). Cf. Genest, X, 283, 287–288.

gentleman, who, having a plentiful estate, keeps open house to all comers and goers, and by his liberality makes himself the country's darling," [1] was intended, it was surmised in the eighteenth century,[2] as a complimentary portrait of some local celebrity. However that may be, he was the only important addition to the personnel of sentimental comedy between 1710 and 1728.

Sir Patrick is surrounded with people who cannot appreciate his philosophy of life. His younger brother Clumsey, " a swinish squire," lives to please himself, and protests against Sir Patrick's kindness to others.

Sir Patrick

'T is in vain for me to hope you can ever have any notion of humanity. Too many like you run after their sordid pleasures, which hinders them from tasting those lasting joys this life affords. Few know the bliss of contemplation, the conversation of a friend, and that delightful attribute of man — the will and power of doing good. Generosity has a delightfulness unbounded goes along with it; and 't is to me undecided which has the greater pleasure in 't, to give or to forgive.

Clumsey

. . . You have a silver tongue, truly. You can always find out a bloody many of my faults, but never think of your own profuseness. . . .

Sir Patrick

Poor weak man! I think myself an earthly steward, deputed by Heaven to distribute that fortune it has intrusted me with, on my fellow creatures. What satisfaction is there like relieving of the poor, giving food and raiment to the miserable, and stopping the current of a deplorable man's condition? [3]

Morose, a retainer in the family, thinks Sir Patrick's generosity useless because men are unworthy of it.

---

[1] Shadwell's description of him, *Dramatis Personae.*
[2] *Biographia Dramatica* (1812), II, 333.
[3] Pp. 214–215.

Morose

Men of honor are not so mean-spirited as to receive your alms; and the mercenary rascals you feed, though never so lavish now in your praise, will for the other sixpence rail at you and cut your throat.

Sir Patrick

It is impossible then to make you think mankind sincere?

Morose

. . . I think every man a knave till I find him honest.

Sir Patrick

Now I believe everyone honest till I find him otherwise.

Morose

That's the way to be deceived.

Sir Patrick

I had much rather be deceived than harbor an ill opinion of my own species.[1]

The last remark is especially noteworthy for its uncompromising sentimentalism.

In the course of the play, Sir Patrick's faith is put to severe tests. He discovers that his son Charles is plotting to seduce the virtuous daughter of one of his tenants, and has already inveigled her into a secret and fraudulent marriage ceremony. He circumvents Charles's designs, induces him to make the girl his wife, and is characteristically confident that "persuading Charles he is good, perhaps may make him so."[2] In this case, however, he meets artifice with artifice. In another, he depends wholly upon generosity to overcome wrongdoing. A rich man of the neighborhood, Sir Wouldbe Generous, who affects liberality out of ostentation, hates Sir Patrick because everybody thinks him the more truly benevolent of the two. So extreme

[1] P. 221.　　　　[2] P. 302.

is his jealousy that he plans to murder Sir Patrick. The latter
is apprised of the danger, but bravely meets his enemy alone
and unarmed, and tries to allay his hostility by an appeal to his
sense of honor.

Sir Patrick

Sure you would not kill a poor defenceless old man? You have more
compassion and generosity than that comes to.

Sir Wouldbe

S' death, I 'll murder thee immediately, darest thou talk to me of
generosity.

Sir Patrick

Indeed, I dare; and since I find your design is upon my life, I am
convinced I have much more generosity than you, for when I had you
in my power, and you had [unwittingly] intrusted me with your intent of
coming hither, instead of surrounding you with all my servants, and
punishing you for your vile attempt upon my person, I have met you
here alone and unattended. . . . Now, sir; strike home: old Worthy's
heart lies here.

Sir Wouldbe

Ha — this act of generosity has indeed disarmed me, and you have
given me convincing proofs that you are the good man I ought to be.

Sir Patrick

Heaven make me good enough for your example. . . .

Sir Wouldbe

Thou wondrous man . . . is it then possible I can be forgiven?

Sir Patrick

With open arms thus into my bosom I receive you. . . . From this
moment I call you brother.[1]

So thorough a benevolist as Sir Patrick had not previously
been created, — not even in Sir Friendly Moral.[2] It was
unfortunate that this play, which might have accelerated the
development of such characters, had no immediate influence on
the metropolitan stage, where it was not performed until 1766.

---

[1] Pp. 292–293.   [2] Chap. vi, above.

In London, the boldest venture in the drama of sensibility between 1710 and 1728 was the production of a domestic tragedy, *The Fatal Extravagance* (21 April, 1721). In its original form it had only one act, but by 1726 it was expanded to a play of regular length. It appeared under the name of Joseph Mitchell, an obscure and impoverished writer. Its real author was Aaron Hill,[1] a typical benevolist, who displays many of the amiable as well as some of the weak characteristics of his kind, and whom Dr. Johnson observed to be "remarkable for singularity of sentiment."[2] By 1721 the earlier domestic tragedy, *The Rival Brothers* (1704), was forgotten; and the title-page of *The Fatal Extravagance* proclaimed that this work was written "in a manner wholly new." Perhaps the favorable reception which had greeted the tragic domestic tales of *The Tatler* and *The Spectator* encouraged Aaron Hill in his experiment. Certainly the critical precepts of Richard Steele are echoed in the preface of *The Fatal Extravagance*, and in the following lines of its prologue:

> None can their pity for those woes conceal,
> Which most who hear perhaps too deeply feel.
> The rants of ruined kings of mighty name,
> For pompous misery, small compassion claim.
> Empires o'erturned, and heroes held in chains,
> Alarm the mind but give the heart no pains.
> To ills remote from our domestic fears,
> We lend our wonder, but withhold our tears.[3]

[1] A bibliography of Aaron Hill is found in Dorothy Brewster's *Aaron Hill* (1913), pp. 279–290. On *The Fatal Extravagance*, cf. besides Miss Brewster's study, H. Beyer, *Edward Moore* (1889), p. 34; and H. W. Singer, *Das bürgerliche Trauerspiel* (1891), pp. 83–88.

The historical importance of *The Fatal Extravagance* is, it seems to me, nowhere sufficiently recognized.

[2] *Life of Savage*, in *Lives of the English Poets*, ed. G. B. Hill (1905), II, 339–340.

[3] Aaron Hill, *Works* (1760), I, 291. Cf. the prologue for the revival of the play in 1729.

In carrying these principles into practice, Hill was guided
by the example of sentimental comedy. He took many hints
for his play, to be sure, from *A Yorkshire Tragedy*.[1] But the
expectation which that fact excites, — that he resurrected the
spirit of Elizabethan domestic tragedy,— is not realized. The materials are similar, but their treatment is different. *A Yorkshire
Tragedy* shows the wicked deeds of one Calverly, a man of
evil habits, unreasonable jealousy, violent temper, and false
pride. Having wasted his means in dissipation, he murders
his wife and children, and is led off to just punishment. In
The Fatal Extravagance, the sternly realistic qualities of the
Elizabethan play have disappeared, the plot is modified in a
significant manner, and the characters are utterly changed.

Calverly, who in the original arouses terror, becomes the
sympathetically drawn Bellmour. His youthful follies, like those
of the prodigals in sentimental comedy, are ascribed to the
allurements of evil companions. He is praised for

> his courage and humanity,
> His fine frank spirit, and his generous nature.
> .   .   .   .   .   Nobly willed,
> His pitying heart flows out in generous purposes;
> But, wanting power to stem the tide of pleasure,
> Irresolute he drives and floats to ruin.

Though he has gambled away his fortune, he is pointed at with
admiration because he grieves not on his account, but on that
of the friend who stands security for his debts:

> Bellmour will never live to sink a friend.
> Look yonder, where in pensive grief he walks,
> Unhoping and disconsolate!

He protests to his wife:

> Think'st thou I am so mean, so lost a wretch
> That my *own* misery stings me? Cruel wound!...

[1] Well known, because included in the works of Shakespeare since 1664.

Thine and thy helpless infants' woes rise to me,
Glare on my apprehension like pale ghosts,
And point me into madness!

It is to save his friend from being thrown into prison for debt
that Bellmour assaults the villain Bargrave, who had "stained
the native whiteness of his soul," and kills him, thereby preventing the execution of the creditor's bond. To spare his wife
and children from a life of beggary, he attempts to poison
them and to commit suicide. They are fortuitously rescued, but
he himself dies. His conduct, which in the Elizabethan play
was frankly abhorred, is here pitied and condoned.[1]

Sentimental characterization is equally noticeable in Bellmour's wife Louisa. For his early dissipation, she has no word
of reproach; and his enormities she fully pardons, clinging to
him throughout with inexhaustible patience and love. In her
brave efforts, she is supported by his uncle, Courtney, a character evidently modelled upon Sir Friendly Moral. It is he who
substitutes for the poison a harmless liquor, and saves Louisa
and the children. At the end he arrives with the report of an
inheritance that will restore the family to wealth. Since this
news comes only a moment too late to prevent the suicide of
Bellmour, the catastrophe is an unnecessary calamity, — an important characteristic of the play which brings it into complete
harmony with Steele's idea of tragedy.[2] Let Bargrave be merely
wounded, have Courtney arrive in time, — and *The Fatal Extravagance* would be, without any changes in the characters or
their motives, a sentimental comedy.[3]

No inconsiderable part of the historical importance usually
attached to *George Barnwell* (1731) justly appertains to *The
Fatal Extravagance*. Aaron Hill was the first author to make

---

[1] Hill, *Works*, I, 296, 297, 301, 305.   [2] Cf. chap. vi, above.
[3] It actually did thus become a sentimental comedy in G. W. Waldron's
The Prodigal (2 December, 1793), published 1794.

the revolutionary attempt to produce sentimental domestic tragedy moderately successful. His play was applauded in its first
season, and was revived in 1722, 1723, and 1730. In ten
years it was published five times.[1] It was, furthermore, largely
borrowed from in Edward Moore's *The Gamester*, the best-
known domestic tragedy of the second half of the century.
Its success in 1721, though not great, was sufficient to show
that after sentimental comedies had flourished twenty-five years,
audiences were prepared to welcome a domestic tragedy conceived in the same spirit.

By 1722 sentimental comedy had become so fixed a type that
even before the first performance of Steele's *The Conscious
Lovers* (7 November, 1722) the characteristics of the play
were foretold. John Dennis, who was defending the methods
of Etherege against Steele's attack, and who opined that the
latter " knows nothing of the nature of comedy," ironically expressed the hope that in the forthcoming piece " the characters
would be always drawn in nature, and a young man not given
the qualities of an old one, that they would be the just images
of their contemporaries, that instead of setting patterns for
imitation Steele would make those follies and vices ridiculous
which ought to be shunned, that the subject of the comedy
would be comical by its constitution, and that the ridicule would
be in the principal incidents and characters."[2] This antici-
patory and indirect criticism proved justified. The young man
in Steele's play was indeed given the qualities of an old one.
The lovers were " conscious "; that is to say, they possessed
sensibility;[3] *The Unfashionable Lovers*, a discarded title, would
less obscurely have indicated their natures. The comic element

---

[1] Dorothy Brewster, *Aaron Hill*, p. 98 note, p. 282.
[2] G. A. Aitken, *Richard Steele* (1889), II, 281; paraphrasing John Dennis,
A Defense of Sir Fopling Flutter (1722), p. 24.
[3] *The Censor Censured* (1723), pp. 9-10.

was found, as Dennis shrewdly surmised would be the case, in the subordinate incidents and characters, — in the fop Cimberton and the ridiculous servants Tom and Phillis.[1]

The main plot is based upon Terence's *Andria*, a work in which, as we have seen, the comic point of view was never abandoned, in which the lovers outwitted their elders, and all the personages were given comic traits.[2] In *The Conscious Lovers*, the chief characters have been sentimentalized. The amusing Pamphilus has become the admirable Bevil, "the most unfashionable lover in Great Britain." He declines to fight a duel, and by patience and generosity reconciles his angry adversary. His conduct in his love affair is exemplary. While on the Continent, he has rescued Indiana from the wiles of an unscrupulous stranger, and has escorted her and her aunt back to England. He knows that his father would object to his marriage with a girl of mysterious origin, and he has a high sense of filial duty. On that account, and in order to spare Indiana any possible embarrassment, he has honorably tried to give her no indication of his deep love for her, which is based " not on external merit, but on merit of the soul."[3] Indiana, who takes a far more prominent part in the action than her original, Terence's Glycerium, is not deceived by Bevil's attempt to hide his feelings, — his " tender confusion " has at times betrayed him ; but she appreciates the delicacy of his

---

[1] As *The Conscious Lovers*, " a full-blown example of the new species " (A. W. Ward, Introduction to Lillo's *Barnwell*, p. xxiv), is universally considered a typical example of sentimental comedy, the large proportion of its comic scenes, which occupy only a little less than half the play, should not be ignored in defining the genre.

[2] Chap. ii, above. Miss Morgan, *The Novel of Manners*, p. 245, says that " a story with much the same plot as *The Conscious Lovers* is *The History of the Marquis de Criton*."

[3] Act I, scene ii; Act II, scene ii; Act IV, scene i. The last of these scenes, in which the duel is prevented, is, according to Steele, the one for the sake of which the whole play was written.

motives, honors him the more for his self-sacrificing conduct, and trusts him fully.

In place of Terence's Chremes, is found the highly estimable Mr. Sealand, a successor to Farquhar's good merchant Fairbank.[1] When Sir John Bevil proposes a match between young Bevil and Mr. Sealand's daughter Lucinda, and talks condescendingly about the advantages of gentle birth, Mr. Sealand proudly asserts the dignity of his class, "a species of gentry that have grown into the world this last century." He judges young men, not by their rank, but by their virtue; and since he has been disturbed by reports of Bevil's acquaintance with Indiana, he goes to call upon her in order to ascertain whether there has been any impropriety in Bevil's conduct. Suspicious of the nature of Indiana's relations with Bevil, he pretends to her that he is a messenger with money for her lover; but her modest bearing undeceives him. Questioning her, he is astonished and much moved by her ingenuous answers, which testify to Bevil's noble conduct and naïvely disclose her own virtues. She confesses that she loves Bevil; and, supposing his marriage to another imminent, she grows distracted with grief, exclaiming:

> What have I to do but sigh, and weep, and rave; run wild, a lunatic in chains; or, hid in darkness, mutter in distracted starts and broken accents my strange, strange story!

"In her disorder, she throws away a bracelet, which Sealand takes up, and looks earnestly on,"—and thereby recognizes her as his long-lost daughter. Of course Indiana is married to Bevil. The words in which their union is approved express the guiding principle of the action: "You have set the world a fair example; your happiness is owing to your constancy and merit."[2]

[1] Chap. v, above.

[2] Act IV, scene ii; Act V, scene iii. Referring to the distracted speech of Indiana, quoted above, the author of *The Censor Censured*, p. 71, asks: "Could any mad princess in a tragedy have said more?"

Leonard Welsted's prologue to *The Conscious Lovers* urged its support as an attempt "to chasten wit and moralize the stage." The redoubtable Dennis, however, roundly condemned it as "built upon several things which have no foundation either in probability, or in reason, or in nature"; and several other critics also expressed themselves unfavorably.[1] In protest, Steele wrote as follows:

> The chief design of this was to be an innocent performance, and the audience have abundantly shown how ready they are to support what is visibly intended that way. . . . This [duelling] incident, and the case of the father and daughter, are esteemed by some people no subjects of comedy: but I cannot be of their mind, for anything that has its foundation in happiness and success must be allowed to be the object of comedy; and sure it must be an improvement of it to introduce a joy too exquisite for laughter, . . . which is the case of this young lady. I must therefore contend that the tears which were shed on that occasion flowed from reason and good sense; and that men ought not to be laughed at for weeping till we are come to a more clear notion of what is to be imputed to the hardness of the head and the softness of the heart. . . . To be apt to give way to the impressions of humanity is the excellence of a right disposition and the natural working of a well-turned spirit.[2]

The weaknesses of Steele's plea were exposed in a long, anonymous pamphlet, *The Censor Censured*, the best passage in which is this:

> That which has its foundation in happiness and success will be allowed the object of comedy, and passions of all kinds may be represented in comedy as well as in tragedy; but then they must be expressed in a different manner, not in the tragical style and tone; nor must the distress be so exquisite as to melt the heart with sympathetic grief and render it incapable of relishing the approaching joy. 'T is unnatural to suppose the mind can fly so readily from one extreme to the other.[8]

[1] John Dennis, *Remarks on a Play called " The Conscious Lovers "* (1723); Anon., *The Censor Censured* (1723). Cf. Aitken, II, 281–284.

[2] Preface to *The Conscious Lovers* (dated 1723).

[8] Pp. 70–71.

Such arguments were overborne by the welcome accorded the play. In its first season, it ran eighteen nights; and for two generations it was a favorite. The king allowed it to be dedicated to him. The popular verdict was expressed, appropriately enough, by Aaron Hill, who said: "There are sentiments so generous in many parts of *The Conscious Lovers* that the noblysighted, one should think, could never look for its errors."[1]

The novelty of the play[2] lay less in its characters and sentiments than in its action. A mysterious improbability, — Indiana's recovery of her parent, — was the foundation of the plot. Terence had used the strange circumstances of the girl's career to strengthen the comic effect; Steele used them to intensify the emotional. In earlier sentimental comedies improbabilities were present, but not prominent. Their personages were ideal, but their action was on the whole realistic. The further development, one of the most important contributions by Steele to the type, was a natural, almost an inevitable, one. That perfectly virtuous people come to a happy issue out of all their afflictions is, alas, a theory not so plausiblv illustrated in a world resembling the real one as in a realm of beneficent coincidence. In such a region the conscious lovers moved; and sentimental comedy, though still affecting truth to life, departed therefrom still further. As Steele's method in this particular was often followed, improbability of plot became henceforth a frequent, though not a constant, attribute of the genre.

[1] Aaron Hill to Benjamin Victor, 21 February, 1723, in Victor's *History of the Theatres of London and Dublin* (1761), II, 172.

[2] Dr. DeWitt C. Croissant, *Studies in Colley Cibber* (1912), pp. 30 and 62, considers that *The Conscious Lovers* represents a second stage in the development of sentimental comedy, one in which "the action is centered around a pathetic situation." I cannot subscribe to this opinion. The central situation in *Love's Last Shift* is pathetic. *The Twin Rivals*, which Dr. Croissant does not mention, in many respects resembles and anticipates *The Conscious Lovers*.

Colley Cibber had not lost his active interest in sentimental comedy. Steele acknowledged that he zealously assisted in the production of *The Conscious Lovers,* and (just how is unknown) "altered the disposition of the scenes."[1] His next and last service to the type he had founded was rendered in revising and completing an unfinished manuscript of a play by Vanbrugh, *A Journey to London.* That Vanbrugh did not live to finish this work is greatly to be deplored; for it gave strong promise of becoming a true comedy of exceptional merit. Cibber, who entitled the produced version *The Provoked Husband* (10 January, 1728), made changes and additions which, though creditable in their way, were in a style antagonistic to that of the original author. He retained much of that part of Vanbrugh's work which is occupied with the satirically drawn figure of Sir Francis Wronghead,[2] a country squire, who stands for Parliament and brings his family up to London, only to find his hopes of preferment vanished, and his wife and daughter made the dupes of a sharper. As Cibber says,

> In his [Vanbrugh's] original papers, the characters are strongly drawn, new, spirited, and natural, taken from sensible observations on high and lower life, and from a just indignation at the follies in fashion.[3]

In the main plot, dealing with the marital troubles of Lord and Lady Townly, Cibber changed the characterization and the intended dénouement. His modifications of the materials, he defended as follows:

> All I could gather from him [Vanbrugh], of what he intended in the catastrophe, was that the conduct of his imaginary fine lady had so provoked him that he designed actually to have made her husband turn her out of his doors. But when his performance came, after his

---

[1] Preface of *The Conscious Lovers.* Cf. Theophilus Cibber, *The Lives of the Poets* (1753), IV, 120; "T. Wilkes" [Samuel Derrick], *A General View of the Stage* (1759), pp. 42–43; Aitken, II, 377; and Croissant, p. 56.

[2] The names of the personages here given are Cibber's, not Vanbrugh's.

[3] Cibber, Preface to *The Provoked Husband, Works* (1777), IV, 107.

decease, to my hands, I thought such violent measures, however just they might be in real life, were too severe for comedy, and would want the proper surprise which is due to the end of a play. Therefore, with much ado (and 't was as much as I could do with probability) I preserved the lady's chastity, that the sense of her errors might make a reconciliation not impracticable; and I hope the mitigation of her sentence has been since justified by its success.[1]

In consequence of this change in the point of view, the corresponding scenes of *A Journey to London* and *The Provoked Wife* exhibit illuminating contrasts between the methods of true comedy and of sentimental. In Vanbrugh, Lord and Lady Townly have a spirited dispute, which shows the husband ridiculously unable to control his witty and pleasure-loving wife. In Cibber, their interviews are serious: Lord Townly is devotedly fond of his wife, tries long and patiently to regain her, and finally by an eloquent discourse on the unhappy destruction of his ideals of domestic happiness, succeeds in moving her to tears and repentance.[2] The difference between Vanbrugh's Lady Grace and Cibber's is likewise significant: in the former the love of quiet domesticity is regarded with some amusement; in the latter, with admiration.[3] Thus Cibber had his revenge for Vanbrugh's *The Relapse*. *The Provoked Husband* was even more successful than *The Conscious Lovers*. It had an initial run of twenty-eight nights, was dedicated to the queen, and remained a stock play for nearly a century. The merits of its style are, however, greater than the novelty of its substance; for it is merely an agreeable variation of a theme that had already been presented in *The Tender Husband* and *The Lady's Last Stake*.

---

[1] Cibber, Preface to *The Provoked Husband*, *Works* (1777), pp. 107–108.

[2] Cf. *A Journey to London*, Act II, scene i, with *The Provoked Husband*, Act I, scene i; Act V, scene ii.

[3] Cf. Act II, scene i, with Act III, scene i. Cf. Anon., *Reflections on The Provoked Husband* (1728).

With *The Provoked Husband*, Cibber's career as a sentimental dramatist came to its end, closing as successfully as it
had begun. The founder of the type in 1696, its rescuer from
early extinction in 1704, he had impressed upon it its most
enduring characteristics, and had contributed to it more works
of lasting popularity than any rival. The contrast between his
personality and his sentimental comedies is astounding, — far
more so than is the case with Steele, whose little weaknesses
are too well known to dwell upon. The creator of those edifying reformed prodigals, Loveless and Sir Charles Easy, per-
sisted in his libertine ways. He who had attacked gambling in
The Lady's Last Stake remained a confirmed gamester. He
who had so often glorified forbearance and benevolence never
forgave his own daughter for offending him, and observed her
distressful indigence without relieving it.[1] His sentimental comedies were not reflections of his experience but excursions of his
imagination. "Mrs. Porter," says Davies, "upon reading a part
in which Cibber had painted virtue in its strongest and most
lively colors, asked him how it came to pass that a man who
could draw such admirable portraits of goodness should yet live
as if he were a stranger to it. 'Madam,' said Colley, 'the one
is absolutely necessary, the other is not.'"[2] To complete the
paradox, it may be added that though he had created a larger
number of serious characters in comedy than any other dramatist, as an actor he excelled in comic parts. But, after all, he
was never so truly an actor as when he played the preacher
of sentimentalism.

Despite the merit and success of *The Conscious Lovers* and
The Provoked Husband, despite the novelty of *Irish Hospitality*
and *The Fatal Extravagance*, the period from 1710 to 1728
fell short of the expectations which a devotee of sentimentalism

[1] *Biographia Dramatica* (1812), I, 104.
[2] Thomas Davies, *Dramatic Miscellanies* (1784), III, 432.

might entertain at its beginning. The drama of sensibility was still far from driving its rivals off the stage, and showed too few signs of vigor and fertility. The ideals that ruled the literary and intellectual world still preponderated against its spirit. Its authors seemed to lack that venturesome enthusiasm which springs from the sincere belief that one's own ideals of life are the only true ones.

CHAPTER VIII

THE RISE OF GEORGE LILLO: 1729-1732

The development of the drama of sensibility proceeded more rapidly in the four years from 1729 to 1732 than in the preceding eighteen. In the non-dramatic literature of that period there were not as many signs of a growing love for sentimentalism. Yet the most important literary work of those years, James Thomson's *The Seasons*, completed in 1730, is the first considerable poem that shows traces of Shaftesbury's influence. His deism somewhat affected Thomson's attitude towards nature, and his optimism inspired such lines as these :

> The moral world
> Which, though to us it seems embroiled, moves on
> In higher order, fitted and impelled
> By wisdom's finest hand, and issuing all
> In general good.[1]

Thomson discerningly praised Shaftesbury as

> the friend of man,
> Who scanned his nature with a brother's eye,
> His weakness prompt to shade, to raise his aim,
> To touch the finer movements of the mind,
> And with the moral beauty charm the heart.[2]

And in harmony with the precepts of the philosophic benevolist, he dwelt often upon the moral and social value of humanitarian feelings.[3] Among the stories he introduced in his poem, at least one — that of the swain perishing in the storm[4] — is

---

[1] *Winter*, ll. 583-587. A deistic passage is *Spring*, ll. 846-863.
[2] *Summer*, ll. 1550-1554.
[3] For example, *Winter*, ll. 330-388.   [4] *Winter*, ll. 276-321.

quite in the manner of Steele's pathetic tales, and his panegyric upon domestic love[1] likewise recalls Sir Richard. Such passages, though perhaps not the most characteristic in *The Seasons*, show that by 1730 sentimentalism was beginning to appear in types of literature from which it had previously been excluded.

Its main outlet, however, was still found in the drama. Between 1729 and 1732, true comedies were surpassed in number, if not in intrinsic merit, by sentimental ones, — and this despite the fact that the leadership in comedy was devolving upon a humorist of genius, Henry Fielding. Those traits of Fielding's nature which predominated in his youth urged him to boisterous satire. He was then, as one of his admirers deplored in the sentimental 1760's, "not fond of copying the amiable part of human life."[2] He looked up to the comic dramatists of the Restoration, but he lacked the patience to follow them at their best. Of the eleven plays that he produced between 1729 and 1732, four were burlesques. Of the seven comedies, none was as good as Cibber's *The Non-Juror*, and most showed a further decline toward the farcical than had marked the plays of Mrs. Centlivre. Much of their dialogue was exuberantly coarse, and their low characters were their best. They were brisk and laughable entertainments, written, as Fielding owned, to make money; and in them the arduous upper ranges of comedy were not painstakingly attempted. Two of them, *The Temple Beau* and *The Modern Husband*, were, to be sure, efforts in high comedy; but it is significant that in each of these cases the author, avoiding the difficulty of sustaining the comic tone, deviated into the sentimental.

The central figure in *The Temple Beau* (26 January, 1730) is the virtuous Bellaria.[3] Her three suitors are attracted to her

---

[1] *Spring*, ll. 1109–1162.

[2] Arthur Murphy, *Essay on the Life and Genius of Henry Fielding* (1762), in Fielding's *Works* (1806), I, 39.

[3] For her character see Act II, scene vii.

from different motives, — Wilding (the Temple beau) by her money, Valentine by her beauty, and Veromil by the perfection of her character. The last, who is himself a model,[1] succeeds after several tribulations in carrying off the victory. In the course of the rivalry, Veromil restrains Valentine from fighting a duel, — an episode obviously imitating the scene between Bevil and Myrtle in *The Conscious Lovers*.[2] Owing to his infatuation with Bellaria, Valentine has deserted his former love; and his reconciliation to her, — " with bleeding heart owning his crime, and with tears asking her pardon," — somewhat resembles the reunion of Richmore and Clelia in *The Twin Rivals*.[3] The comic scenes, which are influenced by Molière, are written with much ease. The sentimental episodes lack even that degree of emotional fervor found in corresponding passages by Steele and by Farquhar. In the history of sentimental comedy, *The Temple Beau* is accordingly not important.[4]

Silvia, or the Country Burial (10 November, 1730) is of peculiar interest as the first work of George Lillo.[5] It was called a ballad-opera, a term which in this case, and many others, signifies little more than that the play is intermixed with frequent songs. These lend it a somewhat artificial or remote atmosphere, slightly like that of a pastoral, but they do not radically modify its essential nature, which is sentimental.

[1] Act I, scenes v and vi; Act II, scene xii; Act IV, scene x.

[2] *Temple Beau*, Act IV, scene x; *Conscious Lovers*, Act IV, scene i.

[3] *Temple Beau*, Act V, scene ii; *Twin Rivals*, Act V, scene ii.

[4] It is usually regarded as a study in the style of Congreve. Cf. Austin Dobson, *Henry Fielding* (1907), chap. i; G. H. Gerould, Introduction to *Selected Essays of Henry Fielding* (1905), pp. xiii, xxxiv; and Felix Lindner, *Henry Fieldings Dramatische Werke* (1895), pp. 14-19.

[5] Cf. Leopold Hoffman, *George Lillo* (1888), pp. 2-3; A. Brandl, *Zu Lillo's Kaufmann von London*, in *Vierteljahrschrift für Litteraturgeschichte* (1890), III, 47-62; and A. W. Ward, Introduction to Lillo's *The London Merchant* (1906), p. viii. The relation of *Silvia* to sentimental comedy is generally ignored.

The plot centers around the attempt of Sir John Freeman, a profligate young squire, to seduce Silvia, the reputed daughter of his tenant Welford. He offers her much wealth if she will consent to become his mistress; but though she loves him, she scorns the proposal; and her father, much grieved by the insult, forbids Sir John any further communication with his daughter. A letter in which her lover has craved forgiveness, Silvia returns unopened. Fearing, however, that his resentment may vent itself upon her father, she afterwards goes to Sir John, begging him not to cancel the lease of their farm. Touched by her devotion and distress, he asks her to marry him; but, lest he think her former refusal of his advances based on merely mercenary considerations, she will now not consent to this honorable proposal. When farmer Welford is apprised of the situation, he rejoices at Silvia's unselfishness and Sir John's reformation. Their virtue finds the just reward of happiness: it transpires that Sir John and Silvia have in their infancy been secretly exchanged for one another, so that she is an heiress and he the farmer's son. Therewith, of course, all obstacles to their marriage are swept away. *Silvia* is thus similar in plot and characterization to Hughes' story of Amanda in *The Spectator*,[1] and in improbability of dénouement recalls *The Conscious Lovers*. In such a work as this, which in all important respects is a sentimental comedy, the most famous author of domestic tragedy obtained his first practice in dramatic composition.

A ballad-opera which was written in the vein of true comedy, and which appears to be partly intended to parody Lillo's, is Fielding's *The Grub Street Opera* (July, 1731). Its prologue mimics the insistent didacticism of sentimental dramatists:

> The author does in humble scenes produce
> Examples fitted to your private use;

[1] No. 375. Cf. chap. vi, above.

Teaches each man to regulate his life,
To govern well his servants and his wife.

. . . .

Teaches young gentlemen do oft pursue
More women than 'they well know how to woo;
Teaches that parsons teach us the right way,
And when we err we mind not what they say.
Teaches that pious women often groan,
For sake of their religion — when they 've none;
Teaches that virtue is the maid's best store:
Teaches all these, and teaches nothing more.

Fielding, like Lillo, shows a young squire pursuing a maid of low degree; but he satirizes him as an odious weakling. His Molly, corresponding to Lillo's Silvia, repulses him, — but in a ridiculous strain, saying:

Oh, fool that I was to think thou couldst be constant who hast ruined so many women — to think that thou ever didst intend to marry me, who hast long been practised in the arts of seducing our sex. Henceforth I will sooner think it possible for butter to come when the witch is in the churn, for hay to dry in the rain, for wheat to be ripe at Christmas, for cheese to be made without milk, for a barn to be free from mice, for a warren to be free from rats, for a cherry orchard to be free from blackbirds, or for a churchyard to be free from ghosts, as for a young man to be free from falsehood.

Though Molly and her scapegrace are finally reconciled and married, Fielding to the very end treats comically the sort of situation that Lillo had idealized.[1]

The Lover (20 January, 1731), by Colley Cibber's son Theophilus, is in some particulars a mere imitation of *The Temple Beau*. Again we have as the central figure a virtuous girl, Inanthe, who is courted by three suitors, and marries him who personifies the ideals of sentimentalism. But in one of these suitors, Granger, an important addition is made to the personnel of sentimental comedy.

[1] Fielding, *Works* (1806), II, 52, 81, 116–118.

As we have seen in previous plays of this type, the gay youth of true comedy had passed into the prodigal reformed,— for example, Valentine in *The Temple Beau*, who repents his desertion of Clarissa and is happily united to her. But Granger, the person who in *The Lover* corresponds to Valentine, is of quite another stamp. Reputed a man of exceptional piety and morality, his real conduct is thus disclosed by his ward Lætitia :

> My guardian had a person has appeared handsome in more eyes than mine. As the outward object is apt to seize young minds, no wonder I was prepossessed in his favor, and thought all just he said. The giving specious titles to the foulest deeds, has ever been fatal to artless virgins, — such was his proceeding. How often has he impiously called Heaven to hear his faithless vows of constancy and love ! What methods did he omit that are usual with designing men ! Virtue and vice his rhetoric confounded. I thought that truth could be found in him alone. Conscious myself of no ill design, I was entirely in his power. I need not say he used it. While I was new to him, our scenes of life were such as cheated my weak mind with shows of pleasure, but as his brutish appetite decreased, the mask fell off, and what has been the consequence? Bitter remorse ! confusion ! horror ! wild despair ! and shame !
>
> *Inanthe*
>
> Heavens, how I pity her !
>
> *Lætitia*
>
> 'T is now ten years almost since I first knew guilt ! A painful time ! About four years since, being then of age, I claimed the fortune which my brother left me. The traitor, smiling, replied he thought himself the properest person still to take care of it, — concluding with an insulting vile reproach that I had proved too weak to be trusted even with myself. . . . All my resentment and my rage were vain, since in the first guilty hours of our dalliance, from a too generous confidence, among other deeds committed to his care, I blindly delivered him the writing which robbed me of my power, and has made me since a wretched dependant on his wicked will.[1]

Granger is guilty not only of this odious seduction, but also of a plot to murder his rival. What is most important, he is

[1] *The Lover*, Act III, scene 1, pp. 48–49.

neither punished by comic means, nor reformed by sentimental.
At the end of the play he is thus denounced :

> The man so base to take advantage of a virgin's wants, — such her
> condition then appeared to you, —
>> To undermine her virtue, exceeds him
>> Who holds a pistol to a man unarmed,
>> To rob him of his treasure. Though our laws
>> Set not such wretches in an equal light,
>> With every man of honour and of conscience
>> Yours is the greatest guilt, since, if successful,
>> How much more dreadful is the consequence!
>> Treasure may be regained, lost virtue never;
>> But gives the loser to despair and shame.
>> .   .   .   .
>> Under the mask of piety you 've performed
>> Actions my nature shudders at. — Remove him;
>> His sight grows irksome to all honest men.

> ### Granger
>
>> You triumph. Do, for you have cause indeed;
>> Yet know I now am only grieved to think
>> I have not been successful as I would.
>> Curse on you all! Your sight 's as hateful to me
>> As mine can be to you. — Come, lead me hence.

In short, Granger is what the heroine of the play calls him
— "an unheard-of villain." Sketches of that type of character
had already been introduced into the drama of sensibility,[1] but
Theophilus Cibber was the first author in that genre to paint
it at full length and in the darkest colors. The villain is, from
the philosophic point of view, an anomaly in the sentimental
world, contradicting by his wilful devotion to vice the fundamental principle of its constitution. He was, however, needed
to provide a sufficiently violent conflict; and the claims of
dramatic necessity thus overcame those of ethical consistency.

---

[1] Benjamin Wouldbe in *The Twin Rivals*, and Bargrave in *The Fatal
Extravagance*.

So far as the episode of Granger and Lætitia is concerned, the dénouement of *The Lover* is unusually pathetic. Betrayed and deserted, Lætitia seems almost a heroine of domestic tragedy. But inasmuch as she regains the property of which Granger robbed her, and has the satisfaction of seeing him arrested on a charge of attempted murder, the issue of her troubles was probably regarded by the audience as a reasonably happy one. Yet the situation that the author leaves her in, furnishes another illustration of the closeness with which the two branches of the drama of sensibility may approach each other.

Fielding detested both the Cibbers, and had his fling at Theophilus in *The Author's Farce*, where the author of *The Lover* figures as Marplay Junior, and is made to speak of his work as follows:

> I did once make a small sally into Parnassus, took a sort of flying leap over Helicon; but if they ever catch me there again — Sir, the town have a prejudice to my family; for if any play could have made them ashamed to damn it mine must. It was all over plot. It would have made half a dozen novels; nor was it crammed with a pack of wit-traps, like Congreve and Wycherley, where everyone knows when the joke was coming. I defy the sharpest critic of them all to have known when any jokes of mine were coming. The dialogue was plain, easy, and natural, and not one single joke in it from the beginning to the end. Besides, sir, there was one scene of tender melancholy conversation, enough to have melted a heart of stone; and yet they damned it. And they damned themselves, for they shall have no more of mine.[1]

As a matter of fact, the play was not damned, though it ran only nine nights; and it is not without humor. Fielding's gibe fairly indicates, on the other hand, the novel-like character of its intrigue and the pathetic intent of its principal scene.

---

[1] Fielding, *Works* (1806), I, 291–292. *The Author's Farce* was performed in March, 1730; but the above passage, Act I, scene vi, was added in January, 1734.

An unquestionable failure was Captain Charles Bodens' *The Modish Couple* (10 January, 1732), which on the first night was overwhelmed by a constant chorus of "hollaing, clapping, hissing, and catcalls," and was performed a third time only because of the persistence of the author's influential friends.[1] The play, in which Cibber is said to have assisted Bodens, was good enough to deserve a fairer hearing, but not to merit success; for it is little else than an imitation of *The Careless Husband*, with a character like Sir Friendly Moral taking an active part in the reconciliation of an estranged married couple. Fielding supplied the epilogue, a humorous plea for supporting the gallant captain's raid on Parnassus; but four years later, in his *Pasquin*, he made Queen Ignorance sponsor the work in these words:

> . . . Take this play, and bid 'em forthwith act it.
> There is not in it either head or tail . . .
> *The Modish Couple* is its name; myself
> Stood gossip to it, and I will support
> This play against the town.[2]

The shafts of sarcasm that Fielding levelled against the sentimental plays of Lillo, Theophilus Cibber, and Bodens, did not signify that he himself would with singleness of purpose devote himself to true comedy. In his next play, *The Modern Husband* (21 February, 1732), one of the plots, which pillories a man who winks at his wife's infidelity,[3] is indeed satiric; but the other is built upon a typically sentimental foundation. In this are presented Mr. Bellamant, who, though at heart a kind and loving husband, has been entangled into an amour with

---

[1] *Biographia Dramatica*, III, 54.

[2] Fielding, *Works* (1806), III, 303. Cf. Genest, III, 329-330.

[3] Is this another attack on Theophilus Cibber, who was rumored to be such a husband? (*Biographia Dramatica*, I, 127.) Lawrence, *Life of Henry Fielding* (1855), pp. 41-42, considers this part of the play a libel upon the social conditions of the age. Cf. Lindner, *Fielding*, pp. 56-61.

Mrs. Modern; and the virtuous Mrs. Bellamant, who is being pursued by a titled rake. At the same time Bellamant discovers his wife's loyalty to him, and she his faithlessness. Sincerely contrite, he says to her:

> Guilt is too plainly written in my face to admit of a denial, and I stand prepared to receive what sentence you please.

Mrs. Bellamant

> . . . You can inflict no punishment on yourself equal to what I feel . . .

Mr. Bellamant

> Oh my angel! how have I requited all your love and goodness? For what have I forsaken thy tender virtuous passion?... I never merited so good a wife. Heaven saw it had given too much, and thus has taken the blessing from me. . . . Thou shalt enjoy thy wish; we will part, part this night, this hour. . . . Henceforth I'll study only to be miserable; let Heaven make you happy, and curse me as it pleases.

Mrs. Bellamant

> It cannot make me more wretched than you have made me. . . . And must we part?

Mr. Bellamant

> Since it obliges you.

Mrs. Bellamant

> That I may have nothing to remember you by, take back this, and this, and this, and all the thousand embraces thou hast given me — till I die in thy loved arms. . . . Oh, I forgive thee all, forget it as a frightful dream. . . .

Mr. Bellamant

> Oh, let me press thee to my heart; for every moment that I hold thee thus, gives bliss beyond expression, a bliss no vice can give. Now life appears desirable again.[1]

Obviously *The Modern Husband* is another sentimental comedy on the "careless husband" theme; but it is not a good play of its kind, for even in crises, as the above passage shows, the emotions of the characters are too faintly expressed.

[1] Act IV, scene x; *Works* (1806), II, 226–228.

That the reluctance to force the emotional note was at this time not peculiar to Fielding, is shown by the last sentimental comedy of these years, — John Kelly's *The Married Philosopher* (25 March, 1732). This play is of historical interest in that it is the English adaptation of the first French eighteenth-century sentimental comedy, Destouches' *Le Philosophe Marié* (1727). The general relation of the French dramas of sensibility to the English will be considered below; here it need only be remarked that Kelly, though he followed Destouches' work closely, produced a play which did not appear foreign, and was on the whole indistinguishable from a typical English sentimental fatal comedy of the 1720's and 1730's. The only differences between his adaptation and the original lay in his occasionally broadening the humorous element and slightly toning down the pathetic. The serious scenes, like those of Fielding and Bodens, were written with so little animation that the play, which attracted no attention, did nothing to stimulate the progress of the genre.

It was domestic tragedy, heretofore the weaker branch of the drama of sensibility, which made the real advance in this period. The best known of all domestic tragedies, Lillo's *The London Merchant, or the History of George Barnwell* (22 June, 1731),[1] has in fact long enjoyed the reputation of being the first of its kind. It certainly was the first to become famous on the Continent, where Diderot and Lessing, who have strongly influenced later historians of English drama, proclaimed that it marked a new epoch. Lillo himself asserted "the novelty of this attempt,"[2] and from his prologue it was easy to draw the conclusion that the only approaches to his work were found in the romantic tragedies of Otway, Southerne,

---

[1] For a bibliography of Lillo, see the best modern edition of *George Barnwell* and *Fatal Curiosity*, A. W. Ward's (1906), pp. 242-247.

[2] Dedication of *George Barnwell*, ed. Ward, p. 6.

and Rowe.[1]   In his choice of a domestic subject for tragedy, Lillo has accordingly been considered highly original.   Probably he had never heard of *The Rival Brothers*; but it is difficult to believe that he did not know *The Fatal Extravagance*, which had by this time gone through five editions, and had been revived for about seven performances in the same year (1730) and at the same playhouse as his own *Silvia*.[2]   Doubtless Lillo knew Aaron Hill.   They were both of the mercantile class, and of similar avocations.   They had a mutual acquaintance in Colley Cibber, who wrote the epilogue of *George Barnwell*, and whose son created the title rôle.   In any case, what Lillo says in the dedication and the prologue of his play, concerning the moral effect of domestic tragedy, echoes the sentiments that Hill had already expressed in the prefatory passages of *The Fatal Extravagance*.[3]

That Lillo was indebted in other respects to the example of predecessors, will appear from a comparison between *George Barnwell* and the ballad upon which it is based.[4]   In the play, George Barnwell, a merchant's clerk, having been led astray by the courtesan Millwood, embezzles money, murders his uncle, and, sincerely penitent, is executed for his crime.   Throughout his troubles he is comforted by Thorowgood, his employer; by

---

[1] Ward, op. cit., p. xxvi, says : " There is nothing in these or in any contemporary productions to deprive Lillo's most important work of its title to originality."   Such is the current doctrine, which I believe inaccurate.

[2] Genest, III, 269, 302.

[3] Cf. *Barnwell*, pp. 3, 8–9; Hill's *Dramatic Works* (1760), I, 289.

[4] I cannot agree with Ward (p. xvii) that Lillo probably " had access to some source or sources . . . besides the old ballad itself."   Lillo himself states that his play was drawn "from the famed old song that bears his name,"— that is, *The Ballad of George Barnwell* (English and Scottish Popular Ballads, ed. F. J. Child (1859), VIII, 213 ff.; reprinted by Mr. Ward, p. 121 ff.).   Mr. Ward thinks that Lillo had access to true records of Barnwell's crime, now lost; and as evidence of their former existence points to the fact that *The Memoirs of George Barnwell* (1810) relates incidents not mentioned in the ballad, but found in the play.   I should conclude that the *Memoirs* were based upon the play.

Maria, his employer's daughter; and by Trueman, his fellow-clerk. In the ballad, neither Maria nor Trueman is mentioned, and Thorowgood appears only as a nameless master for whom Barnwell has no affection. Lillo's Thorowgood is character-ized in detail: he has a high sense of the dignity of the mer-chant class, a fatherly interest in young men, and a pitying and forgiving heart in the hour of Barnwell's distress. As an idealized merchant, he has his prototype in Mr. Sealand of *The Conscious Lovers*; and in his kindness towards the un-happy hero, he recalls Old Bookwit of *The Lying Lover*, who likewise visits a repentant youth in prison.[1] Trueman is the typical faithful and self-sacrificing friend, like his name-sake in *The Twin Rivals*, Latine in *The Lying Lover*, and Courtney in *The Fatal Extravagance*. Maria, who loves Barn-well, and sees in his crimes only innocence misguided, resem-bles Aaron Hill's Louisa, and other devoted heroines of the drama of sensibility. None of these three characters is origi-nal in conception; Lillo modelled them after sentimental types already familiar.

The most important difference between the play and the ballad is that between their respective heroes. The Barnwell of the ballad is not placed in a flattering light. After his first fall, he voluntarily continues his relations with Millwood. It is he himself who thinks of murdering his uncle; and, after en-joying the latter's hospitality, he commits the deed with deliber-ation, and enjoys its fruits without remorse. He brings about the capture of Millwood by his testimony, and subsequently perpetrates another murder.

In the play, such circumstances as tend to aggravate Barn-well's offense are altered with obvious care and singleness of aim. He does not confide in Trueman, because it would be "ungenerous and base" to betray Millwood. When he begins

---

[1] Cf. Fairbank in *The Twin Rivals*.

to confess to Thorowgood, the latter refuses to listen to him. Moved by his master's generous confidence, he determines never to see Millwood again ; and he is regained by her only through an appeal to his sympathy for her alleged troubles. " Compassion and generosity," he explains, were his motives in the second theft. The murder becomes nothing but an accident : Barnwell is about to withdraw, when he drops his pistol, is discovered by the noise, and is forced to stab his uncle to prevent recognition. His remorse is instant; he craves and obtains forgiveness of the dying man, and derives no gain from the deed.[1] Throughout the last two acts, his penitence is extreme ; and his final endeavor is to save the soul of the woman who has so vilely betrayed him.

The other characters help to instil this idea of Barnwell. Whatever his deeds, Trueman and Maria feel certain of the real innocence of his heart.

Trueman

Never had youth a higher sense of virtue : justly he thought, and as he thought he practised; never was life more regular than his; an understanding uncommon at his years — an open, generous manliness of temper — his manners easy, unaffected, and engaging.

Maria

This and much more you might have said with truth. He was the delight of every eye, and joy of every heart that knew him. . . . Truman, do you think a soul so delicate as his, so sensible of shame, can e'er submit to live a slave to vice?

Trueman

Never, never! So well I know him, I 'm sure this act of his, so contrary to his nature, must have been caused by some unavoidable necessity.[2]

[1] *Barnwell*, Act II, scenes iii, iv, xi, xiv; Act III, scene vii; ed. Ward, pp. 36–37, 39, 44–51, 68–70.
[2] Act III, scene iii, p. 56.

Thorowgood lays all the blame on Millwood, whom he denounces as follows :

> I know how step by step you 've led him on, reluctant and unwilling, from crime to crime, to this last horrid act, which you contrived, and by your cursed wiles even forced him to commit, — and then betrayed him. . . . He, innocent as he is, compared to you, must suffer too. But Heaven, who knows our frame, and graciously distinguishes between frailty and presumption, will make a difference, though man cannot, who sees not the heart, but only judges by the outward action.[1]

Barnwell was characterized with such boundless sympathy that Charles Lamb seems justified in protesting that " it is really making uncle-murder too trivial to exhibit it as done upon such slight motives," and Sam Weller in holding that " the young 'ooman deserved scragging a precious sight more than he [Barnwell] did." Lillo, in freeing his hero from responsibility, was, however, taking no new point of view. Aaron Hill had changed the source of his tragedy in accordance with precisely the same principles.

Thus Lillo was firmly rooted in the sentimental tradition. To it he owed his avowed purpose, — of making the moral power of tragedy more widely effective by representing ordinary life. To it he owed those characters which he did not find in his source, and in exact agreement with its conception of human nature he characterized his hero. To it he owed the method of conducting his plot in such a way that the tragic conclusion seemed an accident to virtue. As an innovator, he is not to be classed with the authors of *The Rival Brothers* and *The Fatal Extravagance*, nor with Colley Cibber. He was rather, like Steele, an early follower of the pioneers, one who made notable contributions to the history of a genre already established.

In the courtesan Millwood (just as Steele in Old Bookwit), Lillo added a new figure to the personnel of the drama of

[1] Act IV, scene xvi, p. 83.

sensibility. The male villain had previously appeared in Bargrave of *The Fatal Extravagance*, and in Granger of *The Lover*; and it is interesting to observe that Lillo gave to Millwood almost exactly the same traits as had marked those, her brothers in evil. She has the physical attractiveness and mental ingenuity wherewith to fascinate innocence; her wickedness is unrelieved by any redeeming feature; and she meets her fate imperturbably. She is the first of those adventuresses who were to be dramatically very effective in their sharp contrast to sentimental heroines.

A more important contribution of Lillo's to domestic tragedy was his use of prose instead of verse. Yet even in this respect certain limitations upon his claims to originality are necessary. The pathetic scenes in sentimental comedies had been for years usually, though not invariably, written in prose. Nor was the difference between the movement of Hill's blank verse and Lillo's prose in utterance as great as their printed pages might suggest. In emotional passages, Lillo often reverted, probably unintentionally, into a rhythm not unlike irregular blank verse, as the following lines, printed in his text as prose, may show:

Maria

Why are your streaming eyes still fixed below,
As though thoud'st give the greedy earth thy sorrows
And rob me of my due? Were happiness
Within your power, you should bestow it where
You pleased, but in your misery I must
And will partake!

Barnwell

Oh! say not so, but fly, abhor, and leave
Me to my fate! Consider what you are —
How vast your fortune and how bright your fame.[1]

The oral effect of such a "prose" style could not have been entirely novel. Lillo may, however, be credited with cultivating

[1] Act V, scene ix, p. 102.

an unusually natural diction. It was far less grandiloquent than that of classical tragedy, and much simpler even than that of domestic tragedy as written by Hill.

The environment, as well as the language, of Lillo's tragedy harmonized exceptionally well with the spirit of the genre. In *The Rival Brothers*, the scene was laid among the country gentry, and in *The Fatal Extravagance* among city people of quality. None of the various middle-class environments that Lillo might have chosen could have been more suitable than the mercantile circle. The ideals of life that inspired him were, to be sure, penetrating the nation, high and low; but they seemed peculiarly in accord with those of the merchant class. When a "fine gentleman" like Steele's Bevil moralized sentimentally, he felt himself somewhat at odds with the traditions of his caste; when a Thorowgood pronounced the same views, he seemed true to his station in life.

Though the mercantile setting of *George Barnwell* was a praiseworthy novelty in domestic tragedy, that particular environment did not become the one to which the genre was exclusively confined. Like Steele's introduction of mystery into the plot of sentimental comedy, Lillo's setting was found useful but not indispensable. In future, domestic tragedy chose as its realm the life of the middle classes in the very broadest sense of the term, — from that of the farmer or shopkeeper to that of the gentleman of leisure. So Moore's *The Gamester*, as typical a domestic tragedy as Lillo's, moved, like its source, *The Fatal Extravagance*, amid gentlefolk.

The success of *George Barnwell* was more brilliant and lasting than that of any other eighteenth-century domestic tragedy. Though it was first produced in the dull summer season, it aroused so much attention everywhere that the Queen became interested in it and furthered its fortunes. "At the desire of several persons of distinction and eminent merchants of the

city," Cibber had it performed in the regular season of 1731–
1732;[1] and thereafter it remained a stock piece for several
generations. The story was told that a clerk who was hovering
on the brink of dishonesty was so affected by seeing the play
that he at once reformed, and lived to become a most respectable merchant;[2] but apparently nobody ever inquired how many
of the embezzling clerks after 1731 had seen it without such
edifying results. They must have been numerous, for the
tragedy was commonly given on holidays in order that all
apprentices might see it and thus avoid the pitfalls that Barnwell's innocence had led him into. Perhaps one may, in view
of the limited vogue of other domestic tragedies, indulge the
suspicion that the frequent performance of *George Barnwell*
was encouraged by influential citizens, not because they themselves enjoyed it, but because they thought young people should.
Whether or not the popularity of the play was somewhat arti-
ficially stimulated, Lillo's achievement was a remarkable one.
He completely destroyed the tradition that only a tragedy dealing with great persons could attain enduring recognition. He
had his reward, — not only in money, but in fame. The earlier
effort of Aaron Hill was soon forgotten, and Lillo was hailed
" the herald of a literary revolution."[3]

The immediate successor of Lillo in domestic tragedy was
Charles Johnson, previously mentioned as the author of a sentimental comedy,[4] a facile writer of almost every type of drama,
who had produced eighteen plays in thirty years. The theme
of his *Cælia, or the Perjured Lover* (11 December, 1732)
was well chosen. Its central situation is one that, even more
than the ruin of a promising young man like Barnwell, naturally excites pity, — the seduction and desertion of an innocent
maiden. A pathetic figure of this sort had already been sketched

---

[1] Genest, III, 326.
[2] *Biographia Dramatica*, II, 377–378.
[3] Ward's phrase, op. cit., p. xi.
[4] Chap. vii, above.

in Farquhar's sentimental comedy, *The Twin Rivals*; but the distresses into which Johnson plunged his heroine were of a magnitude unprecedented in the drama of sensibility, and were boldly carried to a fatal issue. They were comparable to those which had been briefly narrated in the tragic *Tatler* and *Spectator* tales that recorded the desperate fortunes of victims of libertinism.[1] To arouse compassion for a typical case of that sort was Johnson's aim; and with some justice he opined that the particular kind of immorality attacked by him had not "been set in so full a light by the dramatic writers."[2]

Johnson's Cælia, the daughter of a genteel family resident in a country town, has been seduced by Wronglove, a city libertine, and under a solemn promise of marriage has eloped with him to London. She is about to become a mother, and does not know that Wronglove, who has tired of the amour, is planning to desert her. She has felt, beneath his courteous and considerate manner, a growing indifference to her; but when he proposes that she shall take refuge with a Mrs. Lupine, who, he assures her, is a respectable midwife, she does not suspect that this is his first step in severing their connection. She urges him to visit her soon, saying:

> I am your child, your ward, your care, your trust; I have no father, mother, friend, relation — none but you. You are my comfort and support: I rest alone on you, and when you leave me, I and your child must perish. O blame me not if I complain to you; and when I see you treat me coldly, almost with indifference, to whom can I complain? I have relinquished all for you, and am by all deserted for your sake. My fame, my character, my once unspotted reputation's gone; no virtuous woman will admit me into her fellowship. Wronglove, I am your slave; do not be too hard a master. I must depend upon your smile or frown. But I will not accuse you; these are only, perhaps, my silly suspicions — I see I make you uneasy.[3]

[1] Chap. vi, above.
[2] Advertisement to the Reader, *Cælia*, p. ii.
[3] Act I, scene ii, p. 7.

On first meeting Mrs. Lupine, Cælia is amazed at the woman's coarseness; but she is temporarily comforted by Wronglove's calling on her at her new lodgings, and when he takes his departure (never, as the audience knows, intending to return) she thus expresses her sense of relief:

> I feel my mind is more at ease; my spirits are grown lighter. There is an irresistible sweetness in Wronglove's manner and expression, when he pleases, — a joy I never felt but in his sight, that softens and for the time suspends my grief and fears.[1]

After a night in which she has been terror-stricken by hearing the noisy revelry of Mrs. Lupine's household, and has determined to ask Wronglove to find her other lodgings at once, she is forced by Mrs. Lupine to endure the company of strumpets, whose conversation outrages her delicacy beyond endurance. Their suggestions that she enter upon a career such as they, in a situation like hers, resorted to, she repulses with contempt. Mrs. Lupine then drops the mask of vulgar affability under which the vilest intentions have been imperfectly concealed, and Cælia at last realizes that she is a prisoner in a house of ill fame. She is still expecting Wronglove's return when she receives from him a letter confessing that, in obedience to his father's wish, he is about to marry another.

A glimpse of hope is afforded Cælia by the arrival of an old servant of her family, who has succeeded in discovering her place of concealment. The letter from her father which he brings, and which assures her that she is forgiven, contains also, however, appalling news. It reads:

> Your poor mother, not having strength enough to support the loss of you, sunk under it. She died last week. Some minutes before she died, she said: "Remember Cælia: I never shall see my poor dear child again; let her not be lost; forgive her, as I do." ... Your affectionate and afflicted Father.[2]

---

[1] Act II, scene ii, p. 23.   [2] Act III, scene i, p. 37.

Cælia faints; and the servant, after restoring her to consciousness and trying to comfort her, rushes out to summon her
father and secure her a safe lodging.

She has to undergo yet greater sufferings and indignities.
Before her father can rescue her from Mrs. Lupine's, the
police raid the house, and carry Cælia with the other inmates
before a magistrate. Believing herself now hopelessly lost, she
has to endure the publicity of court-room proceedings and the
horrors of confinement in prison. The shock of this exposure
crushes her fortitude; and when her father finally reaches her
side, she is reduced to abject despondency. The tenderness of
her father's love only deepens her anguish, and she sinks lifeless into his arms. Momentarily she recovers herself, but again
she is struck down by a new woe. A man of honor, who has
vainly tried to induce Wronglove to marry her, has so offended
the seducer that a duel has resulted. In it Wronglove has been
mortally wounded. Before he dies, he repents; and it is his
last will that Cælia shall be recognized as his wife.

Cælia

> As one bewildered in a maze of woes, troubles crowd fast upon me,
> faster far than my weak spirits can support or suffer. My Wronglove's
> sudden death, as he died mine, repenting, sorrowful, and just at last—
> whatever I have suffered by his unthinking conduct, oh, let me drop
> one tear upon his grave![1]

Thereupon she dies broken-hearted.

The play was a fair and forceful portrayal of the darkest
social evil, and Johnson's Sir Friendly Moral pointedly asked:
"Does it not concern humanity?"[2] The sincerity of his purpose deserved applause, as did his skillful conduct of the action
and the natural yet dignified style of his dialogue. Nor was the
audience that attended the first performance of *Cælia* insensible

---

[1] Act V, scene iii, p. 59.
[2] Bellamy's words, Act IV, scene iii, p. 50.

to its merits and unmoved by its poignancy. It "joined with Cælia in her tears." [1] But just appreciation for the work as a whole was lost in the disgust aroused by the realism of the episodes in which Mrs. Lupine and her lewd company were satirized.[2] These scenes might easily have been avoided or softened, and Johnson had been warned that they might prove too offensive; but he obstinately retained them, deeming it necessary " to show the manners of these people in order to raise the distress of Cælia." He paid the penalty for his boldness. His tragedy was performed only two nights, and he never produced another play. His withdrawal was a great loss to the drama of sensibility; for that very desire "to raise the distress," which had in this case run counter to popular taste, was an instinct in the right direction.

Lovers of domestic tragedy might at this time reasonably infer that the failure of *Cælia* was a mere accident, due to certain traits peculiar to that play, and not auguring a rejection by the public of the genre in its essentials. The misfortune of Johnson would hardly shake their confidence in the future of a genre which was supported by the signal success of *George Barnwell*.

---

[1] Advertisement to the Reader, p. i. The play was commended in *The Grub Street Journal* (8 March, 1733) as capable of arousing pathos and furthering morality. Cf. l'Abbé Prévost, *Le Pour et Contre* (1733), I, 40–44.

[2] This introduction of the comic into domestic tragedy is exceptional; if not unique. It illustrates again the kinship of the two branches of the drama of sensibility.

CHAPTER IX

THE LEADERSHIP IN SENTIMENTALISM LOST BY
THE DRAMA: 1732–1750

Before the fourth decade of the eighteenth century, the drama of sensibility labored under the disadvantage of being out of accord with the spirit that dominated the intellectual life and the literary masterpieces of the time. During the fourth and fifth decades, however, the situation changed notably. Indifference or hostility to sentimentalism still marked, it is true, some of the important publications, — among them the philosophic works of Butler and of Hume, the satires of Pope and of Johnson, the earlier poems of Gray, and the earlier novels of Fielding. But at the same time there were appearing equally important works in which sentimentalism was the keynote. The new interpretation of life successfully invaded two leading forms of literature that had been inhospitable to it, — poetry and the novel.

In the poetry of the 1730's the long-retarded influence of Shaftesbury upon belles-lettres at last manifested itself powerfully. It had reached Thomson, as we have seen, and now spread in many directions, sometimes appearing in places where one would least expect it. It entered, by Bolingbroke's mediation, into what was intended to be a stronghold of orthodoxy and classicism, — Pope's *Essay on Man* (1732–1734), — and so undermined the main positions that the whole work became a chaos of inconsistencies. The poem proclaimed at once the frailty of man and the perfection of the universal order.[1] When the heresy of the second of these irreconcilable notions was

---

[1] The former, for example, in II, 1–18, 93–100: the latter, for example, in I, 276–280; III, 7–8, 109–118; IV, 331–340, 361–369, etc.

called to Pope's attention, he repudiated the obvious meaning of
his words; and, years later, having withdrawn from the dangerous mazes of philosophy to the familiar ground of satire, he
made amends by ridiculing Shaftesbury's rhapsody upon nature.[1]

In less famous poems, Shaftesbury's ideas were more consistently expressed and developed. Henry Brooke's *Universal
Beauty* (1735) ecstatically praised the world order, and urged
mankind to abandon the artificial, and to be guided by natural
(that is, divine) instinct. This confidence in the natural was
transferred into the field of taste by Mark Akenside, whose
Pleasures of the Imagination (1746) presented a sentimental
kind of æsthetics that would have delighted Steele, and amused
Dryden. The same theory was given a lyrical and vaguely
imaginative interpretation in William Collins' *Ode on the Poetical Character* (1746). Other aspects of Shaftesbury's teachings
were developed in J. G. Cooper's *The Power of Harmony* (1745)
and Joseph Warton's *The Enthusiast* (1746), the very titles of
which are terms that the philosopher had harped upon. This
group of poets ardently disseminated nearly every principal
tenet of the sentimental faith, — the moral power of natural
beauty, the innocence of the state of nature, the superiority of
emotion to intellect both in life and in literature, and the
inhumanity of unkindness toward man and beast.[2]

Coincident with the vogue of sentimental poetry, grew the
enormous popularity of the sentimental novel. Its founder,
Samuel Richardson, was an intimate friend of Colley Cibber
and Aaron Hill,[3] who were among his chief encouragers, and

---

[1] *The Dunciad*, IV (1742), lines 487–492.

[2] Besides the works mentioned above, see *A Vindication of Lord Shaftesbury, Gentleman's Magazine* (1732), II, 798; *The Happy Savage*, ibid. II, 718;
the dispute about country life, ibid. (1731), I, 334, 421, 433; Samuel Boyse,
The Deity (1739); Shenstone, *A Pastoral Ballad* (1743).

[3] *The Correspondence of Samuel Richardson*, ed. Anna L. Barbauld (1804).
Cf. Clara L. Thompson, *Samuel Richardson* (1900), pp. 18, 77, 86–88.

whose letters to him are often quoted as well voicing the gushing adulation that greeted *Pamela* (1740) and *Clarissa Harlowe* (1748). These great edifices were built after the smaller models of the sentimental tale[1] and the sentimental drama. *Pamela* was said by Richardson to be based on a true incident; but it is nevertheless a story analogous to Steele's tale of Amanda and Lillo's comedy *Silvia*;[2] and, what is more important, it is recounted in the same spirit. Nor can any reader of Charles Johnson's *Cælia*[3] fail to recognize in that domestic tragedy an anticipation, remarkably close, of *Clarissa Harlowe*. In the choice of his subjects, the nature of his moral appeal, the method of conducting his plots, and the conception of his characters, Richardson was carrying forward the movement that the dramatists of sensibility had begun. Even his opponent Fielding, whose *Joseph Andrews* (1742) was the reduction of *Pamela* to an absurdity, was finally swept into the current: *Tom Jones* (1749) is in important passages[4] somewhat affected by sentimentalism, and *Amelia* (1751) very decidedly so.

While the floodgates of sentimental poetry and narrative were being opened, true comedy was sinking towards its lowest level. The best comedy of the 1730's, Fielding's *The Miser* (1733), owed its merits to the fact that it copied, with inconsiderable changes, Molière's *L'Avare*. In the prologue of his *The Universal Gallant* (1735), an original effort, Fielding complained that the public taste was so capricious that a dramatist was nonplussed:

> If wit he aims at, you the traps can show;
> If serious, he is dull; if humorous, low.
> Some would maintain one laugh throughout a play,

---

[1] Richardson's fondness for *The Spectator* is mentioned in *The Rambler*, No. 97.

[2] Chap. viii, above.   [3] Chap. viii, above.

[4] For example, Book XVIII, chaps. x and xii. Fundamentally it is the story of an amiable prodigal forgiven and reformed.

> Some would be grave and bear fine things away.
> How is it possible at once to please
> Tastes so directly opposite as these?

His play did not violate the aims of high comedy; but, wanting power, it fell short of them. He hoped to please by reconciling the satiric with the pleasant, — by what he termed "tenderly laughing you out of vice." The natural result of this weak-kneed attitude was a dull play that failed. In his *An Old Man Taught Wisdom* (1735), there were some telling satiric strokes; but most of his really lively work at this time was mere farce, burlesque, or libel. The Licensing Act of 1737, which was directed against the licentiousness of personal abuse, served also to discourage the liberty of general satire; yet it aroused the literary world to no determined protest. The widespread fear that the Comic Muse might offend against social benevolence was expressed in Whitehead's memorable couplet:

> That eager zeal to laugh the vice away
> May hurt some virtue's intermingling ray![1]

The kind of comedy that was admired about the middle of the century is exemplified by Benjamin Hoadly's *The Suspicious Husband* (1747). Its principal character is Ranger (one of Garrick's most famous rôles), who participates in each of the three interlaced plots. Two of these are love-affairs, — between the merry Clarinda and Frankly on the one hand, and between the more serious Jacintha and Bellamy on the other. The third plot, which gives the title to the play, is concerned with the suspicious Mr. Strictland, at whose house both girls are living. One evening Frankly has been watching before the house for an opportunity of meeting Clarinda. During his temporary absence, Ranger arrives, sees a rope ladder dangling out of the

---

[1] William Whitehead, *On Ridicule* (written 1743?); Chalmers, *English Poets*, XVII, 208.

window, on a gay impulse ascends it, — and presently the fun begins. The impudent Ranger makes love to the startled Mrs. Strictland. After being dismissed by her, he runs upon Jacintha, whom he first frightens with his ardent advances, and finally on learning that she is his friend Bellamy's beloved, helps to escape from the house. The consequence is a series of ludicrous misunderstandings : Mr. Strictland suspects his wife of infidelity, and both Bellamy and Frankly are indignant at Ranger's intrusion into their affairs. There is much merriment, — some of it not without lubricity (fifty years later the play was scathingly called " a profligate pantomime " [1]) ; but, it should be observed, the basis of the comic effect is a farcical situation.

The characters do not dominate the plot. Bellamy and Jacintha are amiable young persons, but their final happiness is not due to their virtues. Mrs. Strictland is a devoted and patient wife, but it is not her goodness that reconciles her husband to her. The comic spirit rules the action ; in the characterization, however, it is weak. Ranger is a wild gallant like Fielding's Temple Beau, but in the copy all the outlines have been softened. Says Samuel Foote :

> His errors arise from the want of reflection. A lively imagination, with a great flow of spirits, hurries him into all the fashionable follies of the town ; but throw the least shadow of wickedness or dishonor on an action, and he avoids it with the same care that he would a precipice. The natural good qualities of this youth obtain for him on the stage the same indulgence that attends him in the world ; we are blind to his foibles, entertained with his adventures, and wish to see . . . the wild rogue reclaimed.[2]

Jacintha is nominally a prude, and Clarinda a coquette ; but what Mrs. Strictland says to them is true and significant, — "You are both too good for either of those characters." Comedy

---

[1] Bell's *British Theatre*, IV (1797), note on *The Suspicious Husband.*
[2] Samuel Foote, *The Roman and English Comedy Compared* (1747), pp. 28–29.

is still amusing, but its sting has been drawn. "The principal intent," says a contemporary critic of the play complacently,
" is to entertain, and afford the care-tired mind a few hours of
dissipation." [1] In other words, even in plays where the spirit
of merriment still rules, comedy has abdicated its high function
of moral satire.

Some plays of the 1730's and 1740's that were for the most
part comic, showed infusions of the sentimental. Garrick's *The
Lying Valet* (1741) is chiefly concerned with the humorous
predicaments that the intrigues of a servant bring upon his
master, but it concludes with a scene of penitence.[2] Though
nearly all of Fielding's *The Intriguing Chambermaid* (1734)
is farcical, there are moments when the lovers are intended to
be affecting.[3] Fielding's *Miss Lucy in Town* (1742), which the
author calls "a farce with songs," begins with a humorous portrayal of the rustic manners of Thomas, a young squire, and
Lucy, his bride. Towards the end, however, there is an abrupt
change in the characterization of Thomas. When he discovers
that a lord has been trying to steal away his Lucy, he refuses
to be comforted by the assurance that " in all probability, who-
ever the gentleman is, he 'll return her again." " Return her ! "
he exclaims, " ha, stained, spotted, sullied ! Who shall return
me my honor ? " And when this hitherto grotesque country boor
is asked by the lord to resign his wife, he momentarily rises
to the dignity of an English freeman.

Thomas

How, my Lord, resign my wife! Fortune, which made me poor,
made me a servant; but nature, which made me an Englishman, preserved me from being a slave. I have as good a right to the little I
claim, as the proudest peer hath to his great possessions; and whilst
I am able, I will defend it.   [*Draws*] [4]

---

[1] *Biographia Dramatica*, III, 310.
[2] David Garrick, *Dramatic Works* (1798), I, 58–59.
[3] Fielding, *Works* (1806), III, 45–47.   [4] *Works*, III, 452, 457.

The decadence of comedy through sentimental contamination is probably best observable in Fielding's *The Wedding Day* (1743). The basis of the plot resembles that of a typical Restoration comedy. Clarinda is in love with Millamour, an unfaithful gallant, and, despairing of winning him, has consented to marry old Stedfast. Neither Millamour nor Clarinda is idealized. He has betrayed and forsaken Lucinda, whose appeals he ridicules, and who remains deserted at the end of the play. Clarinda, though engaged to Stedfast, is disloyal to him in thought if not in action, and secretly visits Millamour to "take one dear last draught of ruin from his eyes." On the wedding day, after the ceremony, she feigns illness; whereupon Millamour, disguised as a physician, is summoned. It is the comic aspect of this situation that is emphasized. On the other hand, there is much in the plot and characterization that ill accords with true comedy. Millamour owes his final possession of Clarinda not to outwitting the husband, but to the discovery that Clarinda's marriage is null and void. He falls at times into a moral mood; he shakes it off with ease, however, when temptation offers. Supposedly he reforms at the close, but rather because his narrow escape from losing Clarinda has frightened him than because he is really contrite. The author's attitude towards his characters is vacillating, and the harmony of effect is disturbed. The influence of Vanbrugh is counteracted by the influence of Cibber, the result being ethical and artistic confusion.

Never had there been circumstances so favorable to the advancement of the drama of sensibility. Sentimentalism was becoming one of the strongest forces of the age. Its ancient enemy, the comic spirit, was no longer brilliantly sustained or unreservedly admired. The public that was acquiring a taste for the new poetry of Shaftesbury's school, and was devouring the novels of Richardson, would have responded with unprecedented fervor to well-wrought plays composed in the same spirit. On glancing at the dramatic records from 1732 to 1750, one might readily believe that the drama of sensibility was flourishing. The classics of the genre, *Love's Last Shift*, *The Careless Husband*, *The Provoked Husband*, *The Conscious Lovers*, and *George Barnwell*, were being performed season after season. It was not a prolific period in any type of drama, but among the comparatively few plays produced for the first time, seven were sentimental. That these indications of a moderately healthy growth were deceptive, however, will appear on examining the quality of the new dramas of sensibility.

The first of these was *The Lady's Revenge, or the Rover Reclaimed* (9 January, 1734), a sentimental comedy by William Popple. Aaron Hill, who wrote the prologue of the play, seems to have urged Popple, then a treasury clerk, to attempt playwriting. The encouragement was ill bestowed. Popple took the well-worn themes of the deserted mistress and the prodigal reformed, and constructed a plot that was somewhat richer in complications than usual; but he was unable to lend to his scenes or characters any effect of novelty. His play was withdrawn after the fourth night.[1]

There followed two domestic tragedies, the earlier of them being John Hewitt's *Fatal Falsehood, or Distressed Innocence* (11 February, 1734). The sub-title is obviously in keeping with the sentimental idea of the tragic; and throughout the play an effort is made to create sympathy not only for the innocent victims of Belladine, a bigamist and murderer, but also for Belladine himself. The prologue recommends him as "a generous libertine" in whom "no sordid vices his high heart reprove," and after having wrecked two lives he dies with the comforting reflection, "my conscience tells me not I've done amiss."[2] Much is made of the fact that he married

---

[1] *Genest*, III, 427–428.
[2] *Fatal Falsehood* (1734), pp. vii and 41. Cf. p. 26.

his first wife, Louisa, only because his financial dependence would not allow him to disobey his father's command. As soon as he comes into his inheritance, he deserts Louisa, and marries his first love, Maria, telling her the "fatal falsehood" that he is free. On the very day of the wedding, Louisa learns that it has taken place; and, hoping to intervene before the marriage is consummated, she disguises herself as a man, hastens to Maria, and tells the bride the appalling truth. Maria will not believe her, however; and Louisa angrily draws her sword. Just then Belladine rushes in. Not recognizing who it is that threatens Maria, he kills Louisa. He himself is thereupon mortally wounded in a duel with Louisa's brother, and his death drives Maria into madness.

Fatal Falsehood marks a reactionary step in domestic tragedy. Both Lillo and Johnson had written in prose. Hewitt returned to blank verse. His style is painfully bad. The most expressive words that he can put into Belladine's mouth at a moment of intense excitement, are these:

> The flatt'ring scene of joy is fled away,
> And left me plunged in endless misery.
> I'm tortured more than nature can support.

When Hewitt attempts the sublime, he becomes unendurable; witness the following:

> My looks express the dictates of my heart,
> Which is, alas! o'ercharged with silent grief
> That inly swells — like subterraneous winds
> Collecting force and lab'ring for a vent.[1]

The characterization is as unnatural as the dialogue. The plot is full of improbabilities, and is centered in the wrong person, — for it is not Belladine but the pathetic Maria upon whom the interest should have been focused. *Fatal Falsehood* is

[1] Pp. 36 and 2.

doubtless the worst of all domestic tragedies, and it has strong claims to being considered the worst eighteenth-century play of any type. Its failure, unlike that of Johnson's *Cælia*, was richly deserved.

Lillo now came to the rescue of domestic tragedy with his *Fatal Curiosity* (27 May, 1736). In one respect the play was a less bold departure from convention than *George Barnwell*: it was written in verse. The personages are gentry of Cornwall, whose sad history had in 1618 been told in a pamphlet, entitled *News from Perin*.[1] Lillo modified the original story after the customary manner of his school. Young Wilmot, who in the source is represented as an undutiful son, a vagabond, and a pirate, becomes in the play a virtuous hero. Driven from home owing to his father's extravagance, he gains wealth abroad, and after a lapse of years returns. During his absence his heart has remained true to Charlot, the heroine (who, like Barnwell's Maria, is not found in the source). On his sudden reappearance, she does not at first recognize him, whom she had mourned as dead; and he is distressed by the fear that she has forgotten him. When he discloses his identity to her, however, she welcomes him with tears of joy.

His next thought is of his parents, who, he learns, have sunk into extreme poverty. Moved by what is termed "fatal curiosity," he plans to visit them as a stranger. He will on the evening of his arrival lead them to talk of their son, will listen to their words of yearning fondness, and, the next morning, in the presence of friends and neighbors, will gladden their hearts with the revelation of his identity. But in the night the parents, who are facing starvation, murder their guest for the possession of his jewels. Their deed is palliated in the words,

[1] Reprinted in A. W. Ward's edition of *The London Merchant* and *Fatal Curiosity* (1906), pp. 221–238.

> 'T is not choice
> But dire necessity suggests the thought.
>
> .   .   .   .
>
> 'T is less impiety, less against nature,
> To take another life than end our own.[1]

Thus the virtuous life and generous hopes of young Wilmot are destroyed by a calamity for which malign fate is held responsible.

About 1780 *Fatal Curiosity* influenced the rise of the German " Schicksalstragödie," [2] and it consequently came to be regarded as the fountain-head of those modern plays in which " destiny is exhibited as operating to all intents and purposes independently of character." [3] As a matter of fact, destiny had tyrannized over character in all the preceding domestic tragedies of the century. The fatalistic element in their plots was the logical consequence of their authors' sentimental conception of human nature. The virtuous can be brought to an unhappy end only by villainous seduction of innocence or by unmerited bad fortune. That principle we have seen recurrently illustrated in the themes of domestic tragedies : a younger brother unwittingly seduces the bride of the elder ; Bellmour, impoverished by a villain, commits suicide a moment before inheriting wealth; Barnwell, ruined by an adventuress, unintentionally murders his uncle ; the betrayed Cælia, just as her future is brightening, is struck down by two unnecessary deaths ; and Belladine, ignorant of his opponent's identity, kills his wife. Obviously Lillo was not introducing an entirely new method when he showed old Wilmot, driven by necessity to rob an unknown

---

[1] Act III, scene i, pp. 197 and 200. In the source the act is without such reservations stamped as a crime.

[2] Cf. Jakob Minor, *Die Schicksalstragödie in ihren Hauptvertretern* (1883), and A. W. Ward's edition of *The London Merchant*, pp. liii–lv.

[3] Ward, p. liii. Mr. Ward apparently is of the opinion that destiny does not operate thus in earlier domestic tragedies.

guest, murdering his son. It should, however, be added that the author of *Fatal Curiosity*, with a directness and lucidity characteristic of his manner of unfolding an action, exhibited the power of fate more vividly than it had been shown in any previous work of this genre.

Lillo gave further development to another inherent feature of the drama of sensibility when he dwelt upon young Wilmot's yearning for deeply emotional experiences. A light touch of the same longing had been bestowed by Charles Shadwell upon Sir Patrick in *Irish Hospitality*, and by Steele upon Isabella in *The Conscious Lovers*;[1] but Lillo was the first to make the trait a conspicuous one. Young Wilmot cannot rest content with the sudden joy that instant recognition by his parents would bring : he must first exhaust the pleasures of fancying the reunion ; then, by artfully concealing his identity, intensify and prolong the happiness of it ; and finally set the stage for a surprisingly dramatic revelation. " I would fain," he says, " refine on happiness." " Imagine," he cries,

> The floods of transport, the sincere delight,
> That all my friends will feel when I disclose
> To my astonished parents my return ;
> And then confess that I have well contrived,
> By giving others joy, t' exalt my own !
> As pain and anguish in a gen'rous mind
> While kept concealed and to ourselves confined
> Want half their force, so pleasure when it flows
> In torrents round us, more ecstatic grows ![2]

As one of the characters observes, young Wilmot is " luxurious in his mental [or, rather, emotional] pleasures."[3] This tendency, which to unsentimental natures appears weak or morbid, Lillo depicts sympathetically : it is one of the most

---

[1] *Irish Hospitality*, Acts IV and V ; *The Conscious Lovers*, Act V, scene iii.
[2] Act II, scene ii, p. 188.
[3] Act II, scene ii, p. 187.

precious virtues in a man of feeling. So much was it to be emphasized in the future literature of sensibility, notably in the works of Sterne, that it became a very prominent attribute of the typically sentimental character; and, indeed, sentimentalism is to-day frequently understood to signify especially the indulgence of emotions for their own sake.[1] That Lillo should have created a hero with a ruling passion so congenial to the drama of sensibility shows how thoroughly he was in harmony with the temperamental basis of the movement, and how intelligently he tried to guide it towards its proper goal.

Fatal Curiosity attained considerable repute in the literary world, one of its admirers seriously comparing its "terrible graces" with those of *Œdipus Tyrannus*.[2] It was performed, however, only seven times in its first season. Though it was for a brief period retained on the stage by the influence of Fielding, who esteemed Lillo personally, and had written the prologue of the play, it never enjoyed a success commensurate with its intrinsic worth. This circumstance, combined with the failure of the equally meritorious *Cœlia*, confirms the suspicion that the vogue of *George Barnwell* was an exceptional phenomenon, and that, as a rule, the public did not yet appreciate domestic tragedy even when it was well written.

One of the three pieces comprising Sir Hildebrand Jacob's *The Nest of Plays* (25 January, 1738) is a short sentimental comedy called *The Prodigal Reformed*. Its general theme is as hackneyed as the title suggests. An extravagant but amiable young American, who has been sent to England to be educated, dissipates his allowance, is deserted by his false friends, runs in danger of imprisonment, repents, and is forgiven by his

---

[1] "Sentimentalism is the cultivation of emotion for the sake of the thrill, of the subjective experience." — William Allan Neilson, *Essentials of Poetry* (1912), p. 208. Cf. the whole chapter, "Sentimentalism in Poetry," for an illuminating discussion of this aspect of the subject.

[2] A. W. Ward, ed. *The London Merchant*, p. xliv.

good-natured father. The only novelty of the play lies in its approval of the sentimental system of education. The father has directed that the young man shall be given an opportunity to develop without the restraints of severe discipline. He is, in the words of his uncle and guardian,

> to be entirely ignorant of his father's generosity, and at the same time to be constantly supplied underhand by me as his guardian. To be contradicted in nothing that did not immediately tend to his dishonor; but, on the contrary, to be humored in all the expenses he could devise that were not low and shameful.

The principles underlying this programme are explained by the father as follows :

> I considered that according to my notion of things the greatest part of our youth were wrongly, and indeed severely, brought up by their parents, losing much of their most precious time under a kind of imprisonment and tyranny, in acquiring what was afterwards generally soon forgot, and what tended not in reality to make them live more wisely or more happily in the world; that this severity and restraint did but help to oppress a noble and generous disposition.[1] . . .

The resultant crop of wild oats is regarded with complacency, and forgotten because the youth repents. The play closes with a justification of the experiment :

> Harsh parents here may learn how they 're to blame
> Who generous youth by hardships would reclaim.
> Let none to spare his purse spoil such a son ;
> For noble souls are best by kindness won.[2]

Though these doctrines, clearly in accord with the sentimental confidence in human nature, were here preached more distinctly than in earlier sentimental comedies, nothing in the actions of the youth distinguished him in an interesting manner from the prodigals that preceded him. The play was damned on the first night.[3]

---

[1] Scene i, pp. 5–6.   [2] Scene vii, p. 21.   [3] Cf. Genest, III, 551.

Two years later, Samuel Richardson touched sentimental hearts with a deeper emotion than had ever possessed them. The example of his *Pamela* ought to have breathed new life into the drama of sensibility. The novel was, indeed, twice dramatized; but one of the versions was so poor that it was never staged,[1] and the other, James Dance's *Pamela, a Comedy* (9 November, 1741), is disappointing. That searching penetration into the life of the emotions, that sustained pathetic effect, which marks the original, has been lost; only the skeleton of that palpitant being remains. So far as the plot and the large outlines of the characters are concerned, Dance did not modify the story in any important respect. He shows Belvile (Mr. B.) planning to dismiss Pamela's friend, the kindly Mrs. Jervis; the steward Longman, approving Mrs. Jervis' accounts; the coachman John Arnold, displeased with his master's orders regarding the kidnapping; and, of course, Pamela writing to her dear parents. In the third act, the real conflict begins, — between Belvile, Mrs. Jewkes, and Colebrand (the two latter being satirically drawn) on the one side, and Pamela and Williams on the other. After the girl's vain attempt to run away, Belvile makes his odious assault, is by her tears moved to repentance, and "rewards virtue" by marrying her. Subsequent to the wedding, old Andrews, not knowing that it has taken place, comes to take Pamela home, is alarmed by seeing her in silk attire, and is then gladdened with the news that she is Belvile's wife. Finally, the sneering Lady Davers is reproved by Belvile, and Pamela wins the affections of all by her generous forgiveness of the injuries they have done her. It was a summary of the novel in dialogue form, — and the result was a typical sentimental comedy.

---

[1] Anonymous, *Pamela, or Virtue Triumphant* (1742). Cf. *Biographia Dramatica*, III, 126. On French dramatizations, especially Voltaire's *Nanine*, see chap. x, below.

During November and December, 1741, Dance's *Pamela* was often performed. The public enjoyed it, partly because David Garrick, the rising star in the theatrical firmament, acted the comic part of Jack Smatter, and partly because it was a series of pictures illustrating the great novel that everybody was reading. But as a play it offered nothing new; and when it had served its pictorial purpose, it was permanently laid aside and forgotten.

No sign of Richardsonian influence is discoverable in the last domestic tragedy of this period, Thomas Cooke's *Love the Cause and Cure of Grief, or the Innocent Murderer* (19 December, 1743). Cooke, weakly imitating Lillo's method in *Fatal Curiostiy*, based his play upon a true incident, "lifted the principal characters," as he himself says, "a little higher than they are described in the story,"[1] and showed well-deserved happiness destroyed by a fatal coincidence. Young Freeman and his sweetheart, Charlotte Briar, are distressed because his aristocratic mother and her blunt father oppose their marriage. A quarrel arises between the families; but the elders do not remain deaf to the appeal of affection and pity, and presently consent to the union. The idyllic joy of the young couple is, however, dashed to pieces when, the day after their wedding, they learn that Charlotte's father has been murdered; and that Freeman's father, found standing beside the body, holding in his hands the cudgel that struck the deadly blow, is apparently guilty of the crime. At his trial it transpires that he is innocent; but in the meantime the widowed Mrs. Briar has died of grief, and Charlotte and young Freeman begin their life together under the shadow of a bereavement which even their love for one another cannot wholly dispel. The general plan of Cooke's work shows that he understood the elementary principles of domestic tragedy; but his style was neither natural

---

[1] *Love the Cause and Cure of Grief* (1744), p. v.

nor powerful, and thus the play, which was performed only once, seemed an unconvincing representation of an improbable calamity.

The only new sentimental comedy of this period which achieved a fair measure of permanent success was Edward Moore's *The Foundling* (13 February, 1748). Its chief merits are fluency of dialogue and occasional vivacity in the comic passages. The design of the plot was original in the sense that it was a new combination of old themes. Moore took for the basis of his play the central situation of *The Conscious Lovers*, — that of a virtuous maiden whose parentage is unknown, who is under the protection of a young man that loves her, and who is finally found by her parent. This situation he complicated by adding to it two other themes of the drama of sensibility. He had the heroine rescued by her lover from a captivity like that of Johnson's Cælia; and he made the lover, not a model of virtue like Steele's Bevil, but a prodigal who, until he reforms towards the end of the play, is trying to seduce her. Obviously his plot gave him unusually numerous opportunities for emotional scenes.

Moore did not, however, seize those opportunities. In the first two acts, instead of dwelling on his Fidelia's terrifying experiences before she found a refuge in young Belmont's family, he slighted the sentimental, and emphasized the absurd predicaments that Belmont finds himself in as a result of the lies which he told concerning his relations with the fair stranger. Nor are the last three acts much better. Slanderous tongues attack Fidelia's reputation, but her sufferings thereunder are not poignantly expressed. Belmont intrigues against her honor, but the conflict in her heart between her love for him and her resentment at his proposals is very weakly manifested. Too little is made of the mystery of her origin, and her father's appearance at the end comes as an incredible surprise.

Henry Brooke, the sentimental author of the philosophic poem *Universal Beauty*,[1] stated, in the prologue of *The Foundling*, that its author had the following intentions :

> He forms a model of a virtuous sort,
> And gives you more of moral than of sport;
> He rather aims to draw the melting sigh,
> Or steal the pitying tear from beauty's eye,
> To touch the strings that humanize our kind,
> Man's sweetest strain, the music of the mind.

But this fair promise Edward Moore did not fulfill, and *The Foundling* must be added to the list of sentimental comedies that contributed little or nothing towards the advancement of the genre.

The drama of sensibility from 1732 to 1750, despite favorable conditions, was falling into a deplorable state. None of its authors, not even Lillo, produced work artistically comparable to that of Akenside and Collins in sentimental poetry or that of Richardson in the sentimental novel. The leadership in sentimentalism which the drama had held was passing to other forms of literature. It might be argued that in some respects these forms were better vehicles than the drama for the conveyance of those feelings which sentimentalism valued. The novel especially, with its almost unlimited length and its slowness of movement, afforded ample means for the minute recording of the ebb and flow of emotion. An illuminating comment on this point is Pamela's objection to the sudden penitence of Mrs. Clerimont in Steele's *The Tender Husband* : " She reforms," complains Richardson's heroine, "*instantly* on the spot." [2] The reformation of a Richardsonian rake proceeded gradually, and

---

[1] Chap. viii, above.

[2] *Pamela*, letter No. 54. The italics are Richardson's. The whole letter is interesting as a protest against an early sentimental comedy by a mid-century sentimentalist.

therefore more plausibly. Yet the limitations which time imposes upon a playwright are not sufficient to account for the weakness of sentimental dramatists in this period. During the same years, French playwrights were producing many admirable sentimental comedies. A sketch of some of these should manifest, better than mere theorizing, the causes for the temporary stagnation of the English drama of sensibility.

CHAPTER X

THE SUPERIORITY OF FRENCH SENTIMENTAL
COMEDY TO ENGLISH

The French eighteenth-century drama of sensibility was
directly descended from the English. Its history begins in
1727 with a sentimental comedy, *Le Philosophe Marié*, by
Philippe Néricault Destouches.[1] In 1717 Destouches, then a
comic dramatist of the school of Molière, was sent on a diplo-
matic mission to London. He helped to form the Quadruple
Alliance, which established exceptionally cordial relations between France and England that endured nearly half a century.
The negotiations introduced Destouches to Joseph Addison,
then secretary of state; and, as was natural in the case of men
of congenial temperaments and similar literary tastes, their
acquaintance ripened into friendship. Doubtless Destouches
came to know Steele and Cibber. Certainly he acquired during
the six years of his residence in London a knowledge of the
contemporary English drama, and a respect for it, at that time
possessed by no French man of letters. He married an English-
woman, Miss Dorothy Johnston; and as he had converted her
to Catholicism, and did not wish to become *persona non grata*,

[1] The usual doctrine is that French sentimental comedy began in 1733,
independently of English influences, with La Chaussée's *La Fausse Antipathie.*
Cf. Gustave Lanson, *Nivelle de La Chaussée et la Comédie Larmoyante* (2nd ed.
1903); and, especially for the drama of sensibility in the second half of the
century, F. Gaiffe, *Le Drame en France au Dix-huitième Siècle* (1910). A detailed study of the life and works of Destouches forms part of my Harvard
doctorate thesis, *Sentimental and Domestic Drama in England and France*
(presented in 1907, as yet unpublished, but accessible at the Harvard University Library).

he tried to keep the marriage a secret. The equivocal situation brought embarrassments upon him and his bride, and these presently suggested to him the central situation of *Le Philosophe Marié*. It seems singularly appropriate that the first French sentimental comedy was written in London, and that an English-woman was the original of its heroine. The historical connection thus established was never severed : in future most of the important French dramatists of sensibility drew inspiration from the sentimental literature of England.

At its inception, French sentimental comedy differed from English chiefly in obeying those conventions which the Comédie Française imposed, — the exclusion of farcical low comedy, the use of verse throughout, and the observance of the unities. In essential matters, the similarities of *Le Philosophe Marié* to such plays as *The Careless Husband* are more striking than the contrasts. The heroine of Destouches is glorified, like her English prototypes, as a virtuous wife, who wins her husband's affection by her patient submission to his will, who scorns the advances of a lover, and who so touches the hearts of those hostile to her marriage that they come to look upon it as a blessing. The effect in Paris was the same as that of *Love's Last Shift* in London thirty years earlier : the pathetic passages caused the audience to shed tears, — a spectacle that aroused the disgust of conservative critics, whose opposition was, however, soon overborne by the popular approval that greeted *Le Philosophe Marié* and its numerous successors. Neither the history of these plays, nor the correspondencies between them and their English counterparts, can here be traced. The differences that soon developed, and that help to show why English sentimental dramatists were not pursuing the right methods, may, however, be illustrated by outlining a few typical French sentimental comedies.

One of the means by which the French improved sentimental comedy may be observed in the plot of La Chaussée's

La Fausse Antipathie (1733). Twelve years before the play opens, its heroine, Léonore, had been forced to wed a youth named Sainflore, who was unknown to her, and who was as reluctant to marry as she herself. At the church door her husband was attacked by a jealous lover, killed him, and straightway fled the country. After long seclusion in a cloister, Léonore has found a home with her uncle Géronte and his wife Orphise. A stranger, Damon, comes as a guest to their house until his neighboring estate can be made ready for his occupancy. For some reason he prolongs his visit unnecessarily. Orphise, who has a marriageable daughter, is secretly pleased ; but Damon's lingering is really due to the charms of Léonore. His diffidence is marked ; and the maidservant, whose comments are as a rule amusing, is awed by the modesty of his behavior, and describes him as an ideal lover :

> Des soupirs étouffés, des régards indirects,
> Un silence pénible autant qu'involontaire,
> Des désirs, des égards, du trouble, du mystère,
> Un intérêt secret, un soin particulier. . . .
> . . . Tout cela fait en somme
> De l'amour ; et, de plus, un amant honnête-homme.[1]

Orphise, as yet unaware of Léonore's growing interest in Damon, tactlessly asks Léonore to aid in making a match between him and her daughter. Léonore dutifully praises her cousin to Damon. His embarrassed replies plainly indicate that his affections are placed elsewhere, but he mournfully confesses that he cannot avow his passion, — for he is already married. With this startling news, Léonore is left alone, deploring the fact that she, the victim of a merely nominal marriage, should have fallen in love with a man who, like herself, was bound by a previous tie.

---

[1] Act I, scene iii ; La Chaussée, *Œuvres* (1777), I, 75.

When Orphise discovers that Damon is not a bachelor, her disappointment vents itself upon poor Léonore ; and her angry innuendoes impel Léonore to ask Damon to depart. Damon thereupon informs her that he purposes divorcing his wife ; but Léonore will not take advantage of such an opportunity, and spurns his love on the ground that he is dishonoring his wife : " I put myself," she says, " in her place." Just as Damon falls on his knees before her, Orphise enters the room, and taunts her niece with accepting his addresses. Léonore bursts into tears, and bids Damon never to see her again.

In the last act, Léonore is informed by her uncle Géronte that Sainflore, her husband, has asked to be freed from his marriage bonds. Much to Géronte's surprise, she refuses to consent to a divorce, which she considers morally reprehensible.

Géronte

Ma nièce, en vérité, tous ces grands sentiments
Sont des inventions pour orner des romans. , . .

Léonore

Il m'en coûtera cher — que dis-je, malheureuse ?
Mais la nécessité me rendra vertueuse.[1]

Not until she has been thoroughly tormented by her inward struggle between love and duty, does it transpire that Damon is none other than Sainflore himself, and that there is no obstacle to their union.

The main situation of *La Fausse Antipathie*, — that of a long-lost husband returning to his wife, — was, of course, an old theme ; it had been used, for example, in *Love's Last Shift*. But La Chaussée obtained new effects from it by so arranging the details of the action that the emotional values were fully brought out. The element of mystery he touched upon repeatedly ; and he confronted his heroine, not with one great

[1] Act III, scene iv, pp. 117–118.

crisis, but with several of increasing intensity. In a later work, *Mélanide* (1741), he carried this method to its extreme. Again his fundamental theme was the reunion of a long-separated husband and wife; but, to avoid the commonplace, he added many complications. He gave his heroine a son, who is indignant at the father's neglect of her; and, to cap the climax, he made the father and the son fall in love with the same girl, and fight a duel with one another. The harrowing effect of all this upon the mother may easily be imagined. To invent complications was with La Chaussée not an end in itself. Edward Moore introduced complications into *The Foundling*. What La Chaussée, unlike the Englishman, did, was to draw from a situation charged with conflicting forces all the sentimental emotions that it might give rise to.

The French sentimental dramatists did not rest content with modifications of those themes which the founders of the genre had employed. Bolder than the English, they ventured on new — and sometimes unpromising — characters and plots. Christophe Fagan, in his *La Pupille* (1734) presented a love-affair not, as usual, between persons of the same age, but between a middle-aged guardian and his young ward. In *L'Amitié Rivale de l'Amour* (1735), Fagan showed a lover resigning his beloved owing to the obligations of friendship, — a curious action, which the public considered unnatural, but which evidences a praiseworthy effort towards novelty. The general desire to achieve originality in characterization is well illustrated by J. B. L. Gresset's *Sidnei* (1745). Gresset, who was of English descent, and more than once resorted to English subjects, laid the scene of this play in England, and gave its hero a trait considered peculiarly British, — that of suicidal melancholy. Tired of the world, and repenting his disloyalty to a girl whose heart he had won, he withdraws to the seclusion of his country estate. Most of the play is occupied with depicting the attempts of his friend

Hamilton to revive hope and courage in Sidnei,—a struggle which serves to exhibit in considerable detail the workings of a remorseful and dejected mind.

The delicacy with which the French dramatists felt and described sentimental experiences is notable. What the English in too many instances indicated only roughly, the French carefully traced. When John Kelly[1] translated Destouches' *Le Philosophe Marié*, he slurred some of the most sentimental lines in the original. He omitted the outburst of filial affection in which Ariste protests against sneers at his father's poverty. He omitted the following passage, expressive of Mélite's love for Ariste:

> Vous avoir pour époux
> Est un bonheur pour moi si touchant et si doux ;
> Il me flatte à tel point, j'en suis si glorieuse,
> Que s'il était connu, je serais trop heureuse.

He retained only the first half of her proud reply to the man who is trying to seduce her affections:

> Je vous répète ici que mon cœur et ma foi
> Ne sont plus à donner : qu'un prince, qu'un roi même,
> M'aimerait vainement ; que j'estime, que j'aime
> Celui que je ferai ma gloire, mon plaisir,
> D'aimer et d'estimer jusqu'au dernier soupir.

The description of the reconciliation between Mélite and Ariste, given in these words of the maidservant, —

> Si tendre, si touchant, et si rempli de charmes,
> Que notre philosophe en a versé des larmes,
> Et moi qui parle, moi, je ne puis y penser
> Sans sentir que mes yeux sont tout prêts d'en verser
> (*Elle pleure*), —

is reduced in Kelly's version to the bald statement : "They are ten times fonder than ever."[2] Such obtuseness was not peculiar

---

[1] Chap. viii, above.

[2] Compare Destouches, *Le Philosophe Marié*, Act III, scene xiii, with John Kelly, *The Married Philosopher* (1732), p. 37 ; Destouches, Act I, scene vi,

to Kelly; for, as we have seen, English sentimental comedy in the 1730's and 1740's hesitated to respond deeply to the promptings of sensibility.

No English sentimental comedies before 1750 displayed such refinement of feeling as Marivaux's.[1] The theme of his *La Mère Confidente* (1735) is the love of a mother for her daughter. The scene is laid in one of the wooded lanes leading to the villa of Mme. Argante, a widow in moderate circumstances, whose only child is Angélique. She has always urged her daughter to look upon her, not as her mistress, but as her friend and confidante. The crisis in their relations arrives when Angélique makes the acquaintance of Dorante, an estimable youth who, though poor, has out of love for Angélique refused to marry a wealthy widow. Mme. Argante discovers that her daughter, on country walks with her maid, has been meeting Dorante. She gently persuades Angélique to confide in her; and, without a trace of anger, points out to her the folly and danger of cultivating a secret acquaintance. Angélique willingly promises to give the lover no further encouragement. But when she tells him to leave her, and intimates that he has taken advantage of her innocence, Dorante sadly replies:

> Adieu, madame; je vous quitte, puisque vous le voulez. Dans l'état où vous me jetez, la vie m'est à charge; je pars pénétré d'une affliction mortelle, et je n'y résisterai point. Jamais on n'eut tant d'amour, tant de respect que j'en ai pour vous; jamais on n'osa espérer moins de retour. Ce n'est point votre indifférence qui m'accable, elle me rend justice; j'en aurais soupiré toute ma vie sans m'en plaindre; et ce n'était point à moi, ce n'est peut-être à personne à

with Kelly, p. 10; Destouches, Act III, scene iv, with Kelly, p. 30; Destouches, Act II, scene i, with Kelly, pp. 13-14; Destouches, Act V, scene ix, with Kelly, pp. 66-69; and Destouches, Act IV, scene ii, with Kelly, pp. 41-42.

[1] Cf. Gustave Larroumet, *Marivaux*, which contains admirable criticisms of the sentimental comedies of Marivaux, though, underestimating the importance of Destouches, it exaggerates their historical importance.

prétendre à votre cœur; mais je pouvais espérer votre estime, je me croyais à l'abri du mépris, et ni ma passion ni mon caractère n'ont mérité les outrages que vous leur faites.

He withdraws in tears.[1] Angélique is moved to call Dorante back. She begs his forgiveness for offending him, and asks him how he hopes to overcome the obstacles to their union. He timidly suggests that she flee with him to one of his female relatives.

Angélique

Mais ou j'entends mal, ou cela ressemble à un enlèvement. En est-ce un, Dorante?

Dorante

Je n'ai plus rien à dire.

Angélique (le regardant)

Je vous ai forcé de parler, et je n'ai que ce que je mérite. . . . Non, Dorante, laissons là votre dame. Je parlerai à ma mère, elle est bonne; je la toucherai peut-être; je la toucherai, je l'espère. Ah![2]

Yet when she faces her mother again, she dares at first not confess, and merely says that she sent Dorante away. Mme. Argante praises her so highly for it, however, that Angélique cannot bear to conceal from her any part of the truth. She falls on her knees, confesses that Dorante suggested an elopement, and declares herself ready to do whatever her mother wishes, though at the sacrifice of happiness.

Finally Mme. Argante meets Dorante. She asks him whether he has reflected that an elopement would mean disgrace to the girl he loves. Gradually he realizes his error. Angélique declares that she will no longer think of evading the wishes of a mother who has never tried to force her inclinations.

---

[1] Act II, scene iii. *La Mère Confidente* is reprinted in Emile Gossot's *Marivaux Moraliste* (1881), the above passage being found on page 304.

[2] Act II, scene vi, pp. 310–311.

Angélique

Ses bontés, ses tendresses m'y avaient obligée; elle a été ma confidente, mon amie; elle n'a jamais gardé que le droit de me conseiller;
elle ne s'est reposée de ma conduite que sur ma tendresse pour elle, et
m'a laissée la maîtresse de tout. . . .

Dorante

Oui, belle Angélique, vous avez raison. Abandonnez-vous toujours
à ces mêmes bontés qui m'étonnent, et que j'admire. Continuez de
les mériter, je vous y exhorte. Que mon amour y perde ou non, vous
le devez. Je serais au désespoir, si je l'avais emporté sur elle.[1]

Their resignation of one another moves Mme. Argante's heart,
and she consents to their marriage. It is a charming play.
Everything is in harmonious accord, — the sentimental ideal
of the relationship between parent and child, the sensitiveness
of the personages, and the exquisite style of the dialogue.

Marivaux's *Les Fausses Confidences* (1737), like *La Mère
Confidente*, has the twofold merit of treating in a peculiarly
suitable style a subject new to sentimental comedy. It is the
romance of a poor young man. Dorante, the secretary of the
wealthy young widow Araminte, has secretly fallen in love with
her. A law-suit arises between Araminte and a count; and
Mme. Argante, her mother, desires to see it settled by a marriage between the litigants. Speaking to Dorante, she deplores
that Araminte does not seem to regard the plan with favor.

Mme. Argante

Ma fille n'a qu'un défaut; c'est que je ne lui trouve pas assez
d'élévation. Le beau nom de Dorimont et le rang de comtesse ne la
touchent pas assez; elle ne sent pas le désagrément qu'il y a de n'être
qu'une bourgeoise. . . . .

Dorante (doucement)

Peut-être n'en sera-t-elle pas plus heureuse, si elle en sort.[2]

[1] Act III, scene xi, pp. 341–342.
[2] Act I, scene x.

Mme. Argante loftily terms his opinion "une réflexion roturière," and urges him to advise Araminte that her case had best be settled out of court. He modestly but firmly replies that he must first examine the documents, and then tell his mistress the exact truth. Throughout he displays scrupulous honor and unselfish fidelity to Araminte's interests. His love for her he dares not confess ; but his servant Dubois employs many amusing if disingenuous means to increase the growing attachment of Araminte to Dorante. What really arouses her love for him, however, is her admiration for his character, and her pity for his apparently hopeless state.

In the last scene, Araminte and Dorante, both trembling with suppressed emotion, try to confer about the law-suit ; but they are too agitated to keep to the subject. Dorante impulsively asks that a portrait of hers which has been removed from his room be replaced.

Araminte

Vous donner mon portrait! songez-vous que ce serait avouer que je vous aime?

Dorante

Que vous m'aimez, madame! Quelle idée! qui pourrait se l'imaginer?

Araminte (*d'un ton vif et naïf*)

Et voilà pourtant ce qui m'arrive.

Dorante (*se jetant à ses genoux*)

Je me meurs !

Though Dorante has had no part in his servant's little deceits, he is too honorable to owe his happiness in the least to their concealment. He confesses his knowledge of them, and sadly declares :

Voilà, madame, ce que mon respect, mon amour, et mon caractère ne me permettent pas de vous cacher. J'aime encore mieux regretter votre tendresse que de la devoir à l'artifice qui me l'a acquise. J'aime mieux votre haine que le remords d'avoir trompé ce que j'adore.

Araminte (le regardant quelque temps sans parler)

. . . Ce trait de sincérité me charme, me paraît incroyable, et vous êtes le plus honnête homme du monde.[1]

Despite the protests of the scandalized Mme. Argante, she rejects the count, and marries the bourgeois Dorante.

The sentimental tendency to depreciate the value of class distinctions, which is an undercurrent in Marivaux's play, as well as in such English works as *Pamela*, was boldly developed by Voltaire. Though far from being a sincere sentimentalist, Voltaire recognized in sentimental comedy a suitable vehicle for social radicalism. The basis of his *L'Enfant Prodigue* (1736) is, as the title indicates, the commonplace theme of the repentant prodigal; but the play conveys an impression of great originality, because on every possible occasion the note of rebellion against the hard-hearted usages of society is emphasized. When the prudent but worldly brother of the prodigal says that the law, as codified by the jurist Cujas, gives a father the right to disinherit a spendthrift son, the sentimental heroine, Lise, indignantly protests:

> Je ne connais le droit ni la coutume;
> Je n'ai point lu Cujas, mais je présume
> Que ce sont tous de malhonnêtes gens,
> Vrais ennemis du cœur et du bon sens,
> Si dans leur code ils ordonnent qu'un frère
> Laisse périr son frère de misère;
> Et la nature et l'honneur ont leurs droits,
> Qui valent mieux que Cujas et vos lois.[2]

Similarly, in opposition to the established right of parents to dispose of their children in marriage, and to the legally supported tyranny of a husband over his wife, Lise eloquently pleads as follows:

[1] Act III, scene xii.   [2] Act II, scene v.

A mon avis, l'hymen et ses liens
Sont les plus grands ou des maux ou des biens.
   Point de milieu ; l'état de mariage
Est des humains le plus cher avantage
Quand le rapport des esprits et des cœurs,
Des sentiments, des goûts et des humeurs,
Serre ces nœuds tissus par la nature
Que l'amour forme et que l'honneur épure.
Dieux ! quel plaisir d'aimer publiquement,
Et de porter le nom de son amant !
Votre maison, vos gens, votre livrée,
Tous vous retrace une image adorée ;
Et vos enfants, ces gages précieux,
Nés de l'amour, en sont de nouveau nœuds.
Un tel hymen, une union si chère,
Si l'un en voit, c'est le ciel sur la terre.
   Mais tristement vendre par un contrat
Sa liberté, son nom, et son état,
Aux volontés d'un maître despotique,
Dont on devient le premier domestique ;
Se quereller ou s'éviter le jour ;
Sans joie à table, et la nuit sans amour ;
Trembler toujours d'avoir une faiblesse,
Y succomber, ou combattre sans cesse ;
Tromper son maître ou vivre sans espoir
Dans les langueurs d'un importun devoir,
Gémir, sècher dans sa douleur profonde ;
Un tel hymen est l'enfer de ce monde.[1]

At such moments, the sentimental heroine, losing her usual insipidity, became a leader of thought.

Nearly every quality in which French sentimental comedy surpasses English is exhibited in Voltaire's *Nanine* (1749). It was based upon *Pamela*, which had been translated by Prévost in 1742, and dramatized by La Chaussée in 1743. La Chaussée's version was better than the English one by Dance,[2] but Voltaire's rose immeasurably superior to both.

[1] Act II, scene i.
[2] Chap. ix, above. There was also a version by Boissy (1743), now lost.

Its author exercised the liberty of introducing important changes in the plot, and he transferred the scene to France. His Comte d'Olban is not a rake like Richardson's Mr. B., but a man of honor and of sensibility. In consequence the tribulations that his Nanine (Pamela) endures are dissimilar to those of the English heroine, and her character is set in a wholly different light.

Before the play opens, a marriage has been arranged between Comte d'Olban and his relative, Baroness de l'Orme (Lady Davers), "an imperious and disagreeable woman." She complains that he does not seem desirous of hastening their marriage, and accuses him of being in love with the maid-servant Nanine, whom his mother had rescued from destitution, and the baroness herself has educated. The count reminds her that their marriage is not of his seeking, and candidly confesses that her impetuosity of temper repels him. He adds that if he chanced to love Nanine he would make no secret of the fact.

La Baronne

Vous oseriez trahir impudemment
De votre rang toute la bienséance,
Humilier ainsi votre naissance,
Et dans la honte où vos senses sont plongés
Braver l'honneur?

Le Comte

Dites les préjugés.
Je ne prends point, quoi qu'on en puisse croire,
La vanité pour l'honneur et la gloire.
L'éclat vous plaît; vous mettez la grandeur
Dans les blasons; je la veux dans le cœur. . . .

La Baronne

Vous dégradez ainsi la qualité!

Le Comte

Non, mais j'honore ainsi l'humanité!

La Baronne

Vous êtes fou; quoi! le public, l'usage!

Le Comte

L'usage est fait pour le mépris du sage;
Je me conforme à ses ordres gênants
Pour mes habits, non pour mes sentiments.[1]

To them comes Blaise, the gardener, asking permission to marry
Nanine, with whom he has fallen in love as she was gathering
a bouquet for her master, —

Sa vue
Etait troublée; elle était toute émue,
Toute rêveuse. . . .

Le Comte

Ah! mon cœur est trop plein.

The count, deeply moved, leaves the room; and the baroness,
indignant at the thought of "le Comte d'Olban rival d'un jar-
dinier," dismisses Blaise with a promise of her aid, and sends
for the girl.

Nanine enters, carrying an English book, of which she says:

Il est intéressant:
L'auteur prétend que les hommes sont frères,
Nés tous égaux; mais ce sont des chimères,
Je ne puis croire à cette égalité.[2]

The baroness demands that she marry Blaise; and, when
Nanine hesitates, angrily threatens to send her to a convent.
Nanine, falling on her knees, declares herself eager to go, —
that she may be delivered from her own self. The baroness
directs her to come at midnight to her apartment, whence they
will start on the journey at dawn. When Nanine is left alone,
she weeps because of her hopeless and dangerous love for her

[1] Act I, scene i.   [2] Act I, scene v.

master. The count comes to her, commends her English reading, and says that he intends to regard her as one of his family; she begs that he will leave her in obscurity, and is about to say more, when she is suddenly summoned to the baroness.

That night the count, unable to sleep, is walking restlessly up and down, and tries to compose a letter to Nanine. He hears noises in the courtyard, and learns that the baroness is preparing to leave with the girl. He sends for Nanine, and asks her whether she is going of her own will. She explains that she does not want to marry Blaise, and that she is fleeing to a convent, but that she hopes she is not offending him, who has always been so kind to her. He puts her to the proof by offering to provide her a husband, — a young man of rank, wealth, and good character. She thanks him, but declines. Thereupon he begs her to marry him. When she can recover from her amazement, she declares she cannot accept his offer, since to do so would be an ill reward for his goodness. Realizing the unselfishness of her love, he remains deaf to her protests.

In painful perplexity, Nanine decides to write for advice. She asks Blaise to take her message to one Philippe Hombert in a neighboring village. The baroness intercepts the letter, and reads it. What Nanine has written is that she is very glad to know of Philippe's arrival, is eager to throw herself into his arms, and is willing to sacrifice everything for his sake. Delighted to come upon this mystery, the baroness remarks:

> Je m'en doutais que le cœur de Nanine
> Etait plus bas que sa basse origine.

She scornfully addresses the count:

> Homme au-dessus des préjugés du temps,
> Sage amoureux, philosophe sensible, —

and hands him the note.[1] Furious with jealousy, he orders his

---

[1] Act II, scenes vii–viii.

man to send away Nanine and to seize her correspondence.
The servant reluctantly obeys, and brings back this report:

> Hélas, monsieur, elle a déjà repris
> Modestement ces champêtres habits
> Sans dire un mot de plainte et de murmure.
>   ... Elle a pris cette injure
> Tranquillement, lorsque nous pleurons tous.[1]

All that can be discovered from her letters is that she loved
the count and refused him for his own sake; but he remains
jealous of the unknown Philippe.

After Nanine, weeping bitterly, has departed, and the count,
equally unhappy, has resigned himself to the necessity of marrying the baroness, a poor old man begs to see him, and against
the snobbish protests of the baroness, is admitted. He proves
to be the father of Nanine. Long ago misfortunes had compelled him to enlist as a common soldier; and, in view of the
contempt with which that station in life was regarded, he had
deemed it better to let Nanine be considered an orphan. Now
the honest man is much disturbed because Nanine has sent him
valuable presents. He cannot understand how she obtained
them, and has brought them to the count, saying:

> Et si ma fille est criminelle, hélas!
> Punissez moi, mais ne la perdez pas.

The count asks his name: it is Philippe Hombert.

> *Le Comte*
> Si vous savez combien je suis coupable!
> J'ai maltraité la vertu respectable!

The baroness, unaffected by the spectacle of virtuous simplicity,
thinks the mistake can be rectified by a gift of money, and op-
poses the return of Nanine. The count scornfully declares that

---

[1] Act II, scene xiii.

the baroness is welcome to the property which would have been
hers, but that he will never marry her; and she departs, de-
nouncing his choice of Nanine as an indignity to the family.

Le Comte

Non, il n'est point indigne; non, madame,
Un fol amour n'aveugla point mon âme.
Cette vertu, qu'il faut récompenser,
Doit m'attendrir, et ne peut m'abaisser.
Dans ce vieillard, ce qu'on nomme bassesse
Fait son mérite, et voilà sa noblesse.
La mienne à moi, c'est d'en payer le prix.
C'est pour des cœurs par eux-mêmes ennoblis,
Et distingués par ce grand caractère,
Qu'il faut passer sur la règle ordinaire;
Et leur naissance, avec tant de vertus,
Dans ma maison n'est qu'un titre plus.[1]

When Nanine enters, clad in mean garments that contrast
with the elegance of the count's surroundings, she hastens
first to her father, saying "Ah! la nature a mon premier
homage." The count humbly asks her forgiveness for his suspicions, and again begs her to marry him; but not until his
mother approves their union will she accept him. Moving
throughout on a higher level than Richardson's Pamela, Nanine displays her virtues not in a struggle to preserve her
honor, but in a wholly unselfish endeavor to keep her lover,
even at the cost of her own happiness, from making an apparently imprudent marriage. And the "reward of her virtue"
by the hand of the estimable count is of less dubious value
than Pamela's conquest of Mr. B. *Nanine* is more dramatic in
action, more powerful in style, and more outspoken in its bourgeois sentiments, than any contemporary English drama of sensibility. It was almost the only play that Jean Jacques Rousseau
commended in his *Lettre sur les Spectacles* (1758), where it

---

[1] Act III, scenes vi–vii.

is praised because it upholds the principle of innate goodness, and "because in it honor, virtue, and pure natural sentiments are preferred to the impertinent prejudices of rank."[1]

In domestic tragedy, the French did not follow the English lead. Both *George Barnwell* and *Cælia* had been drawn to their attention,[2] and the former was translated in 1748; but the only domestic tragedy they produced in the first half of the century was Landois' one-act *Silvie* (1741), which was not successful. In sentimental comedy, on the other hand, they improved upon the English example not only in quality but in quantity. In over fifty years, fewer than fifty sentimental comedies (most of them failures) had appeared in England; in less than half that time there appeared thirty in France, of which about fifteen are intrinsically as good as the best English ones.

The superiority of French sentimental drama may be partly attributed to the comparatively flourishing state of French dramatic criticism. At the beginning of the movement in England, Vanbrugh, Steele, and Dennis had ably discussed some of the principles of the new drama, but in its further course it had been unaccompanied by enlightened criticism. The prologues and epilogues, as well as the journalistic reviews, between 1720 and 1750, were superficial, repetitious, and perfunctory. In France, the important sentimental comedies were fully and intelligently discussed; and even hostile criticisms were illuminating. In England, criticism had not assisted the drama of sensibility by thoroughly examining its methods and clarifying its aims.

The principal reason why the French excelled, however, was that they more keenly comprehended the sentimental

---

[1] *Lettre sur les Spectacles*, ed. L. Brunel (1896), p. 35, note.

[2] Prévost, *Le Pour et Contre*, I (1733), pp. 40–44; and III (1734), pp. 337–357.

principles upon which the new plays were based. The successive experiments of La Chaussée, Fagan, Marivaux, Voltaire, and Gresset led to an interesting variety of results; but
they were all applications of the same fundamental principle,
— a belief that the natural emotions of average men and women
were virtuous and deserved sympathetic representation. Never
forgetting that principle, the dramatists, in their individual
ways, strove to exhibit those emotions in all their multiformity,
— gentle and passionate, domestic and social, peaceful and
revolutionary. They did not altogether disregard the comic
aspect of life :[1] even *Mélanide*, which is more tearful than
any other comedy of the period, has its amusing passages;
and in most of the plays the humorous element (necessarily
omitted in the foregoing descriptions) is conspicuous. But in
those portions of their plays which were intended to be sentimental, they employed their technical skill to bring that mood
to clear and intense utterance. Their technique was good
because it was guided by a ruling idea.

Thus the English had much to learn from their French
followers. In the first half of the century, only one French
sentimental comedy, Destouches' *Le Philosophe Marié*, was
borrowed by them. After 1750, they adapted many. To what
extent did they profit by this influence?

[1] It is commonly maintained that they did.

CHAPTER XI

THE REVIVAL OF ENGLISH SENTIMENTAL COMEDY: 1750-1767

The first English drama of sensibility in the second half of the eighteenth century, Philip Francis' *Eugenia* (17 February, 1752), was written under French influence. It was based upon Mme. de Graffigny's popular sentimental comedy, *Cénie* (1750). The idiosyncracies of Francis so modified the foreign influence upon him, however, as to make *Eugenia* stand distinctly apart from the normal examples of the genre either in France or in England. Mme. de Graffigny's play was written in prose; Francis wrote his wholly in verse, — and perhaps mainly on that account termed it "a tragedy." He omitted the part of the saucy and intriguing maid-servant who occasionally enlivens the original, and thus produced the only sentimental comedy which actually conforms to the erroneous notion that the mid-century plays of this type entirely lack a comic element. These peculiarities of *Eugenia*, which were really of the author's own invention, led Colley Cibber to exclaim in the epilogue:

In France 't was comedy, but here 't is tragic!

The plot of *Eugenia* turns upon an attempt to destroy the happiness of the kind-hearted widower Dorimond, his supposed daughter Eugenia, her governess Orphisa, and her lover Clerval. Clerval's brother, Mercour, on being rejected by Eugenia, tries to avenge himself by telling to Dorimond that she is not his daughter but a supposititious child stolen by his wife from its real mother, Orphisa. Mercour is in the end unmasked as a hypocritical villain : it transpires that Eugenia's parentage is honorable, and she is happily married to the man of her choice. In order to paint Mercour's character still blacker, and provide another source of pathos, Francis added the circumstances (not found in *Cénie*) that Mercour, before his attempt to gain Eugenia's hand, had seduced Æmilia, an orphan dependent upon Dorimond. It is Æmilia who, by bravely confessing her undoing, exposes Mercour's wickedness and saves Eugenia from being given by Dorimond in marriage to him. Æmilia's plight is melancholy enough for a tragedy, but some consolation regarding her is offered towards the close in the words :

> . . . Know that she is happy, reconciled
> To her sweet peace of mind, by holy vows
> That consecrate her future life to heaven,
> A sister of the saints.

Francis successfully retained, unlike Kelly in the case of *Le Philosophe Marié* twenty years earlier,[1] the best traits of the French original. He learned not to pass over emotional crises hastily. When Orphisa is informed that Dorimond is not her father, her sense of destitution is not expressed in one or two commonplace exclamations, but in a long conversation with Orphisa, to whose consoling words she replies as follows :

> Why should I not despair? Have I not lost
> At once the various charities of nature?
> Her dearest first relations — child and father?
> Do I not stand amid the works of Heaven
> A lonely being, where all creatures else
> Allied by instinct, duty, or affection,
> Find mutual aid and comfort? . . .
>   . . . Am I not rather

---

[1] Chaps. viii and x, above.

> The child of poverty, whose wretched parents
> For some low interest sold her? or perhaps —
> Oh save me from the thought — the hapless offspring
> Of loose, forbidden loves? [1]

Eugenia is slowly passed through the fire of this ordeal before she learns that Orphisa is her mother, and then in turn the possibilities of that situation are exhausted before Orphisa and Eugenia are reunited to her father. Every character who emerges morally triumphant has, as Clerval says of himself, "his heart long upon the rack of terror and of wonder." The play should have made a profound impression upon contemporaries; [2] but it did not receive the recognition that it deserved. Though not an immediate failure, it was never revived after its first brief run, and it exercised no perceptible influence upon later dramas of sensibility. It must therefore be regarded as a kind of *lusus naturae*.

Entirely English in its source and its method was Edward Moore's domestic tragedy, *The Gamester* (7 February, 1753), a free adaptation of Aaron Hill's *The Fatal Extravagance*. Moore's Beverley, like Hill's Bellmour, is depicted sympathetically, as one who falls into the gambling habit under the allurements of a false friend, loses his estate, and despairingly commits suicide. Beverley is not, however, as violent in his remorse as Bellmour: he does not try to kill his undoer nor to poison his own family. The merits of *The Gamester* lie in its forceful but not extravagant action, its lifelike protrayal of the sufferings of the ever hopeful and ever disappointed Mrs. Beverley, and its prose style, which is less rhythmical and more natural than that of Lillo.

The plot is so well designed that the last scene surpasses in suspense that of any earlier domestic tragedy. Beverley has

---

[1] Act IV, scene i, p. 47.
[2] Cf. Lord Chesterfield's *Letters*, ed. Bradshaw (1892), pp. 384, 968, 971.—
A literal prose version of *Cénie* was published, also in 1752.

gambled away his final resource, the reversion of his uncle's estate, and has taken poison. Ignorant of these facts, Mrs. Beverley enters the prison where he lies. She is radiant with the news that he has just fallen heir to his uncle's fortune, and is confident that all their troubles are now at an end. But the greatest test of her already too sorely tried devotion is before her.

Beverley

All this large fortune, this second bounty of Heaven, that might have healed our sorrows, and satisfied our utmost hopes, in a cursed hour I sold last night. . . . That devil Stukely, with all hell to aid him, tempted me to the deed. To pay false debts of honor, and to redeem past errors, I sold the reversion — sold it for a scanty sum, and lost it among villains. . . . Come, kneel and curse me!

Mrs. Beverley

Then hear me, Heaven (*kneels*). Look down with mercy on his sorrows! Give softness to his looks, and quiet to his heart! Take from his memory the sense of what is past, and cure him of despair! On me! on me! if misery must be the lot of either, multiply misfortunes! I 'll bear them patiently, so he is happy: these hands shall toil for his support, these eyes be lifted up for hourly blessings on him, and every duty of a fond and faithful wife be doubly done to cheer and comfort him! So hear me! so reward me![1]

Once more the unfortunate woman's hopes are raised, by the arrest of the villain who misled her husband, and by the discovery that a charge of murder brought against Beverley is false. But the poison which the despondent man has taken now works its effect; and he dies in her arms, pitied by his friends as one whose "life was lovely," and whose errors were of the mind rather than of the heart.

The good qualities of *The Gamester*, less questionable than those of *George Barnwell*, were immediately recognized, and its success was lasting. Down to the times of Mrs. Siddons,

[1] Act V, scene iv, p. 76.

the rôle of Mrs. Beverley was a favorite with tragic actresses.[1] Strangely enough, however, the play did not stimulate further activity in domestic tragedy. Between 1753 and 1780, only one other new work of this kind was performed, — Lillo's *Arden of Feversham*, already discussed in relation to its Elizabethan original,[2] and that was a downright failure. *The Gamester* thus has the paradoxical distinction of being at once the best domestic tragedy and the last for a generation.[3]

It was not until 1762, ten years after the appearance of *Eugenia*, that sentimental comedy again began to flourish. Meanwhile signs of a temporary reaction against sentimentalism had manifested themselves in literature: Burke had written his ironic *Vindication of Natural Society* (1756), and Johnson had made a resolute negation of optimism in his *Rasselas* (1759). The drama of the 1750's showed a strong revival of the comic spirit. A new group of playwrights, — notably Samuel Foote, Arthur Murphy, and George Colman, — raised comedy, not to the high level on which it moved in the days of Vanbrugh, but much higher than in the depressing period between 1730 and 1750. Foote, with dashing and reckless energy, ridiculed contemporary rogues and fools in *The Englishman in Paris* (1753) and *The Author* (1757). Murphy less maliciously satirized types of folly in *The Apprentice* (1756)

---

[1] Cf. Leigh Hunt, *Critical Essays* (1807), p. 18. He speaks of Mrs. Siddons' Lady Macbeth, and "the widow's mute stare of perfected misery by the corpse of the gamester Beverley" as "two of the sublimest pieces of acting on the English stage."

[2] Chap. iii, above. Benjamin Victor's *The Fatal Error* (1776), likewise discussed in chap. iii, was not performed. Hannah More's rather powerful *The Fatal Falsehood* (1779) is not sentimental; it is a true tragedy of domestic life, laid in Elizabethan times.

The Tailors (1767), an anonymous mock-tragedy, in which the hero is condemned to death and visited in prison by his friend and mistress, reads like a parody of *George Barnwell*, though probably not so intended.

[3] Richard Cumberland's domestic tragedy, *The Mysterious Husband*, appeared in 1783.

and *The Upholsterer* (1758). Amusing if not brilliant attempts at high comedy were made by Murphy in *The Way to Keep Him* (1760) and *All in the Wrong* (1761), and by Colman in *The Jealous Wife* (1761). So constant was the production of successful true comedies, and they were on the whole so meritorious, that it seemed about 1760 as if the long campaign of the comic against the sentimental had, so far as the stage was concerned, resulted in a victory for the former.

The regained supremacy of the comic did not appear likely to be disturbed by the three sentimental comedies that were produced in 1759 and 1760. Charles Macklin's popular *Love à la Mode* (12 December, 1759) shows the amiable Sir Callaghan ready to marry the heiress he has been courting, even after her fortune is declared to be lost and her other suitors desert her; but the brief sentimental passages are weak, and the main purpose of the play is to draw a humorous contrast between the Irish wooer and his Scotch and Jewish rivals. Foote, contrary to his custom, made a sentimental situation the basis of *The Minor* (c. June, 1760). In it the sympathy of a prodigal youth is aroused by the pitiable state of a maiden who has fallen into the power of a brothel-keeper, and his chivalrous conduct towards her wins him not only her love but also his father's forgiveness of his previous escapades.[1] Here again, however, it is chiefly the groundwork that is sentimental. What made the play a great success was the author-actor's representation of the rascally broker Shift, and, above all, of Mrs. Cole, with her Methodistical cant and scandalous occupation. A work similar in plan, but much inferior in execution, was Joseph Reed's *The Register Office* (25 April, 1761). Here a virtuous housekeeper, who has resisted her master's improper advances, applies for a position at an intelligence office, and is

---

[1] The real beginning of the sentimental passages is at the opening of Act III. Samuel Foote, *Dramatic Works* (1797), I, 264–272.

exposed by its proprietor to further insulting attacks. She is rescued by her former employer, now contrite and full of admiration for her steadfast character, and is married to him. Though this variation of the Pamela theme is the main plot, it is used merely as a means of exhibiting the harpy who presides over the office, her gullible applicants, and her odious patrons. In *Love à la Mode, The Minor*, and *The Register Office*, sentimental comedy is an ill-chosen frame for humorous portraits.

One of the patrons of the register office in Reed's play is Mrs. Slatternella Doggerel, a dramatic poetess who seeks an amanuensis. Her presence is made the occasion for a passing attack on domestic tragedy. Among the forty-five plays she boasts having written, one, performed by "the best company — of puppets — in England," is *The Tragedy of Betty Canning*, from which she recites, to her own satisfaction, the turnkey's soliloquy pompously extolling that murderess.[1] This stroke of satire, of slight importance in the play, is an exceptional one in the satire of the immediate time, which, as a rule, attacked sentimentalism not in the drama but in the novel.

Colman, in *Polly Honeycombe* (1760), showed Scribble, an attorney's clerk, and his sweetheart Polly, endeavoring, to the rage of her prosaic parents, to imitate in their courtship the ways of sentimental heroes and heroines. Most of the allusions are to *Clarissa Harlowe, Tom Jones*, and *Amelia* ;[2] and the long circulating-library list prefixed to the play consists of works of the Richardsonian school, — which the prologue ironically eulogizes as follows :

> And then so sentimental is the style,
> So chaste yet so bewitching all the while!
> Plot and elopement, passion, rape, and rapture,
> The total sum of ev'ry dear — dear — chapter.

[1] *The Register Office* (ed. 1771), p. 41. Cf. the verses on Mrs. Brownrigg, cleverly parodying Southey, in *The Anti-Jacobin* (1797).
[2] George Colman, *Dramatic Works* (1777), IV, 30, 36, 45, 53–54.

The novel monopolizes the satirist's attention, sentimental comedy appearing so moribund as to be beneath his notice. Indeed the novel, — as represented by Sterne's *Tristram Shandy* (1759–1767), Goldsmith's *The Vicar of Wakefield* (1766), and Brooke's *The Fool of Quality* (1766), — continued during the 1760's to be the chief organ for the sensibility of the age. But better days for sentimental comedy were approaching, though it was never to regain its early pre-eminence; and less than twenty years later Sheridan could not ignore it as Colman had done.

The play which initiated the revival of sentimental comedy was *The School for Lovers* (10 February, 1762), by William Whitehead, who in 1757 had succeeded Cibber as poet laureate. He stated the purpose of his comedy in the following lines of the prologue, which might well have served as the future motto of the genre:

> Plain comedy to-night, with strokes refined,
> Would catch the coyest features of the mind;
> Would play politely with your hopes and fears,
> And sometimes smiles provoke, and sometimes tears.

It was a French play that taught Whitehead how to "catch the coyest features of the mind," — or, better, of the heart.[1] *The School for Lovers* is an adaptation of Fontenelle's *Le Testament*, a closet drama, laid in ancient Greece, but written in the style of Marivaux's sentimental comedies. Besides transferring the scene to modern England, Whitehead made several changes which were in accord with English predilections. Though in dedicating his version to the memory of Fontenelle he subscribed himself — and, on the whole, truly — "a lover of simplicity," he thought the French play contained too little action; and he therefore added a new character (Belmour) to complicate the

---

[1] In the same year, 1762, English knowledge of French sentimental comedy was increased by published translations of Destouches' *Le Dissipateur*, *L'Enfant Gâté*, and *Le Trésor Caché*, in the collection entitled *The Comic Theatre*.

love-affair. He also increased, unlike Francis in *Eugenia*, the comic element. *The School for Lovers* is consequently not quite so faint in tone as *Le Testament*; nevertheless its keynote remains one of unusual delicacy.

Most of the characters of Whitehead's play, even those who have less sensibility than its hero and heroine, are persons of remarkable refinement. The theme is one that Fagan had treated sentimentally in *La Pupille* (1734),[1] and that Garrick had given a comic interpretation in *The Guardian* (1759). Cælia is the young ward of the estimable Sir John Dorilant, a middle-aged bachelor, and with her widowed mother, Lady Beverley (a comic figure), resides at his country house. Her father in his will commended his family to Sir John's protection, and left him his estate in case Cælia, on coming of age, should decline to marry him. Sir John has devoted himself to Cælia's education; and, though in love with her, has never confessed his feelings nor taken advantage of his position to force her inclinations. She on her part is deeply grateful for his care, but looks upon him as an elder brother. Her sister Araminta, whose gayety of temper contrasts with Cælia's gentleness, is engaged to a Mr. Modely; and the latter, shortly before the time appointed for the wedding, comes with his friend Belmour to be a guest at the house. Modely is not a man of bad character, but he has acquired an "idle affectation of success among the ladies." When opportunities for private conversation with Cælia arise, he addresses her in a gallant fashion that disturbs her peace of mind. Her youth causes her to be impressed by his attentions, and her inexperience prevents her recognizing their insincerity.

Cælia's mother makes a ridiculous attempt to bring Sir John to propose to herself; and, piqued by his evident preference for her daughter, intimates that Cælia is interested in another

[1] Chap. x, above. Cf. Fletcher's *Monsieur Thomas* (chap. iii, above).

man. Thereupon the harmony that has dwelt in Sir John's household is fled, and many grievous moments are lived through before it is restored. Sir John at first assumes that Cælia's affections are fixed upon the unattached Belmour. Hoping against hope, he sounds her wishes.

Sir John

Would I could read the sentiments of your heart! Mine are but too apparent. In short, my dear, you know the purport of your father's will — dare you fulfil it?

Cælia

To the minutest circumstance: it is my duty.

Sir John

Ah, Cælia; that word *duty* destroys the obligation.

Cælia

Sir!

Sir John

I don't know how it is; but I am afraid to ask you the only question which, sincerely answered, could make me happy — or miserable.   [*Half aside.*

Cælia

Let me beg of you, sir, to ask it freely.

Sir John

Well then — is your heart your own? — Oh, Cælia, that hesitation confirms my fears. You cannot answer in the affirmative, and have too much humanity for what I feel to add to my torments.

He is thunderstruck when she tells him that it is Modely who has been courting her, and that her mother has been urging her to listen to Modely's addresses on the grounds that Araminta would not be happy with him and that Sir John himself desired the match.

Sir John

Oh, the malicious woman!

Cælia

In that indeed I perceive she greatly erred. And I only mean this as a confession of what is past, and of what is now at an end forever. For the future I give myself to your guidance alone, and am what you direct.   [*Giving her hand to him.*

Sir John

Thou amiable softness! No, Cælia; however miserable I may be myself, I will not make you so; it was your heart, not your hand I aspired to. . . . Nothing but that lovely sincerity — which undoes me — could make me credit this villainy of Modely. — Oh, Cælia, what a heart have I lost!

Cælia

You cannot, shall not, lose it; worthless as it is, 'tis yours, and only yours, my father, guardian, lover, husband!

[*Hangs upon him weeping.*[1]

Sir John, convinced against his desires that she is mistaking gratitude for love, presently gives Cælia documents which place her in unrestricted control of her estate. This magnanimous step, which he has taken in the belief that she will now marry another, opens her eyes to the full meaning of unselfish love, and awakens in her a passion for him never felt before. When Modely again courts her, she tears in his presence the deeds that set her free. Modely, by her goodness recalled to his better self, and desirous of repairing the injuries his inconstancy has given, informs Sir John that Cælia's heart is devoted to him alone. After the remorseful Modely has been dismissed by Araminta, not altogether without hope of a future reconciliation, Sir John, at last convinced of the deep sincerity of Cælia's love, is married to her.

The School for Lovers differs from the typical sentimental comedies of the first half of the century in not being concerned with the wild dissipations of a prodigal youth or the gross infidelities of a husband. The worst offense its characters suffer

---

[1] Act III, scene ii, pp. 46–48.

under is a fickle lover's duplicity. The very slightness of the test to which the hero and heroine are exposed, serves to bring out the refinement of their natures. They are deeply troubled by considerations that to commonplace persons would appear trivial, and Sir John is trying to live up to an ideal which most lovers would find incomprehensible. Araminta rightly says that it would have been easier to bring Sir John and Cælia together "had my brother a little less honor, and she a little less sensibility." To introduce such characters, to write the dialogue between them with a purity and grace corresponding to their fastidiousness, was an achievement for which Whitehead deserves more credit than he has received.[1] His play, which was performed fifteen nights in 1762, and was revived in 1775 and 1794, did not revolutionize sentimental comedy; but its success immediately stimulated productivity in the genre, and some of its best qualities were not wholly without influence upon its successors.

Mrs. Frances Sheridan's *The Discovery* (3 February, 1763[2]), which was even more successful than *The School for Lovers*, is a sentimental comedy with a rather incoherent plot but some well-drawn characters. The comic figures, which are livelier and more prominent than in Whitehead's play, are a quarrelsome young married couple and a formal old courtier who has paid his addresses to eight ladies in thirteen years, but with such absurd solemnity that he "never could get them to be serious." The sentimental characters that first attract attention are Lady Medway and her daughter Louisa, whose affectionate companionship reminds one of that portrayed in Marivaux's *La Mère Confidente*.[3] They "read together every evening," and

---

[1] *The School for Lovers* is never mentioned in modern discussions concerning eighteenth-century sentimental comedy.

[2] Possibly 5 February, the date given by W. Fraser Rae, *Sheridan* (1896), I, 46. Cf. Genest, V, 20.

[3] Chap. x, above.

are said by their frivolous friends to be "such housewives they put us to shame." Louisa is "a sober sort of girl, forever poring over a book or a needle." Both are slaves to the wishes of Lord Medway, and require all their patience to support them under the anxieties that his ill-regulated course of life inflict upon them. Presently it appears that the main plot — if a play in which the center of interest so constantly shifts can be said to have a main plot — is concerned with the infidelities of Lord Medway and the love-affair of his admirable son, Colonel Medway.

Lord Medway's latest adventure of gallantry is frustrated by the tactful warning which his wife gives to the object of his pursuit; but his career of extravagance brings him to a pass where nothing but his son's marriage to a wealthy widow, Mrs. Knightly, offers a means of escape from financial ruin. The Colonel is devoted to a Miss Richly (inappropriately named, for she is rich only in her virtues); and the struggle between his pity for his father's desperate condition and his love is grievous. Perceiving this, Lord Medway considerately withdraws his request, saying:

> I must struggle with ill fortune as well as I can. You have been a worthy son; I acknowledge it. You have done enough; you shall not charge me with making you miserable for life.

Colonel Medway

> ... I cannot bear to hear you talk in this strain. ... I would do anything to prevent —

Lord Medway

> A father's ruin, you would say. I know the tenderness of your nature, Medway, and therefore I will not urge you; your father is not such a tyrant; I have always considered you as my friend. ... I will not wrong you every way. I deserve the ruin I have brought upon myself, and am content to sink under it.

Colonel Medway

> My lord, that must not be while I have power to help it.

Lord Medway

I cannot ask it, son.

Colonel Medway

I 'll give up all, even my love, to save you.[1]

Miss Richly, instead of being indignant at the colonel's act, unselfishly approves it.

Miss Richly

I honor you for the motive, for I am sure that nothing else could have brought about such an event; and I should little deserve that esteem which I hope you still retain for me if I could not give up my feeble claim to your tenderness for ties of so much more importance.

Colonel Medway

Oh, Clara, why did I give you up? what have I got to compensate for your loss!

Miss Richly

Your virtue! the consciousness of having acted right. You have broke no oaths, no promises to me.[2]

The painful predicament is finally relieved when it transpires that Mrs. Knightly is a daughter of Lord Medway. Her generosity enables the lovers to marry; and the discovery of her kinship to Lord Medway, reawakening memories of his youth, increases his remorse and his determination to lead a better life hereafter. The play is written in a style that is not as elegant and tender as Whitehead's; but Mrs. Sheridan did not slur the sentimental scenes, and in conceiving the situation of a son sacrificing his love to save his father from ruin, she displayed originality of the sort that sentimental comedy needed.

Samuel Foote, in *The Patron* (1764), again flung a gibe at sentimental dramatists. His ridiculous Sir Thomas Lofty has written a drama, *Robinson Crusoe*, and thinks the amazed

[1] Act IV, scene i, pp. 70–71 (2d ed., 1763).
[2] Act IV, scene ii, p. 77.

silence in which the audience at first received it "a strong mark of their sensibility." As a matter of fact, his play was "most dull, tedious, melancholy." "The coxcomb," we are told, "has prefaced every act with an argument too, in humble imitation, I warrant, of Mons. Diderot,[1] 'showing the fatal effects of disobedience to parents,' with, I suppose, the diverting scene of a gibbet, an entertaining subject for comedy. And the blockhead is as prolix — every scene as long as a homily."[2] Despite such taunts, the movement grew in strength.

The trend towards sensibility in the drama was further shown when Isaac Bickerstaff, who had in 1760 and 1762 written "comic" operas that on the whole[3] deserved to be called so, produced one that should have been termed sentimental, — *The Maid of the Mill* (31 January, 1765). This is the only English dramatization of *Pamela* that enjoyed great success. Probably under the influence of Voltaire's *Nanine*,[4] Bickerstaff made a radical change in the story by converting Richardson's rakish Mr. B. into a model of propriety, Lord Aimworth. The sentimental situations result, not from any attempt by Aimworth to ruin Patty (Pamela), but from his uncertainty as to whether she is in love with a youth of her own social rank. He hints a suspicion to that effect, and tells her that her esteem "confers a value wheresoever it is placed."

Patty

Pray, pray, my lord, talk not to me in this style: consider me as one destined by birth and fortune to the meanest condition and offices, who has unhappily been apt to imbibe sentiments contrary to them! Let me conquer a heart where pride and vanity have usurped an improper rule; and learn to know myself, of whom I have been too long ignorant.

---

[1] Diderot's *Le Fils Naturel* (1757) was anonymously translated as *Dorval, or The Test of Virtue* (1767).   [2] Foote, *Works* (1797), I, 355-361.
[3] There are touches of the sentimental in *Thomas and Sally* (1760) and *Love in a Village* (1762).   [4] Chap. x, above.

Lord Aimworth

Perhaps, Patty, you love someone so much above you, you are
afraid to own it.   If so, be his rank what it will, he is to be envied;
for the love of a woman of virtue, beauty and sentiment, does honor
to a monarch. — What means that downcast look, those tears, those
blushes? Dare you not confide in me? Do you think, Patty, you
have a friend in the world would sympathize with you more sincerely than I? . . .

Patty

I beg, my lord, you will suffer me to be gone; only believe me
sensible of all your favors, though unworthy of the smallest.

Lord Aimworth

How unworthy? You merit everything: my respect, my esteem,
my friendship, and my love! Yes, I repeat, I avow it: your beauty,
your modesty, your understanding, has made a conquest of my heart.
But what a world do we live in! that while I own this, while I own a
passion for you, founded on the justest, the noblest basis, I must at the
same time confess the fear of that world, its taunts, its reproaches —

Patty

Ah! sir, think better of the creature you have raised than to
suppose that I ever entertained a hope tending to your dishonor . . .
I am unfortunate, my lord, but not criminal. . . .

AIR

Cease, oh cease, to overwhelm me,
With excess of bounty rare;
What am I? What have I? Tell me,
To deserve your meanest care?
'Gainst our fate in vain 's resistance,
Let me then no grief disclose;
But, resigned at humble distance,
Offer vows for your repose.[1]   (*Exit*)

The insipid song which concludes the scene illustrates the
weakness of this form of sentimental drama. Just as the
emotions of the character are reaching an interesting climax, he

[1] Act II, scene xiv.

or she (sometimes both, in duet [1]) must burst out into vocal music — and whatever naturalness the scene has possessed vanishes.

It was the example of Bickerstaff that led Richard Cumberland, later to become one of the best-known dramatists of sensibility, into the sentimental field, which he, like Lillo,[2] entered with a musical comedy, — *The Summer's Tale* (6 December, 1765). It was "a tale," as he himself confesses, "about nothing, and very indifferently told ";[3] but its brief sentimental passages pleased sufficiently to encourage his expanding them into a two-act comedy, *Amelia and Henry* (12 April, 1768). George Colman satirized the vogue of musical pieces in his *New Brooms!* (1776), where Crotchet, a successful playwright, says:

> Operas are the only real entertainment. The plain unornamented drama is too flat, Sir. Common dialogue is a dry imitation of nature, as insipid as real conversation; but in an opera the dialogue is refreshed by an air every instant. Two gentlemen meet in the park, for example, admire the place and the weather; and after a speech or two the orchestra take their cue, the music strikes up, one of the characters takes a genteel turn or two on the stage, during the symphony, and then breaks out —
>
> > When the breezes
> > Fan the trees-es,
> > Fragrant gales
> > The breath inhales,
> > Warm the heart that sorrow freezes.[4]

The sarcasm testified to the popularity of opera, but did not check it.

Mrs. Elizabeth Griffith's *The Double Mistake* (9 January, 1766) showed that its author understood and admired a sentimental heroine without perceiving what kind of plot was

---

[1] See the absurd duet at the end of Act I.
[2] Chap. viii, above.
[3] Richard Cumberland, *Memoirs* (1806), pp. 105–106.
[4] *Works* (1777), IV, 335.

suitable to display the virtues of such a character. The heroine, Emily, on two occasions chances to be found in a situation
reflecting upon her honor. In each case, after she has had to
endure unjust suspicions, it transpires that she was the innocent victim of accidental circumstances. Her mental sufferings
are not badly described, but their causes are such farcical improbabilities as to be out of harmony with the main object of
the play. The fact that *The Double Mistake* succeeded in
spite of its artistic blemishes shows how completely sentimentalism had for the time being recaptured the theatrical public.

The Clandestine Marriage (20 February, 1766), by Colman
and Garrick, marks a surrender to the popular taste on the
part of playwrights who had heretofore been disinclined to
sentimentalism. Garrick had written *The Gamesters* (1757)
and *The Guardian* (1759) in the comic vein; and in *The
Farmer's Return to London* (1762) had jested at Whitehead's
The School for Lovers.[1] Colman had attacked sentimentalism in *Polly Honeycombe* (1760); and his *The Deuce is in
Him* (1763) had held up to ridicule such sensibility as that
of Whitehead's Sir John Dorilant, — "the deuce" in this
case being the anxious desire of a lover that his mistress
should love him solely for his own moral sake and not for
his good looks. Colman had even succeeded in keeping his
extraordinarily popular comedy, *The Jealous Wife* (1761), one
of the plots of which was a love-story based on *Tom Jones*,
almost entirely free from sentimental contamination. *The
Clandestine Marriage*, however, though as usual it contains
comic personages (the commercial Mr. Sterling, his ambitious
sister Mrs. Heidelberg, and the elegant old gallant Lord
Ogleby), is sentimental in its main plot and chief characters.[2]

---

[1] David Garrick, *Dramatic Works* (1798), II, 270.
[2] It has been regarded as a work that maintained the comic tradition. Cf.
G. H. Nettleton, *Drama of the Restoration*, etc., pp. 257–263.

The central situation is similar to that of Destouches' *Le Philosophe Marié*.[1] Fanny Sterling has secretly married one of her father's clerks, Lovewell; and, as she, weeping, says to him, "the indelicacy of a secret marriage grows every day more and more shocking" to her. Constant apprehensions that his stolen visits to her may be discovered, keep her in continual agitation. She dutifully submits, however, to Lovewell's insistence that they must prudently wait until he can find a favorable moment to confess their union to her father. Her distress is increased when Sir John Melvil, who was to have married her elder sister, falls in love with herself, and gains her father's consent to marry her. She has to endure being looked upon by her chagrined sister and her aunt as one who has shamelessly alienated Sir John's affections; and when she appeals to his father, Lord Ogleby, to prevent the match, the old courtier fancies that he has made an impression on her heart.

The height of Fanny's troubles is reached one night when, on the discovery that a man is hidden in her chamber, the entire household calls upon her for an explanation. Still loyal to Lovewell's wish, she can only falter:

> I am at this moment the most unhappy — most distressed — the tumult is too much for my heart — and I want the power to reveal a secret which, to conceal, has been the misfortune and misery of my — my — (*faints away*).

> *Lovewell (rushing out of the chamber)*

> My Fanny in danger! I can contain no longer. Prudence were now a crime; all other cares were lost in this! Speak, speak to me, my dearest Fanny. Let me but hear thy voice; open your eyes, and bless me with the smallest sign of life.[2]

Mr. Sterling, in the first flush of his indignation, threatens to dismiss Lovewell; but after Lord Ogleby, chivalrously pleading

---

[1] Chap. x, above.   [2] Act V, scene ii.

the cause of the lovers, has asked him to pity and forgive them, he does so. The comic portions of *The Clandestine Marriage*, notably those in which the highly entertaining Lord Ogleby figures, are written with more spirit and skill than the emotional, and doubtless helped largely to give it its remarkable vogue; yet the significant fact remains that such expert judges as Garrick and Colman thought it expedient to found the comedy on a sentimental basis.[1]

Colman founded his next play, *The English Merchant* (21 February, 1767), on Voltaire's admirable sentimental comedy, *L'Ecossaise* (1760). The French work, which has the originality of substance and force of style characteristic of its author, deals with an unfortunate Scotch earl, Monrose, who, because of complicity in the rebellion of 1745, has been for years an exile from his country and a stranger to his family. His daughter, Lindane, whom he has not seen since her infancy, and who is now of age, has lost her only protectress, and is living in obscure poverty. The reunion of the father and the daughter is described in a natural and affecting manner, poor Lindane pathetically calling it "the first happy moment of my life." Her joy is short-lived; for her father tells her that he dreads above all the hereditary enemy of his house, Lord Murray, — and it is young Murray who has won Lindane's heart. Now she has good reason to fear that a meeting between her father and her lover will lead to a duel. She is willing to sacrifice her love to her filial affection, and begs her father to flee with her to a remote solitude.[2] The meeting she dreads takes place. Lord Murray, however, so far

---

[1] It may be noted in passing that in this season Charles Shadwell's interesting sentimental comedy, *Irish Hospitality* (cf. chap. vii, above), was revived (15 March, 1766). Its Sir Patrick Worthy must, even at this late date, have seemed an exceptionally thorough benevolist.

[2] Act IV, scene vi. Cf. the corresponding scene in *The English Merchant*, Act III, scene i.

from continuing the family feud, has secured a royal pardon for the exile, and, sword in hand, addresses him thus:

> Father of the virtuous Lindane, I am the son of your enemy; but it is thus (*throwing his sword upon the ground*) that I contend against you![1]

Unfortunately Colman was too set in his English ways wholly to adopt the superior French methods. He increased the proportion of comic scenes. Attracted by one of the secondary figures in Voltaire's play, the merchant Freeport, a humorous character with a kind heart and a crusty manner, he raised him to a position of much importance, — constituting him, rather than the lover, the rescuer of the distressed father and daughter. He omitted the motif of the family feud, and thus lost one of the best scenes in the original, that of the threatened duel. The character of the lover he changed for the worse, making him at first a merely gallant pursuer of Lindane (Amelia), a change for which the youth's subsequent contrition insufficiently compensates. Though these modifications are deplorable, enough of the original work remained to make *The English Merchant* equal in merit to most of the English sentimental comedies of the period. It achieved success, and was during the next twenty-five years several times revived.

William Kenrick's *The Widowed Wife* (5 December, 1767) was not drawn from a French source, but the nature of its plot gives ground for the surmise that its author was acquainted with some of the sentimental comedies by La Chaussée. As in the latter's *La Fausse Antipathie* (1733) and *Mélanide* (1741), the central figure is a deserted wife whose husband returns after a long absence. The circumstances which Kenrick imagined arising out of that situation were novel. It cannot truly be said, however, that they were invented happily. His Mrs. Mildmay,

----

[1] Act V, scene vi.

"the widowed wife," discovers that the young man with whom her daughter has just eloped is apparently a son of her absent husband — and therefore the girl's half-brother. The impression later proves a mistaken one, founded upon a fortuitous identity of family names. The misunderstanding is more improbable than any in La Chaussée, and the plot suffers from its incredibility.

The effect of the situation on the characters is unfolded in a better manner than most of the English dramatists of sensibility had mastered. Mrs. Mildmay is shown in successive states of anxiety that gradually increase in intensity. At first she is worried by her daughter's impetuous disposition, and fears the girl has inherited the temperament that had caused her own troubles. Then she is agitated by happening to see her long-lost husband, and not knowing what his present feelings towards her are. Finally she has to suffer the agony of believing him to be the father of her daughter's lover. At that point, Kenrick impaired the value of his play by dwelling too much upon the pursuit of the lovers and their endeavors to escape. But in the play as a whole, though he never neglected the comic element, he rightly centered attention upon the emotional.

In the six years ending with 1767, the temporary supremacy of true comedy was thus overthrown, and seven successful sentimental comedies were produced. In no previous period had the genre been so dominant and prolific. The spirit of contemporary literature was favorable to sentimentalism, which was not only continuing its course in the novels of the Richardsonian school, but was also finding a new outlet in such works as *Ossian* (1760–1763) and *The Castle of Otranto* (1764). The rise of the French influence on sentimental comedy enriched its substance and improved its methods. Its plots ceased to be slavish imitations of Cibber's and Steele's. Situations

new to English sentimental comedy, and in some cases to
French, were introduced in *The Discovery, The Clandestine
Marriage, The English Merchant,* and *The Widowed Wife*;
and they were infused with more vigor of emotion. Elusive
feelings, heretofore unexpressed, found utterance in *The School
for Lovers.* Most of these plays, however, were not as delicate
in tone as Whitehead's. What the public desired was either
a love-story like Pamela's in the form of an " opera," presenting idealized lovers and humorous characters of rustic
simplicity; or, preferably, a comedy of social and domestic
life which had a sentimental plot with a good deal of action
and some mystery, and which contained at least one prominent
comic figure, — a person whose habits were amusingly odd
or affected but not vicious.[1] Such were the two varieties of
sentimental comedy that between 1762 and 1767 almost
monopolized the stage.

[1] Sir Anthony Branville in *The Discovery*; Lord Ogleby and Mrs. Heidelberg in *The Clandestine Marriage*; Freeport in *The English Merchant*; etc.

CHAPTER XII

KELLY, GOLDSMITH, MRS. GRIFFITH, AND CUMBERLAND: 1768-1772

Between 1768 and 1780 sentimental comedy progressed in a devious manner, difficult to trace. It was rather blindly feeling its way towards a goal that it never fully attained. On several occasions it seemed to meet with decisive defeats, but it invariably resumed its onward movement. By sheer weight of numbers it overwhelmed forces that had brilliant leaders and that were favorably placed. The managerial control of the regular theatres was in the hands of Colman and Garrick, and that of the summer theatre in those of Foote, — men who, though as managers and authors they frequently bowed to the public will, were at heart devoted to the Comic Muse. Goldsmith and Sheridan, whose literary talents far outshone those of the sentimental dramatists, in theory (though not always in practice) upheld the idea that comedy should consist of humor and wit. These forces failed to destroy sentimental comedy ; but they sometimes seemed to be on the point of doing so, and — what is as confusing as important — they often compelled it to compromises inconsistent with its true nature.[1]

Some of the anomalies which characterize the genre in this period appear in Hugh Kelly's *False Delicacy* (23 January,

---

[1] The usual interpretation of the history of sentimental comedy in Goldsmith's time, — an interpretation which radically differs in many respects from the account given in this chapter, — may be found in Austin Dobson's Introduction to Goldsmith's *The Good-Natured Man* (1903), pp. xi ff.

1768). The subplot of the play, and the basis of the main plot, are sentimental; but its title and some of its conspicuous qualities are antagonistic to sentimentalism. In the subplot Sir Harry persuades Miss Rivers, whose father has agreed to bestow her hand on another, to elope with him. The father is grieved by her trying to conceal that intention, but instead of preventing the elopement he hands over her fortune to her. "Pierced to the very soul" by his sorrow and generosity, she relinquishes her plan, and owing to her contrition wins his consent to marry her lover. The main plot resembles Whitehead's *The School for Lovers* in that most of the characters are unusually refined and are placed in a delicate predicament. Lady Betty has a dependent friend, Miss Marchmont. Lord Winworth requests Lady Betty to convey to Miss Marchmont his offer of marriage, and to urge its acceptance. The offer distresses both the young women; for Lady Betty is herself in love with Winworth, though she has formerly rejected him; and Miss Marchmont loves another man, but feels that her obligations to Lady Betty are so great as to make it impossible to disregard her apparent wishes. Lord Winworth presently realizes that it is still Lady Betty whom he loves, but he feels that a withdrawal of his proposal to Miss Marchmont would be dishonorable. Thus the motives of these three characters are of the highest.

Whitehead, in *The School for Lovers*, had exalted delicate sensibility. Kelly wished to show that it had absurd[1] as well as amiable aspects. He introduced into his play the lively widow Mrs. Harley, an amusing personage, not intended by him to be disliked, who exclaims: "Thank Heaven, my sentiments are not sufficiently refined to make me unhappy!"

---

[1] An abstract of an essay, *Hugh Kelly and his Sentimental Comedy*, dealing with the comic capabilities of Kelly, was printed in the programme of the Modern Language Association for 1912.

and "The devil take this delicacy! I don't know anything it does besides making people miserable." Kelly did not perceive that by admitting such a character he had placed a traitor in the sentimental camp. The dénouement is likewise out of accord with the general spirit of the play. Whitehead's lovers are drawn to one another in a sentimental manner; Kelly's, though they are supposed to have unusually sensitive perceptions, are not led by them to an understanding of each other's emotions. They are brought together by a trick on the part of their friends, who fool them into the belief that each has summoned the other. It is a conclusion in the manner of true comedy.

The worst mistake that Kelly made was to abandon the usual method of lending the principal passages a consistently sentimental tone and striking the comic note only in subordinate ones. In scenes of consequence, like that in which Lord Winworth startles Lady Betty with the announcement of his intentions regarding Miss Marchmont, and that in which Lady Betty communicates them to her, there is not only sympathy for the distressful perplexities of the characters but also an undercurrent of amusement at their misunderstandings. Kelly, instead of alternating the gay and the pathetic, tried to blend them, — tried, as it were, to unite the high comedy of Molière with the sentimental comedy of Marivaux, — an effort as vain as it was unusual. Nevertheless, the amiability of his characters, the interest of the situations in which he placed them, and the agreeable ease with which he wrote the sententious parts of the dialogue, greatly pleased his audiences. Such was the success of *False Delicacy*, and such the superficiality of contemporary criticism, that the play came to be regarded as one which carried sentimentalism to an extreme, and was by enemies of sentimental comedy declared to be destitute of humor; when, as a matter of fact, it is a peculiar variation of the type, and sometimes satirizes the very tendency it is supposed to support.[1]

In the preface to *The Good-Natured Man* (29 January, 1768), Oliver Goldsmith expressed his opinion that French comedy had become too elevated and refined, and his fear that a similar tendency in England might banish "humor and character" from the stage. He intimated, doubtless sincerely, that he was leading a return to the comedy of "the last age," that is, to one that was natural, humorous, and, if necessary, "mean" or "low."[2] His historical knowledge concerning comedy of the older school was vague or erroneous; but his practice to a considerable extent conformed to his theoretic ideals. He gave *The Good-Natured Man* a larger proportion of comic scenes than had been customary in sentimental comedies since 1762. Low characters such as had been as a rule excluded from them, he admitted in the persons of two comical bailiffs whose vulgar impertinence in conversation with the heroine disgusted the public. His subplot, though it began with a situation like that in *The Conscious Lovers* and *The Foundling*, he conducted through a series of amusing misunderstandings. He enlivened his dialogue with unforced pleasantry; and drew admirably ridiculous figures in Sir Thomas Lofty, a pretender to political influence, and in Mr. Croaker, a lugubrious borrower of trouble. Yet his main plot was that of a sentimental comedy.

Goldsmith's Sir William Honeywood, like Sir George Wealthy in Foote's sentimental comedy, *The Minor*,[3] is secretly watching the conduct of his prodigal nephew; and to

---

[1] An interpretation of *False Delicacy* very different from the one given above is found in G. H. Nettleton, *English Drama of the Restoration and Eighteenth Century* (1914), pp. 269–271.

[2] In 1759, he had protested against the dominance of high comedy, in *The Present State of Polite Learning*, chap. ix.

[3] Chap. xi, above. In *The Minor*, it is not a nephew but a son.

cure the youth of spendthrift habits, he purposes to "involve him in fictitious distresses." Young Honeywood believes in "universal benevolence," is charitable to the poor, and merciful to offenders.[1] He is so good-natured as to be duped by Sir Thomas Lofty into believing that he is obliged to him for extraordinary services; and, to acquit the obligation, he will even further Lofty's courtship of Miss Richly,[2] whom he himself loves. Miss Richly intuitively understands her lover's true character, overlooks his improvident ways, and is sure that they are atoned for by "his tenderness, his humanity, his universal friendship." [3] She rescues him from the debtor's prison; and, on his acknowledging the folly of his conduct, and convincing his uncle of his repentance, she marries him. In all this there was, except for the limpid simplicity of the style, little else than the commonplace traits of sentimental literature. It was just the kind of play, indeed, which one would expect from the author of *The Vicar of Wakefield,* — humorous but not trenchantly satiric, tender but not strongly emotional. To make a successful revolt against the dominance of the drama of sensibility, it did not suffice to write a sentimental comedy with sprightly comic passages; one must exclude the sentimental entirely. That step, which would really have been a return to "the last age," Goldsmith had not yet taken.

The genre pursued its course as if *The Good-Natured Man* had never been written. Bickerstaff produced another sentimental "opera," *Lionel and Clarissa* (25 February, 1768). To the influence of Goldsmith might be attributed the presence of low comedy characters in the piece, were it not that Bickerstaff, three years earlier, had introduced such characters

---

[1] Act I, scene i.
[2] A kind of inversion of Lady Betty's furthering the courtship of Lord Winworth in *False Delicacy.*   [3] Act III, scene i.

in *The Maid of the Mill*.[1] *Lionel and Clarissa* consists of
two love-stories, one of which is comic. The sentimental one
shows some originality, especially in the characterization of
Lionel, a dependent of Sir William and the tutor of his
daughter Clarissa. Sir William plans to marry Clarissa to his
neighbor's son, but she and Lionel have fallen in love with
each other. She is torn between love and filial affection; he,
between love and gratitude to his generous master. His sense
of honor triumphs over his passion, and he forces himself to
tell Clarissa that he may not think of marrying her against
the wishes of his benefactor. His renunciation is overheard
by Sir William, who had thought him guilty of ungrateful
hypocrisy, but who now, recognizing his worth, gladly gives
him Clarissa. It is Bickerstaff's best work, the affection of
the father, daughter, and lover, as well as their perturbed states
of mind, being painted in clear and agreeable colors.[2]

A sentimental comedy of little intrinsic value is Abraham
Portal's *The Indiscreet Lover* (c. May, 1768), which treats the
familiar theme of a prodigal reformed by arousing his pity for
virtue in distress. Its author was a jeweler, and its *milieu* is
entirely mercantile. The interest of the work lies in the circumstances of its production. It was given for the benefit of
the British Lying-in Hospital, the charitable aims of which
were praised in the prologue. The speaker of the epilogue was
supposed to be a poor soldier whose wife had been an inmate
of the hospital. He pointed to its patrons in the audience, and
said :

> There! look around!
> As generous worthies as ere trod on ground.
> These gents and nobles — blessings on them fall! —
> Relieved their soldier, and preserved poor Moll.

[1] Farmer Giles, Ralph, and Fanny. See particularly the quarrel scene
between Ralph and Fanny (Act II, scene ii).

[2] On Cumberland's *Amelia*, the next sentimental play to be performed
(12 April, 1768), see chap. xi.

.   .   .   .

> And while to serve our king abroad we roam,
> They save our wives from misery at home.
> This play you 've seen was all of their invention,
> To raise supplies to serve their kind intention.

The choice of a sentimental comedy for such a purpose was of course peculiarly appropriate; for the humanitarian movement, which was making such remarkable advances in this age,[1] was inspired by the literature of sensibility.

In imitation of Bickerstaff's sentimental "operas," Joseph Reed wrote *Tom Jones* (14 January, 1769). Fancying that he was improving upon Fielding's novel, he stripped, he says, "its hero of his libertinism, to render him more amiable and interesting." In consequence, the theme is no longer that of a rake reformed, but of virtuous lovers rewarded.[2] Tom, as one of the characters remarks, "would have made a most admirable parson," and not only conducts himself under trying circumstances with the utmost propriety, but also tries to guide his friends into the paths of rectitude.[3] Reed caught enough of Bickerstaff's pleasant manner to ensure the temporary success of the play; but it did not hold the stage, for he was much inferior to his master in depicting the finer shades of emotion and characterization.

At this point sentimental comedy appeared in danger of being turned aside from its true ends. Kelly had tried to merge it with high comedy; Goldsmith had emphasized that element in it which, from the sentimental point of view, should be subordinated, if not suppressed; and Bickerstaff and Reed

---

[1] Cf. C. S. Loch, *Charity and Social Life* (1910), pp. 337–343. An unpublished Harvard doctorate dissertation bearing on this subject is C. A. Moore's *Humanitarianism in the English Periodical Essay and English Poetry, 1700–1760* (1913).

[2] "The hint of legitimating Tom Jones," Reed admittedly took from Poinsenet's opera.   [3] The first and the last scenes of Act II.

had cast it into the less dignified form of "opera." It was brought back into its regular channel, again under French guidance, by Mrs. Griffith. Her masterpiece, *The School for Rakes* (4 February, 1769), is an adaptation of Beaumarchais' *Eugénie* (1767). The manners of her comic personages, — Mrs. Winifred Evans, a Welsh lady proud of the interminable Ap Evans genealogy; and Captain Lloyd, with his bluff nautical speech, — she copied from British life. But fortunately she introduced no important changes in the sentimental action of her source, the result being that in this case she did not display that weakness in plot structure which is the characteristic defect of her other plays.[1]

Especially in the first three acts of *The School for Rakes*, suspense and surprise are well created. An ominous feeling is instilled at the outset, when the heroine, Harriet Evans, accompanied by her father and her aunt, comes to London as the guest of Lord Eustace, to whom she has been clandestinely married.[2] From the remorseful soliloquies of Eustace's dependant, Frampton, we apprehend some mysterious iniquity in the circumstances of this marriage, and are anxiously concerned for the trustful Harriet. Towards the end of the first act, a painful conversation between Frampton and Eustace discloses the fact that the wedding ceremony was conducted by a sham clergyman, Eustace's steward, who had suggested this vile artifice to his master. The goodness and devotion of Harriet have led the conspirators to regret their deceit bitterly: the steward, who lies dying, threatens to reveal the plot; Frampton cannot forbear reproaching his patron; and Eustace himself, still deeply in love with Harriet, would gladly legalize her

---

[1] *The Double Mistake* (cf. chap. xi, above), *A Wife in the Right* (chap. xii), and *The Times* (chap. xiii).

[2] It is said that Mrs. Griffith's own marriage was clandestine. Cf. *Biographia Dramatica*, I, 301.

relationship to him. An apparently insuperable obstacle to that act of justice arises when Eustace's father chooses a wife for him, and directs him to pay his addresses to her.

A clear exposition of this predicament having been given, the second act unfolds the growth of fearful uncertainty in Harriet's mind, and the third shows her realization of the full truth. Among the merits of the action, not the least is the fact that Harriet's agony is caused not merely by her loss of legal right or of reputation, but also by her loss of faith in her lover, who, unaware that she knows all, and still hoping by some means to avert a breach, maintains an attitude of utter devotion to her, and thus in her eyes adds hypocrisy to wrong-doing. In the last two acts, which are not quite so well built as the others, Eustace is challenged by Harriet's father to a duel, and Frampton, through a successful appeal to Lord Delville, brings about a happy reconciliation. Care is taken to provide grounds for Harriet's regaining respect for her lover. She learns that he had determined not to return her father's fire in the projected duel; and that in a letter having all the solemnity of a last will, he had enjoined upon Lord Delville to do justice to Harriet. *The School for Rakes* was the most intelligent adaptation of a French sentimental comedy since Whitehead's *The School for Lovers* (1762). It showed an appreciation of those qualities of character that the sentimentalist values, and told a moving story in a simple yet impressive manner.[1]

It was not a sign of a high standard of public taste that the success of *The School for Rakes* was surpassed[2] by that of

---

[1] The next sentimental comedy, Mrs. Charlotte Lennox's *The Sisters* (18 February, 1769), is, I regret to say, inaccessible to me. From Genest's description (V, 241) I infer that it had few new traits, if any. It was a failure. Cf. Goldsmith's *Poetical Works*, ed. Austin Dobson, in *The World's Classics* (1907), pp. 65–66, 215.

[2] *The School for Rakes* was in its first season performed thirteen nights, and it was once revived; *The Brothers* was performed twenty-two nights, and revived several times.

Richard Cumberland's *The Brothers* (2 December, 1769). This play was the first sentimental comedy, not in the form of " opera," [1] by that author whom fate singled out as the memorable exponent of the genre in his day. It exhibits some of Cumberland's most marked characteristics, but not his best. Among the sentimental comedies of the 1760's it occupies a position similar to that taken among those of the 1740's by Edward Moore's *The Foundling*; [2] for, more than any other work of the kind in its decade, it strives to hold attention by a plot crowded with incidents.

No less than three actions, each sufficient for an entire play, are here combined. One of these, concerning a hen-pecked husband who successfully rebels against his wife, is comic. In the other two may be recognized, notwithstanding considerable differences in details, sentimental themes similar to those of Farquhar's *The Twin Rivals* and Mrs. Griffith's *The School for Rakes*. Belfield Senior has deserted his wife, Violetta, a Portuguese lady; and, through a series of intrigues in which he is aided by his steward Patterson, is proceeding to gain the hand of Sophia, who was engaged to his absent brother but has been led to believe him false. Belfield Junior, in company with Violetta, returns home; and, after some misunderstandings and contentions, he regains his Sophia, and his penitent elder brother is reunited to Violetta. The characters that have conspicuous parts are unusually numerous, and most of them participate in each of the three plots, so that there arise in rapid succession new confrontations of personages. To conduct so complicated an action without confusion was Cumberland's talent.

It is an illuminating fact that the actors found the comic rôles more satisfactory than the sentimental.[3] The boisterous

---

[1] On Cumberland's *The Summer's Tale* and *Amelia*, cf. *supra*, chap. xi.

[2] Chap. ix, above.

[3] Elizabeth Inchbald, *The British Theatre* (1808), vol. xviii, " Remarks " on *The Brothers*.

Captain Ironsides, who roared through his scenes like a south-easter, was a telling part. The ludicrous coward, Sir Benjamin Dove, had a good mock-duel scene, in which his opponent allowed him to impress his termagant wife with his bravery. Such comic effects may be produced by vigor and rapidity; but to convey a deeply sentimental or pathetic impression, time is needed. Cumberland hurries his many sentimental characters through their vicissitudes, and cannot give them leisure to vent their feelings adequately. When Sophia learns that her lover is not, as she had supposed, unfaithful, there are too many complications awaiting disentanglement to allow her to utter her sense of happiness.[1] The trials of the other heroine, Violetta, are grievous; but rarely can she signify her state of mind other than in a few exclamatory sentences.[2] Belfield Senior, Violetta, and Patterson stand in somewhat the same relationship to one another as Eustace, Harriet, and Frampton in *The School for Rakes*; but in Mrs. Griffith's play the motives for their respective actions are developed deliberately, whereas in Cumberland they are indicated in a few downright statements.[3] To Mrs. Griffith it must have seemed that Cumberland's characters were too much engaged in outward activities to reveal the workings of their minds and hearts. To Cumberland it probably seemed that Mrs. Griffith's were too much absorbed in mere conversation; and in this attitude towards sentimental comedy the popular verdict was in the long run to support him.

Hugh Kelly, in *A Word to the Wise* (3 March, 1770), repeated his attempt to blend high comedy and sentimental. The "word to the wise" is a word against libertinism. Captain

---

[1] Act V, scene ii.

[2] Act V, scenes i and ii.

[3] Contrast the sudden reform of Cumberland's Belfield Senior (Act V, scene ii) with the gradual improvement in the character of Mrs. Griffith's Eustace (Acts IV and V).

Dormer loves Miss Willoughby; but when, of her own accord, she flees from her father's house to put herself under his protection, he conceives base designs against her. The anguish of her father, — a benevolent optimist reduced by the loss, years ago, of his infant son, and by the recent flight of his daughter, to "a distressed, unfortunate, miserable old man," — finally leads the captain to reform. In the subplot, Villars (who in the end turns out to be Willoughby's lost son), the impecunious secretary of Sir John Dormer, and the latter's daughter, fall secretly in love with each other, but will not by dishonorable or unfilial means cross her father's plan that she shall marry Sir George Hastings. When Sir John discovers the state of their feelings, and finds his daughter's lover noble in character though not in rank, he gladly sanctions their union.

Obviously sentimental as these plots are, they are conducted with a curious avoidance of the very scenes that from the sentimental point of view should be the principal ones. In that respect the love-affair between Villars and Miss Dormer is inferior to the similar one in Bickerstaff's *Lionel and Clarissa*. In the latter, Lionel figures prominently in scenes with Clarissa and her father, — the persons most concerned. In *A Word to the Wise*, on the other hand, the scenes which bring out the ideal character of Villars have nothing to do with his own courtship: they are those in which he rescues Miss Willoughby from her dangerous situation, and refuses to retain a commission procured for him by her pursuer, Captain Dormer.[1] Again, in the other love story, the sentimental scene which should be conspicuous is absent. Captain Dormer is shown repentant, not under the influence of Miss Willoughby's tears, but after an appeal by her father.[2] It is difficult to account for these characteristics of the plot except on the ground that the playwright strove at any cost to achieve the unexpected.

[1] Act III, scene iii; Act IV, scene iii.   [2] Act IV, scene i.

Because of his persistent desire to present at once the comic and the sentimental aspect of his situations, Kelly gives a confused impression of his attitude towards several of his personages. He allows Captain Dormer, for example, to sneer in a witty manner at Miss Willoughby's imploring letter, and to proceed with his courtship of the Miss Montagu whom his father desires him to marry, in a spirit of gay abandon that recalls the rakes of Farquhar,[1] and that does not harmonize with the sentimental notion of a good-natured prodigal temporarily led astray.[2] Moreover, after the captain has declared his intention to reform, and should by every sentimental precedent appear in a scene of tender reconciliation with his forsaken mistress, he is brought together with her in a comic one. He comes, by his father's commands, to pay his addresses to Miss Montagu. She, knowing that he loves Miss Willoughby, conceals her within hearing, and merrily leads him, after he has paid extravagant compliments to herself, to make slighting remarks about the listener. In the midst of these, Miss Willoughby makes her presence known, and both the young ladies laugh at his confusion.[3]

Kelly not only introduced such incongruous scenes, but also admitted some direct attacks against the sentimental spirit. His Miss Montagu jests at "a very florid winding up of a period, very proper for an elevated thought in a sentimental comedy," and opines that what "makes the men so intolerably vain" is women's "good-nature and sensibility."[4] His Sir George Hastings is a sentimental exemplar satirized as a prig. Sir George is "attentive to every law of justice and generosity," reproves convivial and libertine habits, and boasts his heart "unadulterated, and therefore worth any woman's acceptance." Touched by Miss Dormer's distress,

---

[1] Chap. v, above.   [3] Act V, scene i.
[2] Act III, scene i.   [4] Act I, scene i; Act II, scene ii.

he is persuaded to take upon himself the blame of breaking
off their engagement, — a gentlemanly act, which, however,
brings him not admiration but comic embarrassment.[1] In
short, though the main tendency of *A Word to the Wise* is
strongly sentimental, many cross currents deflect its course.
The play failed because the political enemies of Kelly refused
to allow it to be heard; but in view of its ambiguous nature
this can hardly be considered a misfortune to the genre.

Extraordinary enthusiasm greeted Cumberland's *The West
Indian* (19 January, 1771), which was performed twenty-eight
nights in its first season, and survived longer than any other
sentimental comedy of this period. Its author, conscious that
it would always be considered his masterpiece, recorded in
his *Memoirs*[2] the place and the circumstances of its composition with a particularity and seriousness resembling Gibbon's
on an incomparably worthier occasion. Making some allowance for Cumberland's vanity, one may grant that he had
reason to be proud of his achievement. He surpassed the
merits of his previous play, and repeated its faults only in
a lesser degree. Again he constructed, by borrowing and
ingeniously rearranging old themes, a plot that was thronged
with action. He conducted familiar figures, — an heiress
courted by a poor young man; a father in disguise watching
the career of his son, the issue of a clandestine marriage;
the son reformed through love for a virtuous girl, — through
varying scenes that were never inactive and that seemed
new. As in *The Brothers*, he had not leisure to express
the emotions of his characters in detail. He managed, however, more frequently and forcefully than heretofore, to find
opportunity to voice those emotions in well-worded, though
somewhat platitudinous, sentiments. To the serious characters

[1] Act I, scene i; Act II, scene ii; Act III, scene ii; Act IV, scene ii.
[2] Ed. 1806, p. 114.

he added some that were by turns comic and villainous, including a female Puritan, who, it is interesting to observe, was despised because " her heart is flint." He combined anew those elements which recent history had shown to be popular, and was careful not to repeat any of the unappreciated experiments made by his rivals.

Though a sedulous observer of conventions in vogue, Cumberland was not destitute of originality and enterprise. He perceived that the sentimental dramatists had not carried their idealization of life far enough. He thought that the goodness of human nature should henceforth be illustrated, not only by those types of character which had been repeatedly exalted, but also by those which had been disregarded or treated in comic and disdainful fashion. This programme, an intelligent and sincere one, he described in his *Memoirs* as follows :

> I fancied there was an opening for some originality, and an opportunity for showing at least my good will to mankind, if I introduced the characters of persons who had been usually exhibited on the stage as the butts for ridicule and abuse, and endeavored to present them in such lights as might tend to reconcile the world to them, and them to the world. I thereupon looked into society for the purpose of discovering such as were the victims of its national, professional, or religious prejudices, in short, for those suffering characters which stood in need of an advocate; and out of these I meditated to select and form heroes for my future dramas, of which I would study to make such favorable and reconciliatory delineations as might incline the spectators to look upon them with pity and receive them into their good opinion and esteem.[1]

The purpose thus undertaken resulted in an important forward step in sentimental comedy, and gave Cumberland his securest claim to remembrance.[2] First carried out in *The West Indian*, it guided his subsequent work, and appeared in some of his

---

[1] Pp. 115–116.

[2] This is usually ignored, emphasis being laid upon Cumberland's moralizing, — a tendency which he shares with his rivals.

plays which, like *The Jew* (1794), lie beyond the chronological limits of this book.

"I took," he says, "the characters of an Irishman and a West Indian for the heroes of my plot." The public had not associated the heroic with those types. The Irish had, with inconsiderable exceptions, been portrayed on the stage as utterly ridiculous;[1] but Cumberland's Major O'Flaherty in *The West Indian* was, though humorous, never unattractive. Concerning him, Cumberland wrote:

> The art, as I conceive it, of finding language for the Irish character on the stage, consists not in making him foolish, vulgar, or absurd; but on the contrary, whilst you furnish him with expressions that excite laughter, you must graft upon him sentiments that deserve applause.[2]

O'Flaherty's bravery; his patriotism, voiced in such sentences as, "I am an Irishman; mine is not the country of dishonor"; his ready sympathy, which led him to "share the little modicum that thirty years' hard service had left him" with the destitute; and his fiery scorn of meanness, — these were traits as engaging as they were novel.[3]

The colonials from the West Indies were looked upon in London as ill-bred, violent, and grossly ostentatious. As such they had been lampooned in Foote's Sir Peter Pepperpot in *The Patron* (1764). When Cumberland's play was announced, it was assumed that he too would cast ridicule upon them; and some West Indians went to the theatre "to chastise the author."[4] They found, however, in Cumberland's Belcour a

---

[1] For example, Foigard in Farquhar's *The Beaux' Stratagem*, the Irish apprentice in Murphy's *The Apprentice*, Captain O'Cutter in Colman's *The Jealous Wife*, Patrick O'Connell in Reed's *The Register Office*, and the Irish sharpers in Colman's *The Oxonian in Town*. Exceptions are the comparatively amiable Irishmen in Thomas Sheridan's *The Brave Irishman* and Macklin's *Love à la Mode*.   [2] *Memoirs*, p. 116.

[3] There was difficulty about finding a suitable actor for this rôle. Cf. *Memoirs*, p. 123, and Genest, V, 297-298.   [4] *Memoirs*, p. 122.

young gentleman who did honor to their land, whose passionate temperament was excused on the ground of the tropical climate, and of whom it was said that "his very failings set him off." He was a sentimental prodigal, with all the instinctive goodness of heart proper to such a character, and the additional charm of delightful vivacity. It was not, as Arthur Murphy complained, an accurate delineation of the manners of a West Indian planter; but it was a variation of the sentimental hero that took the town by storm.[1]

The national prejudice which Cumberland tried to overcome in his next sentimental comedy, *The Fashionable Lover* (20 January, 1772), was that against the Scotch. For the benefit of those Englishmen who still nursed a grudge against the nation that had risen against them in 1745, Cumberland had his Colin Macleod utter this appeal:

When you have shad the blude of the offenders, it is na' generous to revive the offense. As for mine awn particular, Heaven be my judge, the realms of England does na' haud a heart more loyal than the one I strike my hond upon![2]

The last words of the play, spoken by its Sir Friendly Moral, protested against those whose charity "never circulated beyond the Tweed," and declared: "I 'd rather weed out one such unmanly prejudice from the hearts of my countrymen than add another Indies to their empire." Colin Macleod stood in marked contrast to the contemptible Scotch characters that had predominated on the stage.[3] In him the niggardliness imputed to the North Briton was shown as unselfish

---

[1] It may be noted in passing that in this year (1771) Charles Jenner published *The Man of Family*, an adaptation of Diderot's *Le Père de Famille*, with a rather interesting preface explaining why the work seemed unsuited to the British stage.

[2] Act III, scene iii.

[3] For example, Macruthen in Foote's *The Englishman Returned from Paris*, Donald Macgregor in his *The Orators*, Johnny Macpherson in his *The*

economy. Colin faithfully guards against extravagance in his
master's household, and bestows the greater part of his wages
upon poor relations. He helps to rescue the heroine of the
play from a precarious situation; and he is favorably contrasted with his master, Lord Abberville, who "in a distinguished rank openly assaults innocence" while Colin "in his
humble post secretly supports it." [1]

The frame into which this kindly portrait of the Scotch
steward is inserted is pieced together from parts of earlier
sentimental comedies like *The Foundling, The Clandestine Marriage,* and *The School for Rakes.* The heroine, Miss Aubrey,
a dependant in a rich merchant's family, is beloved by the
poor but deserving Tyrrel and pursued by the fashionable
libertine, Lord Abberville. In the end the rake reforms; and
the heroine, discovered to be an heiress, is married to her worthy
lover. Most of the scenes, — like that in which Miss Aubrey,
at a moment when Abberville is forcing his unwelcome attentions upon her, is surprised by his fiancée and accused of
giving him encouragement, — are theatrically effective. So
frequent are the turns in the plot, however, and so unusually
numerous the characters with important parts, that only the
greatest care for unity of action could have kept the play from
disorganization. That care Cumberland did in this instance
not exercise, and consequently the work leaves a confused impression.[2] His public, however, though not admiring *The*

Devil upon Two Sticks, the Scotch apprentice in Murphy's *The Apprentice,*
and Maclaymore in Smollett's *The Reprisal.* Later than Cumberland's Colin
Macleod appeared Foote's ridiculous Lady Catherine Coldstream in *The Maid
of Bath*; and the absurd, though not unamiable, Rhodolpha Macsycophant in
Macklin's *The Man of the World* (performed in Dublin in 1760, in London
not until 1781). Macklin's play, however, preaches against provincialism.

[1] Act II, scene i; Act III, scenes i, ii, v; Act V, scene ii.

[2] It was probably against criticisms of this nature that he was replying in
his preface when he said that the British drama, with its traditions of freedom, should not imitate the French.

Fashionable Lover as much as *The West Indian*, overlooked its looseness of structure on account of its many vigorous scenes and appealing characters.

Mrs. Griffith, in *A Wife in the Right* (9 March, 1772), again offered a sentimental comedy which aimed at delicacy of feeling rather than strength and rapidity of action. Her previous play, *The School for Rakes*, had derived much advantage from being founded on the admirable plot of Beaumarchais's *Eugénie*. When Mrs. Griffith now attempted to invent an original plot, she went to the opposite extreme from Cumberland's method, and constructed one which was not merely simple but barren. It is the story of a Miss Melville, who is distressed by being suspected of an intrigue with her friend's husband. The situation is too largely based upon a misunderstanding and there is not sufficient variety of emotion. The play was damned for its dullness. The same fate overtook William O'Brien's *The Duel* (8 December, 1772), a good adaptation of Sédaine's poignant sentimental comedy, *Le Philosophe sans le Savoir* (1765). Thus, unfortunately, a setback was given to the more refined type of sentimental comedy, which English dramatists seemed to be incompetent to write well unless a Frenchman guided their pen.

In the five years ending with 1772, sentimentalism had met with little opposition in either dramatic or non-dramatic literature. It was the dominant note of nearly every notable novel or poem, — of Sterne's *A Sentimental Journey* (1768), Goldsmith's *The Deserted Village* (1770), Beattie's *The Minstrel* (1771), and Mackenzie's *The Man of Feeling* (1771). As for the drama, those plays of the time which were wholly comic, — some farces by Colman, Garrick, Whitehead, and Foote,[1] —

---

[1] Foote, *The Devil upon Two Sticks* (1768); Colman, *Man and Wife* (1769); Whitehead, *A Trip to Scotland* (1770); Foote, *The Lame Lover* (1770), *The Maid of Bath* (1771), *The Nabob* (1772); and Garrick, *The Irish Widow* (1772).

were rightly regarded as not at all equal in importance and dignity with the contemporary sentimental comedies. The dominance of the latter had been, to be sure, occasionally attacked. Foote, in *The Devil upon Two Sticks* (1768), had remarked that the drama was being directed by "the Genius of Insipidity," who had "entered into partnership with the managers of both houses, and they have set up a kind of circulating library for the vending of dialogue novels."[1] In the "whimsical trifle," *A Trip to Scotland* (1770), Whitehead, momentarily revolting against the spirit in which he had written *The School for Lovers*, had satirized an eloping girl whose head was turned by sentimental literature.[2] Goldsmith, in *The Westminster Review* (December, 1772), had berated "weeping comedy" as illegitimate and dull.[3] No really powerful attacks, however, were delivered until 1773.

On February 15th of that year, Foote, — on the whole the most faithful devotee of the Comic Muse, — gave at his theatre, the Haymarket, an entertainment called *The Primitive Puppet-show*. He began it by delivering an oration in which he ironically praised "the pure, the primitive puppet-show" as the highest branch of the dramatic art; fancifully reviewed its history; and recommended its actors as beings infinitely more refined than Punch and Judy, beings from whose mouths "not a single expression shall escape that can wound the nicest ear, or produce a blush on the most transparent skin." He then announced that the puppets would perform a sentimental comedy, *The Handsome Housemaid, or Piety in Pattens*. The curtain was drawn, and revealed puppets of life size, handsomely clothed and well featured. These went, after the usual manner, through the motions of a play, full of platitudinous sentiments, the action of which is described by a contemporary as follows:

---

[1] *Works* (1797), II, 346.   [2] Especially scenes ii and vi.
[3] Reprinted in Austin Dobson's edition of *The Good-Natured Man* (1903).

The piece was of two acts; the story, a servant girl whose master had fallen in love with her, and being offered a settlement by him, is warned by Thomas the Butler, who loves her, and tells her to beware of her master; for if she once loses her virtue, she will have no pretensions to chastity. She takes his advice, and slights her master, who overcome by her honest principles, and the strength of his passion, offers to marry her. She begs Thomas may be by, to hear the reply she gives to such a noble offer; when she immediately bestows her hand on the butler for counselling her so well. The squire, vanquished by such goodness, gives his consent to their junction; when the heroine, out of gratitude for his great condescension, resolves to marry neither, and to live single, although she loves them both.[1]

Evidently this was a parody of the kind of sentimental comedy exemplified by Bickerstaff's *The Maid of the Mill*. Foote, it should be observed, had a larger comprehension of the nature of the genre than any of its other antagonists since Vanbrugh. Most of the attacks upon it, both before Foote's time and thereafter, were directed against its sententious style and serious tone. Foote struck deeper, and made ridiculous the sentimental desire to idealize common life.

The entertainment concluded with some foolery, in which the puppets were arrested as vagrants. The house, which was crowded to the doors, found the production too short, and demanded, by a vote of three to one, a repetition of it, which was accordingly given. Not all the spectators at first realized that the piece was a burlesque; but when it had been revised and lengthened for later performances, it was thoroughly appreciated, and was called "Foote's Mirror for Sentimental Writers."[2]

While Foote was delivering his keen blow against the sentimental dramatists, Goldsmith was renewing his attempt to revive true comedy. In *She Stoops to Conquer* (15 March, 1773), unlike *The Good-Natured Man*, the spirit of merriment is never extinguished. Even when Marlow, carried away by his

---

[1] *Biographia Dramatica* (1812), III, 154.
[2] *Biographia Dramatica*, III, 150–156.

admiration and love, proposes marriage to Miss Hardcastle, whom he still thinks a servant, her beguiling manner, and the perplexity of the eavesdroppers, keep the situation comic.[1] The characterization of Miss Hardcastle, to speak of only one of the well-known personages, is a notable departure from that of the contemporary sentimental heroines, including Miss Richland of *The Good-Natured Man*. Her frank delight on being told that her prospective lover is handsome; her chagrin because he is shy and reserved; her failure to be shocked by his scandalous reputation, or even by the innuendoes which he addresses to her in ignorance of her identity; her ennui in the "sober, sentimental interview" with him; and the zest with which she deceives him: all these traits of mischievous girlhood were as uncommon as vivacious. Nobody is idealized, reformed, or wept over. Nearly everyone is amused by the actions of the others; and all, without exception, are amusing to the audience.

On the other hand, no character in the play is satirically lashed after the manner of the comic dramatists of the Restoration. The power of sentimentalism stayed the hand of its antagonist. Instead of deriding faults, Goldsmith smiles at foibles. He laughs *with* Tony Lumpkin, not at him. The only approach he makes to the kind of motif that Wycherley, Congreve, and Vanbrugh founded their comedies upon [2] may be seen in the circumstance that the mother-wit of Tony upsets the plans of those who look upon him as their intellectual inferior; and this point Goldsmith does not emphasize. He is even less inclined to a sarcastic criticism of life than his master, Farquhar. His Comic Muse is not a social satirist, but a merry jade who descends to practical jokes. High comedy, almost as much as sentimental, is uncongenial to

---

[1] Act V, scene iii.
[2] Chap. iv, above.

him. He would dispel seriousness from comedy by raising peals of innocent laughter, regardless of the means; and he attains his object by a farcical action and agreeable humorous characters. He thinks to destroy sentimental comedy without offending the kindly attitude towards human nature which is the basis of its existence.[1]

The success of *She Stoops to Conquer* was so great that its enthusiastic admirers declared it had "banished triumphantly those mawkish monsters of fashion," — the sentimental comedies; and that Goldsmith, together with Foote, had "laid the ghost" of sensibility.[2] Whether these claims, — which imply the sudden overthrow of a genre that had almost monopolized the stage for a decade, and that was developing in new directions, — were justified, the events of the next few years will show.

[1] Goldsmith's good-natured portrayal of Mr. and Mrs. Hardcastle and Tony should be compared with Foote's maliciously satiric characterization of Mr. and Mrs. Aircastle and Tony in *The Cozeners* (1774).

[2] *Biographia Dramatica* (1812), III, 293; and William Cooke, cited by Genest (V, 376). A modern judgment on the question is Austin Dobson's: "Sentimental comedy may be said to have received a deadly if not fatal blow" (Introduction to *The Good-Natured Man*, p. xxvii). Cf. G. H. Nettleton, *English Drama*, pp. 289–290.

CHAPTER XIII

SHERIDAN AND THE FINAL TRIUMPH OF
SENTIMENTAL COMEDY: 1773-1780

She Stoops to Conquer, despite its popularity, did not give rise to a school of "laughing comedy." It was followed by three plays of the sentimental type. Goldsmith must have felt discouraged on observing that two of these were produced at the theatre of his ally Foote, and that Foote himself was the author of the first, — *The Bankrupt* (21 July, 1773). In this an honest merchant scorns the opportunity of avoiding business losses by engaging in corrupt practices; and his daughter, harassed by an anonymous letter-writer, happily overcomes the suspicions aroused against her. Robert Hitchcock's *The Macaroni* (September, 1773) contains an unusually large number of the stock sentimental characters, and its diction is remarkably gushing. The natural son, so often referred to in previous sentimental comedies, here actually appears on the stage, — a boy of four years, holding the hand of his deserted mother, and described as her "little rose-lipped comforter." A better play was Charles Dibdin's *The Deserter* (2 November, 1773), an "opera" adapted from the French, and written in the manner of Bickerstaff. Its simplicity and naturalness gave it, alone among these three works, permanent success.

The public, after damning an attempt to dramatize Fielding's *Amelia* in the comic manner,[1] gave a hearty welcome to Hugh Kelly's sentimental comedy, *The School for Wives*

[1] William Kenrick's *The Duellist* (20 November, 1773).

247

(11 December, 1773). Kelly, who regarded Goldsmith's influence as endangering the value of both true comedy and sentimental, concluded *The School for Wives* with the following remarks on that subject:

Lady Rachel

Why, the modern critics say that the only business of comedy is to make people laugh.

Belville

That is degrading the dignity of letters exceedingly, as well as lessening the utility of the stage. A good comedy is a capital effort of genius, and should therefore be directed to the noblest purposes.

Miss Walsingham

Very true, and unless we learn something while we chuckle, the carpenter who nails a pantomime together will be entitled to more applause than the best comic poet in the kingdom.

While maintaining the importance of a moral purpose, Kelly attacked, as in his earlier plays,[1] excessive sentimentality. His Lady Rachel Mildew is an old maid who writes sentimental comedies. She moves among the serious characters, taking notes on their emotions and behavior, and expresses her gratification when they are greatly distressed, as well as her disappointment when they are not quite as wretched as the circumstances would allow.[2] In praise of one of the virtuous personages, she has written a play, which, for popularity's sake, she has enlivened with silly farcical scenes.[3] Kelly's own aim, stated in his preface, was "to steer between the extremes of sentimental gloom and the excesses of uninteresting levity."

The School for Wives shows that Kelly had learned much from the example of Cumberland. He no longer tries to blend the comic with the pathetic,[4] but interchanges them, and subordinates the former to the latter. His theme is that

[1] Chap. xii, above.
[2] Act III, scenes ii, iii; Act IV, scene i.
[3] Act I, scene iii.
[4] Chap. xii, above.

of the prodigal husband reclaimed, the dénouement being a
decorous modification of that in *Love's Last Shift*; but he
complicates and diversifies the action by involving the husband in more than one affair of gallantry. He advances even
beyond Cumberland in idealizing the Irish character, his
Conolly being drawn without that propensity to quarreling
which Major O'Flaherty of *The West Indian* retained. His
most noteworthy contribution to the progress of sentimental
comedy, so far as this play is concerned, lay in the characterization of the admirable lawyer Mr. Torrington, whose profession had heretofore been regularly exposed to scorn, even
by Cumberland himself.[1] Mr. Torrington, though his testiness
and his legal jargon occasionally render him humorous, is a
noble and benignant figure, "a downright Parson Adams in
good-nature and simplicity," who in the end finds his confidence
in human nature justified by the conduct of those whom he
trusts. The main object of the play, to exalt the power of se-
rene virtue, was attained in an appealing and interesting manner;
and *The School for Wives* held the stage for a generation.

A work less ambitious in its aims but equally popular was
the sentimental "opera," *The Maid of the Oaks* (5 November,
1774), by John Burgoyne.[2] It dwells insistently upon the advantages of rural simplicity over urban luxury and affectation.
Mr. Oldworth, a country gentleman whose benevolence has
made his neighborhood "a region of perfect innocence," fears
that if his daughter knew she was an heiress it would have
a bad effect upon her character, and therefore brings her up

---

[1] For example, Sergeant Flower and Counsellor Traverse in Colman's
The Clandestine Marriage (1766); Furnival in Kenrick's *The Widowed Wife*
(1767); Sergeant Circuit in Foote's *The Lame Lover* (1770); Varland in
Cumberland's *The West Indian* (1771); Pillage and Resource in Foote's
The Bankrupt (1773).

[2] The general whose boastful proclamations, a few years later, led to his being
derisively termed "the Chrononhotonthologos of the American Revolution."

as a poor orphan in his household. His hopes are realized when her unsophisticated graces lead to her being courted by a noble youth, who loves her solely for her own sake, and who is willing to risk foregoing his inheritance in order to marry her. Mr. Oldworth, on revealing the true situation of affairs, rejoices because he has succeeded in finding in this world "successful merit and disinterested love." The public thought the play just what Mr. Oldworth termed the wedding fête, — "a feast for the heart."

In view of the favorable reception given to these sentimental plays, it temporarily seemed as if the genre were again to progress without formidable opposition. When Goldsmith died, in March, 1774, the reaction he had tried to lead with *She Stoops to Conquer* had brought forth only one other true comedy that was not unimportant or entirely unsuccessful. This was Colman's *The Man of Business* (31 January, 1774), a satiric portrayal of a young banker who neglects his affairs, and of an old one who is a hypocrite. It was performed, however, only nine nights, and was never revived.

Among the last verses that Goldsmith wrote were the lines in *Retaliation* describing Cumberland as follows :

> The Terence of England, the mender of hearts,
> A flattering painter who made it his care
> To draw men as they ought to be, not as they are
> His gallants are all faultless, his women divine,
> And comedy wonders at being so fine ;
> Like a tragedy-queen he has dizened her out,
> Or rather like Tragedy giving a rout.
> His fools have their follies so lost in a crowd
> Of virtues and feelings that folly grows proud ;
> And coxcombs, alike in their failings alone,
> Adopting his portraits are pleased with their own.

How astonished Goldsmith would have been, could he have lived to learn that the first tolerably successful effort in the comic vein, subsequent to *She Stoops to Conquer*, was made by him whom he had thus consigned to the sentimental niche! In *The Choleric Man* (18 December, 1774), Cumberland for once drew men as (from the comic point of view) they really are. His chief personages were an irascible old gentleman who is cured of his temper by a trick, a pair of lovers who are never sentimental, and a country boor who is satirized for lack of good breeding. So far, in fact, did Cumberland for the time being adopt an attitude opposed to sentimentalism, that he derided the liberal system of education which it favors.[1] The play was not a masterpiece of wit; but it met with a better reception than Colman's; and once more the Comic Muse seemed to have been granted a reprieve.

Such was the situation when Richard Brinsley Sheridan began his career as a playwright. The spirit of sentimentalism was mighty, but another reaction against it was under way. Opportunity beckoned to a satiric genius: what Goldsmith had left undone, and what lesser artists were unable to do brilliantly, — namely to write high comedy untouched by sentimentalism, — Sheridan might have fully accomplished. He possessed extraordinary skill in producing dramatically comic effects by bringing amusing characters into contrast with one another, and by tirelessly maintaining between them a natural yet witty dialogue, upon which criticism long ago exhausted its vocabulary of praise. In the second prologue of *The Rivals* (17 January, 1775), he attacked

> The goddess of the woeful countenance,
> The sentimental Muse.

[1] To complete the sum of anomalies, it may be added that the preface of this true comedy is a defense of sentimental comedy against the strictures that Goldsmith had passed upon it in *The Westminster Review* of December, 1772, — strictures which incidentally alluded to Cumberland's *The Fashionable Lover*. Cumberland apparently did not know that it was Goldsmith who had written the article.

He exorcised her from that portion of the play which is centered about the courtship of Captain Absolute and Lydia Lan-
guish, where wit and humor rule. But Sheridan was not a
Congreve or a Vanbrugh. He failed to take a consistently
comic attitude towards life. When he converted Vanbrugh's
The Relapse into *A Trip to Scarborough* (1777), he changed
the original dénouement and the satiric point of view precisely
as Cibber had done in the case of Vanbrugh's *A Journey to
London:* [1] he caused Loveless and Berinthia to be reformed
by overhearing Amanda's noble expression of confidence in
their honor. And in *The Rivals* itself he conducted the subplot, dealing with Faulkland and Julia, according to sentimental
principles.[2]

The same kind of courtship as that of Faulkland and Julia
had been depicted in Arthur Murphy's *All in the Wrong*
(1761). Murphy's Belinda, like Sheridan's Julia, has a lover
of such "extreme sensibility" that on the most trivial occasions he troubles her with jealous suspicions. Murphy, dwelling wholly on the absurd aspects of the situation, plunged
the lover into ridiculous embarrassments and endowed the
mistress with gayety. Sheridan, though capable of far ex-
celling Murphy in that method of treatment, chose to present
the theme after another fashion. His Faulkland's hypersensi-
tiveness is excused as originating in the admirable "delicacy
and warmth of his affection"; [3] and the agony it causes him
is regarded rather sympathetically. Julia, who "can never be
happy in his absence," does not consider absurd his notion
that "the mutual tear that steals down the cheek of parting
lovers is a compact that no smile shall live there till they

---

[1] Chap. vii, above.

[2] This is sometimes forgotten, because modern stage versions omit large
parts of the Faulkland-Julia plot. Cf. G. H. Nettleton, "Mr. Joseph Jeffer-
son's Acting Version of *The Rivals*," in *The Major Dramas of Sheridan* (1906),
pp. 323–325.   [3] Act V, scene iii.

meet again."[1] When he pretends to be a fugitive from justice, she offers to flee with him, saying:

> Then on the bosom of your wedded Julia, you may lull your keen regret to slumbering; while virtuous love, with a cherub's hand, shall smoothe the brow of upbraiding thought, and pluck the thorn from compunction.[2]

The guiding idea of the action is that his "unhappy temper" is reformed by "her gentleness and candor."[3] Contemporary critics observed that "there are various sentiments in the piece which demonstrate the author's no stranger to the finer feelings," and that the characters of Faulkland and Julia are "the most *outré* sentimental ones that ever appeared upon the stage."[4] What Sheridan had reverted to was not the comedy of the Restoration but the earliest type of sentimental comedy, in which (as, for example, in Steele's *The Tender Husband*[5]) one of the plots was comic and the other sentimental.

It was rather the extraordinary brilliance of the comic portions of *The Rivals* than the conventional sentimentalism of its sub-plot that commanded admiration. The success of Sheridan's play encouraged the production of a few farces and short comedies, but none of these was of notable merit. Among them was *Bon Ton* (18 March, 1775), a satire against fashionable gallantry, by Garrick, who in the same year attacked sentimental comedy in *The Theatrical Candidates* (23 September). In this, Tragedy laid the following accusation against Comedy:

> You . . . a thief can be,
> Wise with stale sentiments all stolen from me,
> Which, long cast off from my heroic verses,
> Have stuffed your motley, dull, sententious farces:
> The town grew sick![6]

---

[1] Act III, scene ii.   [2] Act V, scene i.   [3] Act V, scene iii.
[4] *The Public Ledger* (18 January, 1775) and *The Town and Country Magazine* (January, 1775), cited by G. H. Nettleton, *The Major Dramas of Sheridan* (1906), pp. 313, 316.   [5] Chap. v, above.   [6] *Works* (1798), III, 248.

and Apollo charged the Muses to keep strictly within their respective spheres. If Sheridan had now struck while the iron was hot, if he had provided for the season of 1775–1776 a wholly comic play, he might have instituted a genuine revival of true comedy. He let slip the opportunity, however; and Colman's attempt to aid the cause by producing an alteration of Jonson's *Epicene* (13 January, 1776) resulted in failure. Thereupon a sentimental comedy was offered; and the welcome it received clearly showed that the genre which Sheridan, Garrick, and Colman had tried to ridicule out of fashion was to the public as dear as ever.[1]

The sentimental comedy referred to is Mrs. Hannah Cowley's *The Runaway* (15 February, 1776). Both in its rural setting and somewhat in its theme, it resembles Burgoyne's *The Maid of the Oaks*; but it is sufficiently original in treatment. Written in an effusive style, it exalts the ardent and uncalculating love of the hero and the heroine (played by Mrs. Siddons), and the triumph which they win over the worldly designs of their elders. In their courtship they are aided by Mr. Drummond, a middle-aged benevolist, who is one of the best-drawn characters of this sort in the whole genre. His tenderness of heart is always appropriately manifested. He cannot mention his wife, dead many years ago, without being overcome with emotion; and his object in life is to alleviate the sorrows of all sorts and conditions of men. Wealth and rank he despises, and meanness of spirit he outspokenly condemns. Unlike most men of his years, he admires the young lover whose ardor is so strong that he will marry in defiance of prudence. "I like," Mr. Drummond

---

[1] In 1776 was published Benjamin Victor's domestic tragedy, *The Fatal Error*, an adaptation of Heywood's *A Woman Killed with Kindness*. Cf. chap. iii, above.

Hugh Kelly's *The Man of Reason* (9 February, 1776) was probably a sentimental comedy. It was not published.

exclaims, "to see a man romantic in his love and in his friendships : the virtues of him who is not an enthusiast in those noble passions will never have strength to rise into fortitude, patriotism, and philanthropy."[1] He sees to it that the lovers are not allowed to be, as he says, "sacrificed to the ambition and avarice of those on whose hearts nature has graven duties which they willfully misspell " ;[2] and he finally wins the admiration of those who at first thought him absurdly idealistic. There are tolerably amusing passages in *The Runaway*, and its plot is well enough constructed to hold the attention ; but its especial merits proceed from Mrs. Cowley's thorough understanding of the sentimental views about life, and from her enthusiasm in expressing them.

The effort to destroy the popularity of sentimental comedy was renewed in the season of 1776–1777 by Arthur Murphy. In *News from Parnassus*, a dramatic "prelude" performed at the opening of Covent Garden (23 September, 1776), he satirized Rebus, an author ignorant of "men and manners," who is supposed to have written a pathetic comedy. Sophy Goodchild, its heroine, steals a loaf of bread to save her father from starvation, weeps at her trial, is acquitted by the jury, and is duly rewarded by gaining a wealthy husband. It is, Rebus proudly says, "very generous and improbable ; and so the audience go away crammed with sentiment, and highly delighted with so pathetic a piece."[3] Murphy followed this attack with his *Know Your Own Mind* (22 February, 1777), a true comedy which shows him, unlike Sheridan, indisposed to make any important concessions to sentimentalism. One of the characters, to be sure, a poor girl dependent upon a tyrannous old woman,

---

[1] Act IV, scene iii, ed. 1776, p. 50.
[2] Act V, scene iv, p. 69.
[3] *Works* (1786), IV, pp. 405–408.

occasionally arouses sympathy; but on the whole Murphy is obviously desirous of avoiding serious or emotional scenes.[1]

The chief female character in *Know Your Own Mind*, Lady Bell, is the most vivacious young woman (Goldsmith's Miss Hardcastle not excepted) that had appeared on the stage for at least one generation. In comparison with her, Sheridan's young women are tiresome. Her outspoken delight in the art of captivating men's hearts, her mischievous joy in teazing her lover, her mockery of grief at his fickleness, are depicted with a gayety recalling the traditions of seventeenth-century English and French comedy.[2] Lady Bell does not escape the satirist: having laughed at the follies of others, she herself, presently tricked into a display of unwarranted jealousy, is laughed at in her turn.[3] The irresolution of her lover, the moralizing hypocrisy of another youth, and the bold scandal-mongering of a third, were the principal objects of Murphy's satire; and he managed the plot in such a way as to place these various propensities in a ridiculous light. He thus conformed to the demand of the classical school of criticism that comedy should be " comical by its constitution " as well as in its characterization.[4] *Know Your Own Mind*, though written in marked disregard of the recognized preferences of the public, proved a successful venture. It was Murphy's misfortune that the merits of his play were soon overshadowed by the *éclat* of Sheridan's masterpiece.

Though *The School for Scandal* (8 May, 1777) is, needless to say, far wittier in its dialogue than *Know Your Own Mind*,

---

[1] Miss Neville's distress on learning that she is in grave danger (Act V, scene ii) is passed over as quickly as possible. Observe the avoidance of opportunities for sentimentality in the omission of the scene in which the lover receives the slanderous letter (Act IV, scene i), and of that in which the lovers are united (Act V, scene ii).

[2] One of the sources of the play is Destouches' true comedy, *L'Irrésolu* (1717).   [3] Act IV, scene i.

[4] John Dennis, *A Defense of Sir Fopling Flutter* (1722), cited in chap. vii, above.

it is decidedly not as free from sentimental tendencies. Those passages of Sheridan's play which are, like Murphy's, devoted to an attack upon detraction and hypocrisy, are composed in a wholly comic manner : the Scandal Club is excoriated ; and Joseph Surface, the pharisaical man of sentiment, hoist by his own petard, is made an object of aversion. But Sheridan did not maintain an attitude of mockery or scorn towards other and equally important characters. Charles Surface and his uncle, as well as Sir Peter and Lady Teazle, however amusing the scenes in which they figure, are designed to be amiable. "Lady Teazle," a contemporary complains, "is more likely to excite imitation than disgust."[1] In his conception of these characters, Sheridan resembles mid-eighteenth-century playwrights like Hoadly, with their amusing but lovable personages,[2] rather than Congreve or Molière. He either could not or would not boldly revolt against his age. The fact was that as long as the general spirit of the time was so kindly disposed towards human nature, as long as there was so little support for the sterner ethical point of view, true comedy of character must remain an occasional *tour de force* and could not flourish abundantly. Sheridan kept within the bounds to which sensibility had confined the Comic Muse. A spirited satirist of manners, he is, as a satirist of morals, hesitant and superficial.

The plot of *The School for Scandal*, like the characterization, shows Sheridan no thoroughgoing opponent of sentimentalism. Motives which the sentimentalist admires, determine the crucial acts of the main personages. It is because the prodigal Charles Surface is charitable to the distressed, and affectionately grateful to "the old fellow who had been very

---

[1] Communication to *The Gentleman's Magazine* (February, 1778) cited in G. H. Nettleton's *The Major Dramas of Sheridan* (1906), p. 327.

[2] Cf. chap. ix, above.

good to him," that he wins the hand of Maria and gains his uncle's forgiveness for his extravagances. What cures Lady Teazle of her flightiness is her overhearing that Sir Peter, despite the vexations she has caused him, still loves her so deeply that he intends to provide most generously for her future comfort. After being discovered behind the screen, she says to him:

> The tenderness you expressed for me, when I am sure you could not think I was a witness to it, has penetrated so to my heart that had I left the place without the shame of this discovery, my future life should have spoken the sincerity of my gratitude.[1]

These plots are not "comical by their constitution." They have the motivation and the dénouements of sentimental comedy. Nothing testifies more strongly to the power which the genre exercised over those theoretically opposed to it than that Sheridan, the wittiest genius of his day, should have followed its methods in one of the plots of *The Rivals* and borrowed its favorite themes for the groundwork of *The School for Scandal*.

Most of the lesser playwrights between 1777 and 1780 who tried to imitate the humor of Goldsmith or the wit of Sheridan vulgarized the comic spirit instead of invigorating it. Only one of them, Mrs. Cowley, produced a meritorious true comedy. This was *The Belle's Stratagem* (1780), a lively but decorous treatment of the same theme as that of Wycherley's *The Country Wife*, combined with a farcical love-story involving a satire upon a youth who considers English girls dull. The other comic dramatists seemed determined to arouse laughter by any means, however extravagant. They produced many trivial farces, some of which, like Colman's *Suicide* (1778) and Pilon's *The Invasion* (1778), dealt with subjects ill suited for humorous treatment. Sheridan did not point the way to

---

[1] Act IV, scene iii.

better things in the comments on comedy that he introduced into *The Critic* (30 October, 1779). The tenor of his persiflage was to belittle not only "genteel comedy . . . taken from the French . . . written in a style which they have lately tried to run down, the true sentimental, and nothing ridiculous in it from beginning to end," but also true comedy with a moral purpose;[1] and to support the frivolous and pernicious notion that the theatre should be merely a place of entertainment. In contrast with such trifling, Mrs. Dangle's defense of sentimental comedy on the ground that "there was some edification to be got from those pieces," though doubtless meant to provoke derision, seems sound good sense.

The successive waves of opposition to sentimental comedy did not overwhelm it,[2] but they retarded some of the developments in the genre that seemed promised by its career from 1762 to 1773. The tendencies, shown by Cumberland and Kelly, to increase the personnel of sentimental comedy, and to extend its idealization to despised nationalities and professions, were temporarily checked. Any further reduction in the proportion of the comic element was likewise inhibited; and sentimental dramatists felt impelled to intensify that element, sometimes by admitting broadly farcical scenes or characters. But these effects of the reaction, though they unfortunately discouraged the genre from realizing its own nature to the full, did not modify its character as already established. It resumed its normal course, and soon regained its supremacy.

[1] See Sneer's remarks on *The Reformed House-breaker*, Act I, scene i. The fact that Sheridan is attacking two different kinds of comedy seems to be disregarded in G. H. Nettleton's note on this passage, in *The Major Dramas of Sheridan*, pp. 302-303.

[2] For an opinion to the contrary, see G. H. Nettleton, *The Major Dramas of Sheridan* (1906), pp. xliii–xlv, where Sheridan in *The Critic* is spoken of as raining "parting blows upon the well-nigh extinct body of Sentimental Comedy."

Between 1777 and 1780, there were published two sentimental comedies by Henry Brooke,[1] and translations of Voltaire's *L'Enfant Prodigue*, *Nanine*, and *L'Ecossaise*.[2] Three
new sentimental comedies were performed, one of them —
Robert Hitchcock's *The Coquette* (1777), a dramatization of
Mrs. Heywood's *Betty Thoughtless* — at provincial theatres,
the author himself acknowledging it too poor for the London
stage. At Drury Lane, of which Sheridan was now the manager, there appeared Mrs. Griffith's last work, *The Times*
(2 December, 1779). The failure of her previous play[3] having
shown Mrs. Griffith her inability to invent a good plot, she
advisedly borrowed (from Goldoni's *Le Bourru Bienfaisant*,
1771) the outlines of the action of *The Times*. Its comic
element is provided by the idiosyncracies of Sir William
Woodley, an impetuous and domineering old gentleman, who
avers that he "never said anything in jest since he was born."
He desires his niece to marry his middle-aged friend Counsellor Bedford; but that estimable man of sense, on discovering that the girl's affections are placed elsewhere, withdraws
his suit, and, with some difficulty, succeeds in mollifying the
wrath of Sir William. In order to soften the satire against
the latter, in the usual manner of the genre, we are informed
that "his foibles are natural and unsophisticate," and that he
is "quite as singular for goodness of heart as for that outward
varnish which too often supplies the place of it."[4]

The main plot of *The Times* is concerned with Sir William's married nephew, Woodley. He and his wife have been
living beyond their means, and have fallen a prey to fashionable sycophants. Sir William thinks that it is Mrs. Woodley

---

[1] *The Contending Brothers* and *The Charitable Association*, based respectively on Farquhar's *The Twin Rivals* and Terence's *Hecyra*.
[2] Cf. chaps. x and xi, above.
[3] *A Wife in the Right;* cf. chap. xii, above.
[4] *The Times*, ed. 1780, pp. 6, 34, 46.

who is to blame for their follies; but, in point of fact, Woodley, proud of seeing his wife shine in social life, has encouraged her career of extravagance while concealing the impending ruin of his fortune. He resists the temptation to use her jointure for the relief of his necessities, and his deepest sorrow is the thought that she will have to forego those luxuries to which she has become accustomed. When his predicament becomes known, his false friends desert him; but his wife rises nobly to the occasion.

Woodley

Could every pang I now endure be doubled to save you from the shock which you must feel, I 'd bear them all without complaining. But ruin comes on apace! and that you must share it aggravates my distress.

Mrs. Woodley

Ungenerous Woodley! to think I would shrink from any misery that attends on you! But speak your meaning clearly — suspense is torture — what misery awaits us?

Woodley

Our fortune 's gone, my Mary; we are undone!

Mrs. Woodley

Gone! Not all — my jointure still is left. Dispose of that, and let me go into retirement with you. With pleasure I 'll renounce all the fantastic gayeties of life, and find true happiness in your society.[1]

Sir William finally comes to their rescue, confident that Woodley's reform is permanent since, despite his follies, he has "a generous mind" and "no baseness in his nature." Though *The Times* was in every respect typical of the genre which had been subjected to derision, though it offered nothing strikingly admirable, it was not regarded with disfavor by the public. Sentimental comedy gave it a pleasure so agreeably familiar as to be indispensable.

[1] P. 63.

After Sheridan, theoretically opposed to sentimental comedy, had as a theatrical manager, bowing to the public demand, sanctioned the appearance of a play of that genre at Drury Lane, Colman, avowedly of the same hostile party, followed suit by producing at Covent Garden Miss Sophia Lee's *The Chapter of Accidents* (5 August, 1780). It is a work of more vigor and variety of interest than *The Times*. Miss Lee, unlike Mrs. Griffith, utilized for the comic effects of her play farcical incidents and characters, — a method justified by the precedent of Goldsmith.[1] A valet in *The Chapter of Accidents*, discovering that the heroine is an heiress without knowing it, schemes to marry her; but his intrigue ends in his discomfiture, for he finds himself married instead to a roguish maidservant who impersonated her. The "lowness" of this subordinate portion of the play was combined with strong sentimentality in the main plot, — a combination that became very common in the subsequent history of the genre. Both elements were defended by Colman in the prologue as follows :

> Let each would-be critic know
> That sentiments from genuine feelings flow.
> Critics in vain declaim, and write, and rail;
> Nature — eternal nature — will prevail.
> Give me the bard who makes me laugh and cry,
> Diverts and moves, and all I scarce know why.
>
> .   .   .   .
>
> To-night our author's in a mixed intent —
> Passion and humor — low and sentiment;
> Smiling in tears — a serio-comic play —
> Sunshine and shower — a kind of April day!

Cecilia, the heroine of *The Chapter of Accidents*, is the daughter of Governor Harcourt.[2] Her mother, who died

---

[1] Prologue. A detailed account of the way in which the play was composed is given in the preface.

[2] This part of the play was drawn from Marmontel's tale of Lauretta, the character of the Governor being taken from Diderot's *Le Père de Famille*.

young, carried, in the Governor's opinion, sensibility and refinement to fantastical extremes. Fearing that a town education would develop the same traits in Cecilia, he consigned her as a child to the care of Mr. Grey, a poor curate in a Welsh village, whom she is taught to believe her father, and who brings her up under the influence of "nature and simplicity." When she has arrived at the age of about eighteen, her beauty and unaffected graces arouse the love of Lord Glenmore's son, Woodville. His intentions are honorable; but, aware that his father will object to his union with a girl of no wealth or social position, he persuades her to elope to London with him. She yields to his passion. The author is at pains to exculpate their conduct: Woodville, filially desirous of not offending his father by downright disobedience, is justified in his words, "I sinned from virtue"; and Cecilia, whose innocence and affection lead to her misstep, in hers, "My sensibility ruined my virtue." In such paradoxes the sentimentalist saw nothing absurd.

Woodville hopes by some means to gain his father's consent to marry Cecilia; and, unlike the betrayers in earlier sentimental comedies, never wavers in his love for his mistress. The natural purity of Cecilia's heart, however, soon awakens in her a realization of the wrong she has committed; and such is her sense of her own unworthiness that she tells Woodville they must break off their relationship.

Cecilia

My dear Woodville, I am an altered being. Why have you reduced me to shrink thus in your presence? — oh, why have you made me unworthy of yourself? (*leans against his shoulder weeping*) . . .

Woodville

Will you never be above so narrow a prejudice? are we not the whole world to each other? Nay, dry your tears; allow me to dry them (*kisses her cheek*). What is there in the reach of love or wealth, I have not sought to make you happy?

Cecilia

That which is the essence of all enjoyments, — innocence. Oh, Woodville, you knew not the value of the heart whose peace you have·destroyed. My sensibility first ruined my virtue, and then my repose. But though for you I consented to abandon an humble happy home, to embitter the age of my venerable father, and bear the contempt of the world, I can never support my own. . .

Woodville

Give me but a little time, my love! . . . Let me if possible be happy without a crime; for I must think it one to grieve a parent hitherto so indulgent. . . I long for the hour when the errors of the lover will be absorbed in the merits of the husband.

Cecilia

No, Woodville. . . I love you too sincerely to reap any advantage. . . . Love cannot subsist without esteem, and how should I possess yours when I have lost even my own? . . . I solemnly swear never to accept you without the joint consent of both our fathers, and that I consider as an eternal abjuration. But may the favored woman you are to make happy have all my love without my weakness! (*Exit in tears*).[1]

The unhappy Mr. Grey arrives in London, searching for Cecilia. He informs Governor Harcourt of her flight and seduction. When the irate Governor threatens to abandon all interest in her, he protests:

Moderate your passion, sir! Reflect, when age is frail, what can we expect in youth? shall man desert humanity? . . .

Governor Harcourt

By Heaven, I abjure the audacious little wretch forever! . . .

Mr. Grey

I will sooner want a shilling than suffer her to waste her youth in a state which will render her age an unsupportable burden. Fear not, sir, ever seeing her or me again; for the bosom which reared will joyfully receive her, nor further embitter her remaining days with the knowledge she was born the equal of her undoer. . .[2]

[1] Act II, scene i, ed. 1780, pp. 21–23.   [2] Act III, scene ii, pp. 46–47.

Before Mr. Grey succeeds in finding Cecilia, who has taken refuge with friends, she (by one of the "accidents" which give the title to the play) has become acquainted with Lord Glenmore. The latter, without knowing who she is, conceives the highest admiration for her character; and when he learns that it is she whom his son wants to marry, he gladly sanctions the union, saying:

> My prejudice in favor of birth, and even a stronger prejudice, is corrected by this lovely girl. Of her goodness of heart and greatness of mind, I have had incontestable proofs.[1]

She still protests that she is unworthy; but her objections are overborne when Governor Harcourt, now revealed as her father, joins Lord Glenmore in approving the marriage; and when Mr. Grey, on at last finding her, reconciles her to herself by his words of forgiveness, blessing, and encouragement.

As Cecilia stands before us in the final scene, — a woman who has been led to commit the gravest of errors, yet one whose purity of heart gains her the sympathy and admiration of all, — she seems to personify the culmination of the sentimental faith in the goodness of humanity and the glory of benevolence. It was a daring venture on Miss Lee's part to defy prejudice by presenting what the world calls a "ruined" woman as a heroine; but it succeeded brilliantly. *The Chapter of Accidents* was enthusiastically received in its first season, "the most lavish applause" being given to the serious parts,[2] was revived in 1781 and 1782, and held the stage at least as late as 1823. It marks the final triumph of sentimental comedy over its enemies.

With two plays of less importance, the history of sentimental comedy in the period with which we are concerned comes

---

[1] Act V, scene ii, p. 95.

[2] Preface, p. v. The theatrical manager Harris had refused to produce the play unless Miss Lee would consent to omit the serious portion.

to its close. In these works the influence of French sentimental literature continues to manifest itself : Thomas O'Beirne's *The Generous Impostor* (1780) is based on Destouches' *Le Dissipateur* (1736), and John Burgoyne's *The Lord of the Manor* (1780) on Marmontel's *Silvain* (1770). Both of the English authors modified the original according to the usual fashion, Burgoyne in the preface of his "opera" remarking that "continued uninterrupted scenes of tenderness and sensibility" would not succeed in London. Sensibility dominates nevertheless the main action of *The Lord of the Manor*, which, like Burgoyne's previous "opera," extols the moral superiority of country life over city life. A wealthy gentleman's son, revolting against convention, has married for love, renounced his inheritance, and become a farmer. His daughter Sophia develops all the virtues deemed appropriate to her rural surroundings. She finds a worthy lover in Truemore, the son of a poor curate, who endowed him, in lieu of worldly possessions, with learning, modesty, and enthusiasm for natural scenery. Truemore rescues Sophia from a city libertine ; and when her father falls in great need of a sum of money, offers to procure it by enlisting as a soldier. With the love-story are interwoven some attacks on the game laws and the press gangs as discriminative and tyrannous, — an indication that the possibilities of making the genre serve as a vehicle of democratic sentiment were not wholly forgotten. The main purpose of the play, however, was to recommend natural innocence and to show virtue rewarded. The cordial welcome it received demonstrated that the popularity of sentimental "opera" was likewise enduring.

During the rest of the century no attacks upon sentimental comedy were made that are comparable in strength to those delivered between 1773 and 1777. Foote had died in the latter year, Murphy did no work of importance thereafter, and

Sheridan withdrew from the comic field in 1779.[1] The ablest dramatic satirists had departed, leaving no worthy followers. True comedy was dead. The comic spirit, driven from its highest function, — an amusing and sagacious criticism of character and manners, — either sought a mean refuge in farce or lived a slavish existence as the subordinate element in sentimental comedy. The leadership devolved upon Cumberland (who resumed his work in the 1780's), Thomas Holcroft, and the younger George Colman, — all writers of the sentimental school. Usually they tried to enliven their comedies with some laughable situations and one or two humorous personages, but it was their sentimental conception of life that determined the main action of their plays and the motives of their chief characters. As late as the middle of the nineteenth century, Boucicault complained that the only kind of comedy desired by the public was "a sentimental pathetic play" with broadly humorous touches. And to this day no comedy that antagonizes the sentimental ideas and hopes regarding human nature can gain (whatever its success among the "intellectuals") really popular support.

[1] His *The Stranger* (1798) was drawn from no less sentimental a dramatist than Kotzebue. How are the mighty fallen!

CHAPTER XIV

THE STRENGTH AND THE WEAKNESS OF THE DRAMA OF SENSIBILITY

AN IMAGINARY CONVERSATION BETWEEN MASTER SOFTHEART AND SIR HARDHEAD

Mr. Softheart

Don't you think, Sir Hardhead, that our dramas of sensibility deserve greater recognition?

Sir Hardhead

They deserve the recognition that history should accord to all influential works, whether good or bad.

Mr. Softheart

I esteem them good as well as influential. They are written in a more natural manner. You will recall that similar plays appeared in the sixteenth century, both in England and in France. It is in such periods of spontaneity, when the ancient classics have not yet subjected the human mind to the bondage of rigid rules, or when (as in our time) their grasp has been somewhat weakened, that a drama which is the effusion of natural feelings has a chance to develop.

Sir Hardhead

The sixteenth-century dramas you refer to seem to me the accidental outgrowths of a period of artistic confusion. Weeds will flourish until the ground is better cultivated. As our drama outgrew its immaturity, such plays were interdicted. The seventeenth century is the century of real greatness, in the drama as in so many other ways; and from Shakespeare to Congreve that century discouraged your dramas of sensibility.

Mr. Softheart

I would not belittle Shakespeare, — nor even Congreve, though I cannot read the latter without disgust. Yet I have sometimes wondered why Shakespeare's mind, which we call universal, seems not to have comprehended the possibility of moral grandeur in the plain people, why he represents them as more or less ridiculous. As for Congreve, his intellect was, to be sure, ingenious; but his feelings were corrupt, — like those of all the Restoration playwrights. How clearly justified is the drama of sensibility by its bitterest enemies! The cynic, the misanthropic theologian, the neo-classicist who thinks the last word has been spoken in the dead languages, have always been blind to its charm. Their perverted taste found satisfaction only in comedies which libelled human nature and in tragedies which tediously insist that we are weak creatures whose passions cannot follow the dictates of our understandings.[1] Cibber, Steele, Hill, Lillo, and the others who rebelled against the dominance of such dramas have deserved well of the lovers of humanity.

Sir Hardhead

Do you mean to imply that sentimental domestic tragedies are successfully established on our stage? In seventy-five years, less than a dozen have appeared; and only one or two of these are performed as frequently as the great tragedies of the past. Your friends foster the yearly production of *George Barnwell* to keep their apprentices honest, and tragic actresses like the rôle of Mrs. Beverley in *The Gamester*; but the other ventures of the sort are dead.

---

[1] Master Softheart is versed in the cant of sentimental literature. The words " we are weak creatures," etc., are Sir Richard Steele's. See p. 111, above.

Mr. Softheart

Though the cases of lasting success are indeed deplorably few, it was a notable achievement to destroy the fixed rule, founded on aristocratic error, that only the misfortunes of princes are of tragic interest.

Sir Hardhead

I recognize that error, but I submit that it is possible to write a tragedy about middle-class people without making them fault-less. No one is faultless, not even the lower classes. — Why was Johnson's *Cælia*, so good of its kind, damned by the public? Why did *Fatal Curiosity*, despite Lillo's reputation, fail? Is it not because common sense revolts against tragedies which dote upon the morally weak, flatter the foolishly sensitive, exonerate the criminal, and represent them as virtuous, helpless victims of fate?

Mr. Softheart

I am coming to believe that the so-called criminal is not born but made by circumstances, and I fancy that some day men like Aaron Hill, George Lillo, and Edward Moore, will be admired for having opened our eyes to this new truth. The man of feeling weeps over the misfortunes of those against whom a cruel penal tradition would have us retaliate. But he is of too hopeful a disposition to relish a frequent succession of dramas which end unhappily. He loves to see the good, their misfortunes past, reap the reward of their constancy and merit.[1] Hence it is that sentimental comedy, rather than domestic tragedy, flourishes. And what a salutary change is this comedy from that of a hundred years ago! Then the comic playwright vaunted himself when he had attributed all imaginable follies and vices to his fellowmen and had thus brought down upon them the unsympathetic laughter of his audiences. Their laughter was the

---

[1] Mr. Sealand's words in *The Conscious Lovers.* See p. 134, above.

despicable offspring of hate and pessimism. It sprang from the same anti-social feeling which begot that abominable saying: "In the misfortunes of our friends, there is something not wholly displeasing to us."

Sir Hardhead

An unpleasant truth is more salutary than a pleasing fiction. Stinging ridicule may cure a fool of his folly, or at least prevent others from addicting themselves to it.

Mr. Softheart

Our poet-laureate has well said:

> That eager zeal to laugh the vice away
> May hurt some virtue's intermingling ray![1]

Sir Hardhead

You speak as if sentimental comedies never meant to make us laugh. Surely —

Mr. Softheart

Ah, but they make us laugh in a different spirit nowadays. Cibber and the other pioneers, though they took the first steps in the right direction, could not wholly cut themselves loose from the malicious habit of mind of the Restoration, and in the comic portions of their plays the satiric vein is still lamentably manifest. But since the middle of the century sentimental playwrights have shunned bitter satire even in their sub-plots. Their Comic Muse is not the scandalous jade of old, but

> a little blue-eyed maid,
> With cheeks where innocence and health 's displayed.[2]

She enjoys wholesome fun, and smiles at the harmless oddities of human character; but she never wounds anyone's feelings.

---

[1] William Whitehead. See p. 166, above.
[2] Prologue of Mrs. Cowley's *The Runaway*.

As Sir Peter Teazle says, "True wit is more nearly allied to good-nature than you are aware of."

Sir Hardhead

I shall always admire the pat reply : "True, Sir Peter, — I believe they are so near akin that they can never be united." [1] To write true comedy in a wholly good-natured mood seems to me as impossible as to write true tragedy in an optimistic one. What you term malice is that scorn of man's moral and mental pettiness which inspires the great comic genius. Your sentimental playwrights, afraid of being called malicious, have descended to the lower levels of the comic, — to the practical jokes of farce, or to such preposterous singularities of conduct as are not seen in actual society.

Mr. Softheart

The comic passages of our plays are of subordinate importance, intended merely to relieve the serious parts.

Sir Hardhead

A public which craves "comic relief" in a sentimental play betrays feebleness of mind, — an inability to give two hours' sustained attention to one mood and point of view.

Mr. Softheart

Such attention is unnatural. Our comedies are a combination of
Sunshine and shower — a kind of April day.[2]

Sir Hardhead

An April day is not a work of art. Your metaphor confesses that sentimental comedies lack unity of tone.

---

[1] *The School for Scandal*, Act II, scene ii.
[2] Prologue of *The Chapter of Accidents*. See p. 262, above.

Mr. Softheart

They have something better, — an entertaining variety of effect, like real life.

Sir Hardhead

If the confusion of real life in itself gave us good dramatic art, I surmise that we should need no theatre. — However that may be, I hold that though your playwrights profess, by banishing satire, to elevate humanity, they have really lowered it. They demean the dignity of the human mind when they ask us to laugh only at farcical situations and caricatures of personality.

Mr. Softheart

They have immeasurably elevated humanity by exemplifying and encouraging noble conduct. They have led us out of the valley of bitterness. They have helped to restore mankind to confidence in itself.

Sir Hardhead

They have produced not a single work of genius, none that will be played or even read a century hence, none that has the intrinsic merit of the sentimental novels of Richardson.

Mr. Softheart

The novel is a form that lends itself better to the delicate analysis of emotion. That circumstance should not lessen our respect for those dramatists who opened the way for the entire literature of sensibility.

Sir Hardhead

The sentimental dramatists of France did not find the restrictions of dramatic form a barrier to really artistic achievement. The plays of Destouches, La Chaussée, Marivaux, and Voltaire in most cases surpass those of our writers. Their plots are more absorbing, and their characterization is more subtle.

Mr. Softheart

They were pupils who surpassed their masters : first and last, their inspiration came from England. Ours is the land of freedom in literature. But, though we do not fear change, we change slowly. The French, once they are persuaded to adopt a new style, carry it more rapidly forward than we are apt to. We have in our turn learned from them. Their influence since 1750 has been beneficial, as is seen in the charming delicacy of *The School for Lovers* and in the well-built plot of *The School for Rakes.*

Sir Hardhead

That many of the best of our sentimental plays are based on French works does not speak well for the originality of our present authors. The French are more venturesome in the choice of themes and characters.

Mr. Softheart

Originality has not left us. Richard Cumberland's welcome effort to place the Irish, Scotch, West Indians, and other victims of national, professional, or religious prejudices in an attractive light, shows originality as well as benevolence.

Sir Hardhead

The English have attempted no such attack upon what you are sometimes pleased to term the outworn conventions of society, as Voltaire's *Nanine.*

Mr. Softheart

I repeat, we overturn slowly and without offensiveness. Little by little we are creating a state of public opinion before which the old errors shall fade away. The French would overturn in a day the long-established order of society, and I fear that in their enthusiasm they may cause an explosion that will destroy the good with the bad. We are surer of attaining the goal of human brotherhood because we move toward it more slowly.

Sir Hardhead

You make the very shortcomings of our dramas of sensibility plead in its favor. But will you not admit that its history has been one of lost opportunities? Your favorite philosopher, Lord Shaftesbury, candidly owned that an optimistic faith in human beings cannot be well founded solely upon one's observation of their social life, — that it demands a broad appreciation of the harmonious beauty of nature, and of the fellowship of all created things. Yet which of your sentimental dramatists seems to have grasped the sentimental philosophy? Have they not given us commonplace personages with a tincture of sentimentalism, rather than thoroughgoing sentimentalists? Where in their entire gallery do you find a character who is an impassioned enthusiast, a nature-worshipper, a humanitarian reformer, a scorner of all the conventions of society, a rebel against the established institutions of civilization?

Mr. Softheart

Sir Patrick Worthy in *Irish Hospitality* and Mr. Drummond in *The Runaway* are true benevolists.

Sir Hardhead

They are exceptional, and not particularly celebrated; and most of the Sir Friendly Morals do not go even as far as these do. The typical characters of your sentimental plays seem to act upon motives they have not fathomed, and to drift toward goals they cannot see.

Mr. Softheart

Like their creators, they are not philosophic intellects. They are natural characters, instinctively obeying good impulses that will in time lead them to the vision of higher things. The soundness of the sentimental movement is attested by its unforced and unacademic response to the spirit of the age.

Sir Hardhead

It is an age of half-measures and irresolute inconsistency.

Mr. Softheart

Sentimentalism has, I grieve to say, not developed in the drama as straight a course as it might have. One difficulty has been that our writers of sentimental comedy have not devoted themselves to the new spirit persistently. Some, like Philip Francis, Edward Moore, and William Whitehead, after producing one good play of the kind, ceased to write in that genre. Others, like Cibber and Farquhar in the early days, or Mrs. Griffith and Mrs. Sheridan in our own time, have vacillated between the older type of comedy and the new. Still others, notably Hugh Kelly, in one and the same play deride the feelings they in the main approve. Even Cumberland, writing *The Choleric Man*, temporarily deserted the genre with which his name will be inseparably linked.

Sir Hardhead

Does not all this betray lack of conviction and shallowness of mind?

Mr. Softheart

It may show inconsistency in each of the several playwrights. Perhaps if they had been supported by critics competent to interpret the deeper meaning of their plays, and urging them to further efforts in the same direction, they would have more clearly perceived their destined goal and pressed toward it with less hesitancy. I grant they have not formed a school of philosopher-dramatists, issuing literary creeds and manifestoes, and consciously carrying on an ethical propaganda. They have not been master-minds, dominating the public. For my part, I like to think that it is the public and not a school of playwrights that has created the drama of sensibility. Garrick and Colman wrote sentimental comedies like *The Clandestine Marriage* and *The English Merchant* not because they themselves loved the genre but because their audiences insisted upon having it. Even Foote and Sheridan have bowed to a popular demand for the sentimentalism they theoretically condemn. The drama of sensibility has a great future because it does not originate in academic theory but springs from the heart of the people.

Sir Hardhead

The people enjoyed Foote's parody of sentimental comedy, and seemed to approve Goldsmith's and Sheridan's protests against it.

Mr. Softheart

Temporarily they did. Their dying prejudices were reawakened. But after all the only real effect that such opponents have produced has been to postpone that fuller development of sentimentalism which we were discussing.

Sir Hardhead

In my opinion, if someone had the courage to write a sentimental play frankly expressing its radical ideas, it would prove a worse blow to the genre than any of its opponents have inflicted. If the full meaning of sentimentalism were thus revealed, British common sense would revolt at it.

Mr. Softheart

Say rather, British prejudice, the effect of generations of false education in opposition to nature[1]. We are overcoming those prejudices little by little ; and the public of to-morrow will acclaim what would have offended that of yesterday. Our latest

[1] Shaftesbury's phrase. See p. 117, above.

success, *The Chapter of Accidents,* won popular sympathy for a character who would have been looked at askance by even the most liberal minds in the age of Cibber and Steele.

Sir Hardhead

It won sympathy for a girl who abandoned the path of virtue. In real life she would not thereafter have remained the faultless character that Miss Lee paints her. That is how your friends capture the emotions of the public — by giving them the pleasing notion that folly, weakness, or even sin are mere mistakes, which will readily be pardoned by a charitable world, and which, instead of resulting in serious consequences, will not interfere with the achievement of happiness. *Mundus vult decipi.* How untrue to the facts and laws of life sentimental plays have always been! That paragon of insincerity, Colley Cibber, betrays the whole process of deception which he and his followers practise when he explains why he did not bring down upon the outrageous Lady Townly the punishment that Vanbrugh had intended for her. " Such violent measures," he says, " however just they may be in real life, are too severe for comedy." The difference between Cibber's angelic Lady Easy and her model, the notorious Mrs. Brett, typifies to my mind the difference between the Sentimental Muse and the Goddess of Truth. What tragic disappointments will those experience who are led to believe the world a realm of loving-kindness and all mankind virtuous!

Mr. Softheart

I had much rather be occasionally deceived than harbor an ill opinion of my own species.[1] The wickedness which unfortunately looms so large in your view of society will disappear as the emotions of benevolence and pity are restored to their natural dominance in human character. Because the sentimental dramatists

---

[1] Sir Patrick Worthy's words. See p. 127, above.

cultivate those emotions, they are bettering the world. Their favorite themes, — the reclaiming of an errant husband by the loving patience of his noble wife, the reformation of a prodigal youth by the moral influence of his beloved, the triumph of persecuted innocence over villainy,— are a series of edifying illustrations of the sweetness and power of the unsophisticated human heart. They have softened the mind of man and made the heart better.[1]

Sir Hardhead

To soften man's mind seems to me a dubious way of bettering his heart. I have observed that the keenest minds in sentimental comedies are invariably villains. Why do you so distrust the intellect, by which alone we can distinguish between good and evil ?

Mr. Softheart

There is a surer guide than the intellect, — the moral sense, the feeling of delight in the presence of noble deeds and sentiments, which is instinctive and worth all your ethical rationalizing.

Sir Hardhead

I fear we shall never agree upon the value of the drama of sensibility until we are come to a more clear notion of what is to be imputed to the hardness of the head and the softness of the heart.[2]

[1] Steele's words. See p. 110, above.
[2] Steele's words. See p. 135, above.

INDEX